Access Points

ACCESS POINTS

An Institutional Theory of Policy Bias and Policy Complexity

Sean D. Ehrlich

OXFORD
UNIVERSITY PRESS

OXFORD
UNIVERSITY PRESS

Oxford University Press, Inc., publishes works that further
Oxford University's objective of excellence
in research, scholarship, and education.

Oxford   New York
Auckland   Cape   Town   Dar es Salaam   Hong Kong   Karachi
Kuala Lumpur   Madrid   Melbourne   Mexico   City   Nairobi
New Delhi   Shanghai   Taipei   Toronto

With offices in
Argentina   Austria   Brazil   Chile   Czech   Republic   France Greece
Guatemala   Hungary   Italy   Japan   Poland   Portugal   Singapore
South Korea   Switzerland   Thailand   Turkey   Ukraine   Vietnam

Published by Oxford University Press, Inc.
198 Madison Avenue, New York, NY 10016

www.oup.com

Oxford is a registered trademark of Oxford University Press

Library of Congress Cataloging-in-Publication Data

Ehrlich, Sean D.
Access points: an institutional theory of policy bias and
policy complexity / Sean D. Ehrlich.
p.   cm.
Includes bibliographical references and index.
ISBN 978-0-19-973753-6 (hardback: alk. paper)
ISBN 978-0-19-973754-3 (pbk.: alk. paper)
1. Pressure groups.   2. Lobbying.   3. Trade regulation.
4. Fiscal policy.   5. Banks and banking—Government policy.
6. Environmental policy.   I. Title.
JF529.E37   2011
324'.401—dc22   2011005901

10 9 8 7 6 5 4 3 2 1

Printed in the United States of America
on acid-free paper

TABLE OF CONTENTS

PREFACE

This book investigates one of the fundamental questions of political science: how do political institutions influence policy outcomes? A large literature has flourished to answer this question in recent years, and we have learned much about how different institutional forms lead to systematically different types of policy, whether it be that democracies tend to fight wars against each other less often than non-democracies or how central banks can help curb inflation. A recent trend in this literature has examined how a broad swath of institutions each influences some underlying political feature and how this feature leads to certain types of outcomes. For instance, Veto Player Theory (Tsebelis 2002) argues that different institutions provide a different number of veto players—policymakers whose approval is necessary for policy to pass—and that more veto players lead to more policy stability. Also, Selectorate Theory (Bueno de Mesquita et al. 2003) argues that different institutions influence the size of a leader's selectorate and winning coalition—the people involved in selecting the leader and those members of the selectorate necessary for the leader to stay in power—which, in turn, influences the relative mix of public and private goods provided.

While these and other theories have provided valuable answers to the puzzle of the effects of institutions, *Access Points* argues that they do not provide a full account of how institutions influence policy outcomes. Primarily, this is because existing theories, and particularly the prominent Veto Player and Selectorate Theories, treat policymakers' induced policy preferences as exogenous. By not explaining what determines the outcomes that policymakers want, existing theories are unable to provide detailed explanations of the effect of institutions on the *content* of policies, rather only providing explanations for the stability of those policies or whether those policies will be more or less oriented toward providing private benefits to the rulers or providing public benefits to the population at large. Access Point Theory argues that institutions influence the policy preferences of policymakers which helps determine the particular policies they will support. In particular, Access Point Theory argues that different institutions provide different levels of access to interest groups. The more access provided, the more interest groups will lobby, and the more this will shift policymakers' preferences in line with interest group preferences. As a result, if one side has an easier time lobbying, providing more access will lead to policy that is biased in favor of that side. Further, if interest groups are each lobbying for particularist policies that benefit a narrow portion of the population, more access will lead to more complex policies as policymakers add specific provisions to laws to benefit these interests. In sum, Access Point Theory provides an explanation for how political institutions, through their influence on the number of points of access to the political system, influence how biased and complex policy is across a wide range of different types of policy, something that no existing theory is able to do. As such, Access Point Theory combines with existing institutional theories to provide a richer picture of the policymaking process.

The development and testing of Access Point Theory has been a long task, and I have accumulated many debts over the years. Mentioning the people and groups who have helped me complete this book in its preface may be small repayment on these debts, but that is better than no repayment. First and foremost, I wish to thank my editor at Oxford University Press, David McBride, for having faith in this project and helping me see it to fruition, and also thank everyone else at Oxford University Press who helped me through the process.

The intellectual roots for this book go back to my days in graduate school at the University of Michigan, and I must express my gratitude to the political science department there for the training and support they provided. Many individuals then at Michigan also helped me develop Access Point Theory, and I wish to single out a few of them here, recognizing that I must be leaving out numerous people who, nonetheless, have my deepest gratitude. In particular, I would like to thank the following people: Chris Achen, Matt Beckmann, Anne Davis, Alan Deardorff, Laura Evans, Rob Franzese, Michael Hanmer, Jude Hays, Corrine McConnaughy, James D. Morrow, Yoshikuni Ono, Won-Ho Park, Clint Peinhardt, and Ismail White.

The actual writing of this book has taken place at Florida State University, and I thank the political science department here for not only providing me a job but also for creating an extraordinarily welcoming and productive research environment. This book would surely not be the same, and may not even exist, if I had not joined FSU's political science department as an assistant professor six years ago. As such, the department as a whole and everyone who has been in it has my everlasting thanks. Some individuals in the department, though, have provided particular help in the writing of this book. Will Moore read nearly all of the book and provided honest and helpful feedback at many steps along the way. John Ahlquist provided challenging feedback on the theory chapters; John "Scooter" Ryan provided helpful comments on a number of chapters; Chris Reenock helped immensely with my understanding of environmental politics; and my many conversations with Brad Gomez, Cherie Maestas, and Dave Siegel helped me greatly when I ran into a number of problems. I am sure I tried their patience, as well as the patience of the rest of my colleagues, and I thank them all. In addition, this book benefited from the research assistance provided by a number of fantastic graduate and undergraduate students at FSU, including Brian Crisher, Eddie Hearn, Lindsay LaSasso, Aaron Parsons, and JP Turner. I would like to specifically thank Brian who proofread the entire book and caught many potentially embarrassing mistakes, even if he was a bit too enthusiastic about adding commas throughout the text.

In addition to the people affiliated with Michigan and Florida State, many others have provided advice, encouragement, or help along the way. I would like to thank Daniel Kono and Julia Grey for sharing their data, respectively, on tariff complexity and flat tax adoption. A discussion with Jim Alt inspired the chapter on tax complexity and the idea of using the length of the tax code as a measure for complexity. Xun Cao and Tobias Hoffmann both provided useful feedback on the environmental policy chapter as did Quang Zhou on the tariff complexity chapter. I presented the main elements of this book to the Political Science Department and the Graduate School of Public and International Affairs at the University of Pittsburgh, and their thought-provoking questions greatly helped the project. I would also like to thank the following individuals who read parts of the book, provided me with helpful advice, or in some other way helped me in the writing of this book: Marc Busch, Bill Clark, John Freeman, Matt Golder, Sona Golder, Lucy Goodhart, Charles Hankla, Irfann Nooruddin, Angela O'Mahony, Tasha Philpott, Stephanie Rickard, David Andrew Singer, and Frank Zagare. I am sure I am leaving people out, and I hope they will forgive me for my oversight.

On a personal level, I would like to thank my family for the many years of support and encouragement they have given me and for their inexhaustible patience in putting up with me. To my parents, Mike and Carol, to my sister and brother-in-law, Kim and Elliot, and to my nieces, Mollie and Violet, I can never thank you enough for being a part of my life.

Access Points

PART I

Access Point Theory

CHAPTER 1

Political Institutions, Policy Bias, and Policy Complexity

W hy do the policies of a country sometimes favor one group over another? Why are some policies relatively simple while others are quite complex? For instance, the United States has weak environmental regulations that favor industry as well as a tariff code that favors producers over consumers and that is highly complex, with different tariff rates for most products. On the other hand, Norway has many environmental regulations and low tariff levels while New Zealand has a simple tariff structure that favors consumers. What can explain why we see such similar patterns across multiple policy areas across multiple countries? Whom policy favors and how policy is designed are fundamental questions of political science and yet, despite a recent resurgence in institutional theories of policymaking, we do not yet have general and systematic explanations of how institutions might influence these features of policy.

This book provides just such an explanation by presenting Access Point Theory, a general institutional theory that argues that a single underlying feature of many different types of political institutions provides answers to both the questions of whom policy favors and whether policy is complex or simple across a wide range of different policy areas. The central insight of Access Point Theory is that the more points of access provided to interest groups, the more complex policy will be, and if one side of the debate has an advantage in lobbying, the more biased policy will be toward the side with the advantage. In other words, increasing the role of interest groups in the policymaking process enables them to insert special provisions into policy that make policy more complex, and if the interest groups are predominantly coming from one side of the debate, these provisions will yield overall policy that favors this side more.

Why? The key to the process is the number of policymakers who can be lobbied and that have influence in a policy area. I refer to these policymakers as "access points" because they provide interest groups access to the policymaking process. Increasing the number of these access points decreases the costs of lobbying by increasing the supply of access and, thus, increasing competition among policymakers for the resources provided by interest groups. With access cheaper, interest groups are more likely to be active in their attempts to influence policy outcomes. Thus, they will be more likely to approach policymakers asking for special benefits such as elements of the tax code that benefit them or protection for their industry from foreign competition or changes to regulations. The more requests that policymakers receive for these benefits, the more likely they are to narrowly tailor policy for these particular groups, leading to a more complex policy outcome than if policymakers were free to consider one-size-fits-all policies. Complexity will be defined in more detail below, but, briefly, simple policies are ones that treat all individuals and situations the same while complex policies include special exemptions for certain individuals or groups and contingencies for different situations. Policies that are more complex may be harder for citizens to understand, which might make it harder for them to hold policymakers accountable. Further, complex policies might be harder to enforce, leading to more inefficiency or even corruption. On the other hand, more complex policies might be fairer as different circumstances might demand different policies.

In addition to this complexity effect, access points might also lead to bias, defined here as how much policy outcomes favor one side over another. This bias effect will only occur when one side of a debate is inherently better at lobbying or has some advantage that makes lobbying easier. For instance, one side of the debate may be richer than the other and better able to afford to lobby; or one side may care more about the policy area, because the effects of the policy are highly concentrated, while the other side cares less because the effects are dispersed over a large population. This latter situation is the case, for example, in trade policy where opponents of free trade passionately care because increased imports might cost them their jobs or their profits while the largest block of potential supporters of free trade, consumers, care very little because the impact of protection on final prices is relatively small. Thus, as more opportunities to lobby open up, the side with the lobbying advantage will be in a better position to take advantage of this and press for policy that favors them. As a result, this will lead to policy that is more biased in favor of the advantaged side.

Both of these processes can be seen by returning to the examples discussed above. The United States, with a bicameral legislature with numerous legislators in both branches and low party discipline such that every member of Congress has some potential power in a policy area, has a relatively high number of access points and we therefore tend to see highly complex policies that are highly biased in favor of the side with the lobbying advantage. On the other hand, Norway, with a relatively small number of electoral districts and high party discipline, such that very few policymakers have actual power over policy, has a low number of access points and we therefore tend to see simpler policies that are less biased toward the side with the lobbying advantage. This can, therefore, help explain the difference between both trade and environmental policy in the United States. and Norway.[1]

The rest of this chapter will introduce and explain the main concepts discussed in this book—political institutions, policy bias, and policy complexity. In addition to providing precise definitions of these concepts, the chapter will summarize the current state of our knowledge of these topics and describe how Access Point Theory advances this knowledge. Finally, this chapter provides a road map for the rest of book, summarizing its main arguments and findings.

POLITICAL INSTITUTIONS

The study of institutions has long been a central preoccupation of political science. From the founding of the discipline, scholars have addressed questions of how differences in formal political institutions might explain differences in political outcomes. Recently, a new trend in this literature has emerged: identifying single underlying causal processes by which many different institutional structures affect policy-making outcomes. Thus, instead of studying institutions in isolation or comparing two different forms of an institution, scholars have begun to

---

1. Complexity and bias can exist independently of each other. In other words, policies can be simple but biased (a trade policy that includes no protection is quite simple and also very biased in favor of free traders) and can be complex but unbiased (a trade policy that contains equal amounts of tariffs and import subsidies would be unbiased but complex). When access points increase bias, they will also tend to increase complexity, though the reverse, as will be discussed in chapter 8 with regards to tax policy, is not always true.

examine how multiple institutions, like electoral rules and federalism and party systems, simultaneously affect, for instance, the time horizons or the clarity of responsibility of policymakers and then link these processes to important outcomes, such as the quality of representation or the effectiveness of policy. Access Point Theory contributes to this recent trend by identifying an additional underlying institutional feature and by linking this feature to policy outcomes that previous theories have ignored. This section discusses the main existing institutional theories and how Access Point Theory yields additional insights on the policymaking process.

The two most prominent examples of this recent trend are Tsebelis's (2002) Veto Player Theory and Bueno de Mesquita at al.'s (2003) Selectorate Theory. Veto Player Theory argues that the more veto players—policymakers or groups whose approval of policy is necessary for it to pass—there are, the more stable policy will be. If policy is set by one person, then that policy is easy to change: if the policymaker changes her mind, or if the identity of the policymaker changes, then the policymaker can make whatever policy changes she wants. If more policymakers are needed to approve policy, for instance, if you have a coalition government where party leaders from both parties must support a policy for the coalition to pass it, then only policies that meet with the agreement of both players will pass; that is, only policies that both players prefer over the status quo can replace the status quo. The more such veto players there are, and the more their preferences diverge, the fewer policies will be able to defeat the status quo and, thus, the more likely the status quo is to continue. As a result, policy will be stable when a system has more veto players. Tsebelis measures the number of veto players by examining basic institutional differences between countries and determining if they add additional actors that can veto policy. For instance, each additional party in government is a veto player; a federal system adds subnational veto players; and an independent judiciary adds a veto player.[2]

Selectorate Theory argues that political leaders' first priority is their own survival as leaders and that the types of goods they provide their

---

2. As will be seen in chapter 2, there is substantial overlap between institutions that add veto players and institutions that add access points. For instance, both government parties and federalism add both access points and veto players. However, the measures do not perfectly overlap and the theoretical concepts are distinct. Chapter 7 returns to the issue of combining Access Point Theory and Veto Player Theory as the two can be seen as complementary in that the latter explains whether policy change is possible and the former explains the direction and magnitude of policy change if it is possible.

country depends upon the political institutions in that country, most importantly the size of the winning coalition relative to the size of the selectorate. The selectorate is all members of a country who have a "formal role in expressing a preference over the selection of the leadership . . . though their expression of preferences may or may not directly influence the outcome" while the winning coalition is those members of the selectorate "whose support is essential if the incumbent is to remain in power" (Bueno de Mesquita et al. 2003, 38). When the winning coalition is small and the selectorate large, such as in a single-party autocracy where all party members have a formal role in the selection process, but only a small number of power brokers are necessary to maintain the leader's power, the leader is likely to provide mostly private goods, that is, goods that can be enjoyed exclusively by the members of the winning coalition. When the winning coalition is large, as in democracies, private goods are too expensive to provide to everyone. Thus, the leader must provide more public goods that everyone can enjoy in order to maintain the support of the winning coalition. Selectorate Theory therefore predicts that various political institutions can affect the relative size of the winning coalition and selectorate which will affect the amount of public goods, like security or education or economic prosperity, that a leader provides.

Access Point Theory follows in the tradition of these new literatures. Rather than explain the impact of particular institutions or directly compare institutions, such as in the Presidentialism versus Parliamentarism or plurality versus proportional representation (PR) literatures, Access Point Theory identifies an important underlying feature upon which these and multiple other institutions can be categorized, in this case the number of access points. The number of access points is then linked to the amount of lobbying that occurs which helps us explain which policy outcomes are most likely: Will policy be biased toward one group or another and by how much? Will policy be simple or complex? For instance, will trade policy favor industries desiring protection from imports or consumers wanting cheap goods? Will environmental policy favor polluting industries or promote a clean environment? Will banking regulations provide strong consumer protection or privilege the ability of banks to make profits? Will tax codes be simple or complex, with multiple rates and with deductions and exemptions for multiple things?

Neither Veto Player Theory nor Selectorate Theory can answer these sorts of questions because neither provides detailed explanations of how policymakers determine their preferences over different policies, which limits the ability of either theory to provide answers to the question of what final policy will look like and, in particular, whether that policy will be complex or biased. Veto Player Theory only answers the question of how stable policy is, and Selectorate Theory only provides an explanation for the ratio of public-good to private-good provision. In Veto Player Theory, the only way to determine final policy is to assume exogenously what the veto players' policy preferences are and the theory provides no guidance on what might influence these preferences. Selectorate Theory assumes that the leader is survival-oriented, and this will lead to her providing public goods to the whole country or private goods to the members of the winning coalition depending on the size of the coalition relative to the selectorate. But which public goods are provided and how are they provided? Which private goods are provide and to whom? To the extent that policymaking is more complicated than a dichotomy between public and private good provision, Selectorate Theory cannot provide explanations for what the policy outcome will be.

Access Point Theory is most similar to Veto Player Theory, in that both theories argue that a number of a certain type of policymaker is the crucial underlying feature of institutional configurations. Further, as will be seen in chapter 2, there is substantial overlap between institutions that add veto players and institutions that add access points. For instance, government parties and federalism each add both access points and veto players. However, the measures do not perfectly overlap: the number of electoral districts contributes access points without contributing veto players while independent judiciaries contribute veto players without contributing access points.[3] Further, the theoretical concepts are distinct as the two theories focus on different elements of the policymaking process: Access Point Theory focuses on the preference formation and agenda setting stages while Veto Player Theory focuses on final voting stage. However, there will be occasions where both theories make the same prediction. For instance, if the status quo is biased policy, then veto player theory predicts that the more veto players there are, the more likely biased policy is to persist while Access Point Theory predicts that the more access points there are, the more policy will be biased.[4] At other times, such as if the status quo is unbiased policy or if the status quo differs between countries or if policy change is possible in multiple directions, the two theories yield different, though not necessarily

---

3. In fact, the correlation between the summary measure of access points described in chapter 2 and Henisz's (2010) political constrain variable (a commonly used measure of veto players) is only about 0.6.

4. On the other hand, Veto Player Theory provides no explanation for *why* the status quo is biased policy while Access Point Theory would suggest it was because of preexisting access points biasing policy in the previous time period.

incompatible, predictions. As will be discussed in more detail in chapter 8, most of the time Access Point Theory and Veto Player Theory are complements to each other—in that the latter explains whether policy change is possible and the former explains the direction and magnitude of policy change if it is possible—and not competitors. Thus, the two theories could be combined to produce a more powerful explanation of how institutions influence policymaking.

In summary, Veto Player Theory and Selectorate Theory, while extremely useful and having given us answers to many important questions, are also limited because of their treatment of policy preferences. Access Point Theory more directly models the preference formation stage of the policy-making process and, thus, can provide more detailed explanations of the final policy outcome.[5] The theory does this by focusing on how much access different institutions provide to interest groups and, thus, focuses on the interaction between institutions and lobbying. Lobbying is not the only influence on policymakers' preferences as they likely have their own ideological preferences on many issues and are also influenced by party leaders or their own constituents.

However, lobbying can play an important role in the determination of policy outcomes and a large literature exists to document and explain this role. While this literature will be explained in greater detail in chapter 2, the important point to take from it here is that lobbying can take many different forms but that the goal of lobbying, regardless of form, is to influence policy change, either by winning over undecided or even hostile policymakers or by activating supportive policymakers to work harder on your behalf. To have influence, an interest group must first get in the door. Policymakers have limited time and cannot listen to every interest group or address every issue they may care about and so must make choices about who is allowed to lobby them. As Hansen (1991, 2) phrases it, "Lobbies achieve influence in Congress to the degree that legislators choose their counsel, to the degree that legislators grant them access." Interest groups that have an easier time gaining access are more likely to have influence. Further, institutional systems that allow for more access make it easier for interest groups to influence policy preferences. This, then, is the key insight of Access Point Theory: institutions

---

5. This focus on the preferences of policymakers places Access Point Theory squarely within the Liberal Theories of International Relations, as described in Moravcsik (1997). This book therefore demonstrates the power of such preference-oriented theorizing for understanding international political economy outcomes.

that provide more access will encourage more lobbying which will move policymakers' preferences closer to interest group preferences. If one side of the policy debate has an easier time gaining access, then providing them more access will enable them to push policy more in their favor, that is, to bias policy in their direction. If interest groups lobby for specific policy provisions that benefit some narrow group, then providing them more access will lead to more of these provisions and, thus, more complicated policy.

Thus, the more access provided to interest groups, the more biased and complex policy will be. Access Point Theory argues that one crucial determinant of the amount of access is the number of access points. As will be explained in more detail in the next chapter, the number of access points increases the supply of access which decreases the costs of access. Since policymakers have scarce time, they cannot listen to every interest group, even if they support the policies of the interest group. As Hansen suggests, policymakers must choose to give access to interests for those interests to be effective. If access is a scarce good, then it probably has some sort of market component; that is, the more demand there is for that good, the higher the price, while the less demand there is for a good, the lower the price. Increasing the number of access points (holding constant the amount of interests demanding access to policymakers) increases the supply of access, which increases the competition for lobbying dollars or information or subsidies, which lowers the price policymakers can charge interest groups to get in the door. In sum, increasing the number of access points lowers the cost of lobbying which should increase the amount of lobbying and, thus, the influence of interest groups on policy outcomes.

The theory's focus on how more access to policymakers increases the influence of interest groups builds upon some of the classics of political science, like Hansen (1991) above, but also Truman (1951) and Wilson (1989), who explicitly build theories of politics based on this insight. This book makes a number of novel and important additions to these classic works. First, it focuses attention on the number of access points as one crucial feature that determines the ease of access. Second, it explains how a wide range of different institutional features influence the number of access points in the system. Third, it argues that increased access benefits the side with a lobbying advantage whereas previous research, such as Wilson (1989), suggests that the disadvantaged side benefits from increased access. Fourth, it explains how increased access influences two broad and important features of policy outcomes, policy bias and policy complexity. Finally, it provides systematic cross-national and over-time tests of these arguments across a wide range of policy areas. Thus, this book builds on the existing literatures on institutions and interest groups to greatly expand on our understanding of how these features of politics interact to influence the outcomes of the policymaking process, namely how they contribute to the level of policy bias and policy complexity, two broad concepts that are explained in more detail in the next two sections.

POLICY BIAS

The level of bias in policy is one of the most frequently analyzed aspects of politics, although it is rarely called bias. Rather, different studies will examine, in isolation, whether trade policy is protectionist or free; whether environmental or banking regulations are strong or weak; whether the welfare state is large or small; whether the tax code is progressive or regressive; and so on for virtually any policy that social scientists examine. Each of these studies is discussing the level of policy bias, or how much policy favors one side of the debate over the other. If politics is, in the famous words of Harold Lasswell (1958), "who gets what, when, and how," then policy bias is how much of that "what" one side gets relative to the other. Bias, therefore, is not meant here in the statistical sense of deviation from some expected value nor is it meant in a pejorative sense, despite the negative connotations often inherent in the word. Rather, bias is meant in the more straightforward sense as inclination toward one group or against another group and is similar to Schattschneider's (1960) usage of the term in *The Semisovereign People*, where he argued that "organization is the mobilization of bias," in that political organizations attempt to move policy outcomes in directions that benefit them.[6]

The term "bias" is used here in a value-neutral way, and the reader should not assume that biased policies are inferior. In fact, biased policy may actually be the better policy in some cases. For instance, economic theory suggests that free trade is superior to protectionism: eliminating all tariffs might, therefore, be the correct policy for a country to choose but doing so would still yield policy that is biased in favor of those who support free trade and against those who support protection. Indeed, the higher the tariff levels (or other instruments of protection), the more biased policy will be in favor of protectionists while the lower the tariff levels, the more biased policy will be in favor of free traders.

---

6. Steinmo (1993) and Rogowski (1999), for instance, also define bias in this sense.

Policy bias is, therefore, a measure of which side wins and by how much in the policymaking battle. If we view policy in abstract spatial terms[7] and assume that there is a single issue dimension with two actors that have divergent preferences, then neutral policy would be an outcome that is exactly halfway between the ideal points of the two actors. Each actor is equally satisfied (or dissatisfied) with this outcome. An outcome which is closer to one side would be biased in favor of that side and against the other. Moving policy further in that direction would increase the amount of absolute policy bias; moving it in the other direction would decrease the absolute bias until it moves past the neutral point and becomes biased in the other direction. In relative terms, though, moving the policy to the left increases the amount it is biased toward the left, relative to the original policy, even if it is still toward the right of the neutral point. In other words, the new policy is still absolutely biased to the right but is relatively more biased to the left than the original policy was. In practice, without perfect information about every actor's preferences, it is difficult to locate this "neutral policy." Thus, this book focuses on relative bias: is a policy relatively more or less biased toward one side (and against another) than some alternative policy?

While most studies of bias are issue specific—and vast literatures exist studying bias in the particular policy issues examined in this book which will be discussed in the relevant chapters—we can glean some insight into the general factors that affect the level of bias from these issue-specific studies as well as the few works that examine the topic more generally. For instance, and most relevant to the analysis conducted herein, Mancur Olson's *Logic of Collective Action* (1971) and *Rise and Decline of Nations* (1982) illustrate how the ability to overcome the collective action problem might bias policy in one direction or another. Public goods, which are non-excludable and non-rival, that is, you cannot prevent someone from enjoying the good even if they did not contribute to its creation and one person's enjoyment of the good does not limit another's enjoyment, are usually underprovided if collective action is necessary to create the good. This is because everyone has an incentive to attempt to free ride on the efforts of everyone else since once the good is created they get to enjoy it regardless. Olson points out numerous ways to overcome the collective action problem:

---

7. Spatial theory analyzes politics by assuming that we can locate an individual's preferences (their ideal point) in a space and that the farther away a policy proposal is from this point, the less they prefer that proposal. The individual will be indifferent between two policies that are equally far away from this ideal point, regardless of the direction. See Enelow and Hinich (1984) for an introduction to spatial theory.

for instance, if one or a small group of individuals receive so much benefit from the good that they are willing to assume the whole cost of providing it—that is, they are a "privileged actor"; or if a group is small enough that members can monitor and, perhaps, enforce contributions; or if selective incentives can be tied to contributions to the public good that one only receives if one makes such a contribution.

Since lobbying can be seen as a collective action problem (it is often impossible to tailor a policy such that only those who contributed to lobbying for it receive the benefit), if one side can overcome the collective action problem more easily—because they have a privileged actor, because they are small enough to monitor and enforce compliance, because they are better able to provide selective incentive—then they will be more powerful in the policymaking process. As Olson argues, this will often be the case when the effects of policy are concentrated on one side but dispersed on the other, for example, when the costs of a regulation are concentrated on the regulated industry but the benefits are dispersed across all consumers of the regulated good. Policy should therefore be biased in the direction of the side with the collective action advantage. Access Point Theory builds on this insight from Collective Action Theory by suggesting that the size of this bias is partially determined by the number of access points: the more access points there are the more bias will result from a collective action advantage.

The study of bias is also quite common in the fields of international and comparative political economy, and the empirical sections of this book draw heavily on these literatures as Access Point Theory is tested here on economic policymaking. For instance, as discussed in Franzese (2002a), policy bias may follow a partisan or electoral cycle: when left governments are in power, they should be expected to bias policy toward leftist interests while right governments should do the opposite; and when elections are nearing, all governments should be expected to bias policy in the direction of short-term growth rather than long-term investment. Similar logic suggests that when the economy is in crisis, policymakers will bias policy in favor of short-term growth. This suggests the importance of including measures of partisanship, electoral timing, and economic conditions in the study of bias in democracies.[8]

---

8. As it turns out, electoral cycles are not apparent in the policy areas studied in this book and, thus, for the sake of simplicity, are not included in the analyses in later chapters. This should not be too surprising for the regulatory chapters, as the benefits of regulatory change are rarely felt immediately and are, thus, unlikely to generate much short-term electoral benefit. This is slightly more surprising for

With the exception of electoral timing, none of the above explanations describes the effect of institutions on general bias. Only one other existing account contains this focus, although it provides an account of bias on a somewhat narrow range of policy areas: Lijphart (1999) argues that "consensus" democracies will have "kindler, gentler" policy outcomes than "majoritarian" democracies. More specifically, democracies in which power is broadly shared (through multiparty governments, federal systems, independent judiciaries, and other means) will have better outcomes in a number of areas than democracies where power is concentrated on whoever wins a majority, such as better protection of minority and women's rights, better environmental performance, less domestic violence, more welfare spending and social expenditures, less frequent use of the death penalty, and more foreign aid and less military spending, since consensus democracies should show more concern for protection of minorities and marginalized groups than majoritarian systems that can more easily implement their potentially narrow agenda. It is hard to a priori define what policies are "kinder" and "gentler," so it is hard to rigorously test this argument, but to the extent that some of the indicators of consensus or majoritarian democracies also influence the number of access points, one might want to bear in mind the possible overlaps or inconsistencies between the theories when addressing "kinder" policies. This point will be addressed in more detail in the environmental regulation chapter, as this is the only policy area studied here that is also mentioned by Lijphart (1999).

In summary, while policy bias may be one of the most studied elements of policy, it is almost always done so in policy-specific ways, leaving us with little in the way of general explanations for why multiple policies may be simultaneously biased in similar ways. What general explanations we have, further, tend not to focus on the role of institutions, despite the many studies on the effects of institutions on policy outcomes. This book will address these shortcomings in the existing literatures by explaining how institutions, by way of the number of access points they provide to interest groups, can explain how far policy will be biased in favor of different groups.

trade policy, though, where increased tariffs can immediately lead to fewer imports and growth in the protected industry, and Gallarotti (1985) had previously found a business cycle operating in tariff rates. Though not included in the chapters presented here, other studies of bias would be wise to test for the possibility of an electoral effect.

Complexity is a less frequently analyzed aspect of policy than bias but is no less important. Complex policies may be difficult for citizens to understand and, thus, may make it harder for them to hold political leaders accountable for the effects of policies. Complex policies may also be harder to enforce, leading to worse policy outcomes and increased corruption. On the other hand, simple policies may unfairly treat everyone the same or may not be sufficient to regulate and govern a complex world. While the normative merits of complexity may vary by situation, the empirical effects of complexity are potentially large, but few studies have examined either the causes or the effects of complexity. This book will provide the first systematic analysis of the causes of complexity across different policy areas and will hopefully spur additional interest in both the causes and effects of complexity.

What is policy complexity? Policy complexity is defined in this book in a straightforward way: complex policies have many additional provisions or exceptions and provide many details about implementation while simple policies are straightforward and less detailed, often with a single provision that applies the same way to everyone. The best way to explain the continuum from simple to complex policy is with an example, in this case a country's tax code. Perhaps the simplest possible tax policy is a straightforward head tax[9] whereby every citizen of a country is charged the same amount. Here, the tax policy is simply: "Everyone pays X dollars." Slightly more complex tax policies would be flat sales or income taxes where all purchases or incomes are taxed at the same rate. Part of the additional complexity here would involve defining what a purchase or income is and how to collect the tax. These taxes could be made more complex by having variable rates, such as higher sales tax rates for items such as alcohol or tobacco or lower sales tax rates for food or clothing or a progressive income tax with higher rates for higher income levels. The income tax can be made even more complex by adding deductions or credits for dependents or mortgages or charitable giving or separate tax rates for different types of income, like investment income or inheritances. And an even more complex tax policy might include both types of taxes, plus others like payroll deductions and property taxes. The differential rates or deductions in these taxes often provide benefits to specific groups. For instance, lower sales tax rates on

---

9. Steinmo (1993) provides the definitive discussion of the political determinants of tax policy and this example is inspired by examples used in his book.

clothing will lower the price of clothing, thus increasing the demand for it and increasing the profits for clothing manufacturers. Mortgage credits increase the benefit of owning a home, not only benefiting homeowners over renters, but mortgage brokers and real estate agents over rental sales managers. If these benefits to specific groups are all aligned to benefit broad categories of individuals or those with the same ultimate policy goals, then this will also lead to more bias. An example might be if all of the special tax provisions benefited the rich, then the tax code becomes more regressive. However, if the special benefits cancel out in the aggregate, such as if some provisions benefit the rich and others benefit the poor, then complexity can increase without any change to the overall bias of policy.

Why might we care about policy complexity? Although there might be specific reasons why we might care about complexity in particular policy areas which will be described in the relevant chapters for trade and tax policy, there are also more general reasons why complexity is important. The first is that complex policies might hinder the ability of citizens in democracies to hold their elected leaders accountable. If policies are complex, they may be harder for most citizens to understand and it may become more difficult to determine if the policies and, therefore, the politicians who enacted or who support them, are responsible for good or bad outcomes. If this is the case, then complex policies pose a problem for democratic accountability and democratic performance more generally. This is an issue explored in trade policy by Kono (2006), who argues that complex nontariff barriers (NTBs) like regulations make it harder for citizens to blame trade policy for rising prices rather than simpler tariffs, where the connection is more obvious. As a result, Kono argues, democracies, which have an incentive to respond to industry interest groups who want protection but which also have an incentive to avoid being blamed for higher consumer prices by the general electorate, are more likely to protect industries with NTBs while autocracies, which are less responsive to the general electorate, are more likely to protect with tariffs. In other words, complexity could reduce the transparency of policies.

A second general effect of complexity is that complex policies may be harder to enforce. Not only might citizens have trouble understanding complex policies, but so might administrators of the policies, leading to more error. Even if a policy is implemented error-free, it might still require a large administrative apparatus to implement complex policies. For instance, a complicated tax code with multiple exceptions and deductions and rebates needs a larger number of auditors to ensure compliance than a simpler flat tax. This could lead to more inefficient outcomes than simpler but more easily enforced policies. As will be discussed in chapter 7 in more detail, some economists believe that complicated tax systems lead to more shirking and reduce overall tax receipts. Complex policies could also lead to more corruption as bureaucrats can selectively enforce complex policies more easily than simple ones. For instance, as will be discussed in more detail in chapter 6, a complex tariff schedule where similar products are taxed at different rates allows customs agents discretion to reclassify imports to either more or less favorable tax rates which could lead to the possibility of accepting or soliciting bribes.

Complexity need not be a negative feature of policy, though. A complex world may demand complex policies to govern and regulate it and simple policies may not be sufficient for the task. Complex policies also might be more efficient: for instance, in economic analyses of taxation, the Ramsey Rule (Ramsey 1927; Holcombe 2002) suggests that it is more efficient to tax goods at different rates than to have a uniform sales tax on all goods. Since different goods have different elasticities (how responsive quantity purchased or sold is to changes in the price), a flat tax will lead to different consumption distortions on different products, which will not only interfere with the market more but also might lead to less tax revenue than one where a lower tax is applied to elastic products—where raising the price would lead to few purchases—and a higher tax applied to inelastic products—where consumers will keep purchasing the product even at the higher price. If there are decreasing returns to scale on a tax such that increasing any one tax rate brings in less and less revenue as taxpayers shift their activity to other endeavors, as Franzese (2002b) argues, then a complex tax structure where multiple sources of taxation are all employed might be more efficient than a simple one.

In addition, depending on one's normative perspective, a complex policy could be fairer than a simple policy. For instance, a flat tax, with a single rate applied to all income, would be simpler than a progressive tax with different, higher rates for higher income brackets. However many individuals (and most developed countries) seem to believe that a progressive tax, which shifts a higher tax burden on the wealthy, is a fairer tax system. In other words, beliefs about the fairness of tax systems differ, and scholars tend to discuss two different types of fairness, vertical and horizontal equity, both of which are, to some degree, controversial. Vertical equity refers to fairness between those at different income levels: most countries have instituted a progressive tax system whereby those who earn or have more are expected to pay a higher percentage of their income than those who have less, though some countries have moved toward a flat tax where everyone is taxed the same regardless of income. Horizontal equity suggests that even those who make the same amount of money should be taxed differently if their circumstances differ, for instance, if they have more children or if they give more to charity or whatnot. Vertical equity might be achieved with only minimal complexity, but horizontal equity will likely need a highly complex tax code.

Although complexity is less frequently studied than bias, literatures on the topic do exist in multiple issue areas. In chapters 6 and 7, I provide more detail on the literatures on trade and tax complexity. Both of these literatures, though, can be categorized as having a normative component based in economics that examines whether complex or simple policies are preferable from an economic efficiency standpoint (this literature is quite sizable in tax policy and much smaller in trade policy) and then a smaller positive component, largely in political science, that examines the causes and effects of the complexity of policy. These literatures provide some baseline expectations about why some countries have more complex policies than others, but there are limited systematic studies upon which the chapters in this book can build. However, this means that chapters 6 and 7 represent the first attempts to explain the institutional roots of complexity in these two important policy areas.

In addition to the literatures relevant to these two chapters, another literature exists examining complexity within welfare policy, largely comparing the U.S. welfare system to European welfare systems and seeking to explain why the U.S. system, which relies on multiple targeted programs and tax incentives, is more complex than its European counterparts, which usually rely on more direct and general transfer payments. This literature, for the most part, offers answers that are compatible with Access Point Theory, typically arguing that the reason the U.S. system is more complex is because of the system of checks and balances within U.S. policymaking that creates additional policymakers who can be lobbied by various interests or who have their own pet projects to insert into welfare policy.[10] Many of these checks are access points, and the logic offered in this literature mirrors the logic underpinning Access Point Theory; thus, this literature is essentially arguing that the U.S. welfare system is more complex because there are more access points in the United States than in most other countries.

In summary, policy complexity is an important aspect of policy that has been understudied, both in general and in policy-specific realms. Access Point Theory provides the first general theoretical account of what causes complexity, and part III of this book conducts some of the first

---

10. See Hacker (2002) for an introduction to this literature.

systematic empirical analyses of the causes of complexity. Hopefully, the research in this book will encourage more scholarly attention to the causes and effects of complexity, as complexity in numerous other policy areas not examined in this book are potentially quite important, such as in all spheres of regulatory policy as well as in health care, budgetary, and probably many other policies.

OUTLINE OF BOOK

Part I of the book describes Access Point Theory in detail, explaining what access points are, why they matter, and how to measure them. Chapter 2 discusses the mechanics of Access Point Theory. Here, access points are defined in detail as policymakers who are susceptible to lobbying, have power in the relevant policy area, and are either independent or represent a distinct constituency. Then, the link between the number of access points and increased lobbying is described under a variety of different policymaking processes. After that, the chapter describes how increased lobbying leads to more complexity and, when there is an inherent lobbying advantage, increased bias. In this discussion, the chapter also explains when and why inherent lobbying advantages might exist, focusing mostly on Collective Action Theory as a guide. The chapter then discusses how to measure access points. This book employs two different measurement strategies. First, it links different institutional features to the number of access points, such as the more electoral districts there are, the more distinct policymakers there will be and, thus, the more access points there will be on average. Increased party discipline, on the other hand, reduces the number of independent policymakers and, thus, the number of access points on average. Chapter 2 discusses in detail these and other institutional effects and describes why the preferred empirical strategy is to include variables measuring these features separately. Second, when necessary because of sample size or other issues, the book also uses a summary measure of access points, collapsing the institutional variables in a single variable. The appendix to chapter 2 also describes the datasets used in the rest of the book, describes how each of the institutions are measured, and provides summary statistics for the number of access points in different countries.

Part II of the book begins the empirical testing of Access Point Theory with a series of chapters examining policy bias in a number of different policy areas. Chapter 3 examines bias in trade policy and, after describing the existing literature exploring the effects of institutions on trade policy bias and describing why protectionists have a collective action advantage and, thus, should benefit from increasing the number of access points, conducts three different tests of Access Point Theory. The first test examines the effects of access points on tariff rates cross-nationally in a sample of developed democracies after World War II, finding that the access point variables are positively associated with higher tariff rates. The second test examines in more detail U.S. tariff rates, hypothesizing (and confirming) that the delegation of trade power to the President in 1934 should have led to lower tariff rates. The third test examines the microfoundations of Access Point Theory, finding that delegation also led to less lobbying of Congress and a narrowing of the gap between protectionist and free-trade lobbyists, as expected by the theory.

Chapter 4 applies Access Point Theory to bias in environmental politics. In general, regulations impose concentrated costs on those who are regulated while providing dispersed benefits to large numbers of people, such as all consumers of a particular product in the case of consumer safety regulation or everyone on the planet in the case of certain environmental regulations. As a result, we would expect the opponents of regulation to have a collective action advantage such that any increase in access points will yield policy that is more biased toward fewer regulations. Thus, this chapter investigates whether increased access points lead to fewer environmental regulations since regulated industries that produce pollution or other negative environmental effects should oppose regulations that increase the costs of production. This hypothesis is tested on a large time-series cross section of postwar developed democracies using environmental treaty data as a proxy for level of environmental regulations. In addition, a more direct measure of environmental policy, level of taxation for environmental purposes, is examined in a smaller panel.

Chapter 5 completes the examination of policy bias by examining the effect of access points on banking regulations. As in environmental regulations, we should expect banks to have a collective action advantage as banking regulations will typically increase the costs of banking and, thus, decrease their profit margin while the benefits of regulations, that is, more investor confidence and lower systemic risk, are dispersed across the entire economy. However, if one bank takes on undue risk and collapses, this could spread consumer panic to other banks, even if those banks are actually safe. Thus, "good" banks have an incentive to create regulations that force "bad" banks to conform to the standards that the good banks already adhere to, but these "good" banks also have an incentive to oppose regulations that would limit the ability of the good banks to do what they want to make the profit they wish to make. In recent decades, this has meant that banks support capital adequacy standards that force all banks to keep a certain amount of cash on hand to prevent bank runs but that banks oppose, among other regulations, restrictions that limit the type of investments activities they can engage in. Chapter 5 finds, across a broad cross section of democracies at all levels of economic development, that countries with more access points tend to be more likely to have capital adequacy standards but less likely to have activity restrictions and strong regulators, thus supporting Access Point Theory.

Part III of the book continues the empirical testing of Access Point Theory by examining policy complexity. Chapter 6 begins this examination with trade policy complexity, complementing the examination of trade policy bias in chapter 3. This chapter examines the tariff schedules that countries negotiate during General Agreement on Tariffs and Trade (GATT) and World Trade Organization (WTO) negotiating rounds, which set tariff rates for different products. The chapter finds that countries with few access points tend to have simpler tariff schedules with more uniform tariff rates across product classes while countries with many access points have complex tariff schedules with many different tariff rates. The chapter also finds that complex tariff schedules tend to be associated with declining future trade, suggesting that complexity might have important and tangible consequences. Chapter 7 examines complexity in the tax code to demonstrate a situation where access points might not lead to more bias but still lead to more complexity. This chapter uses two measures for tax code complexity. First, the length of the tax code is a proxy for complexity, under the assumption that more complicated policies will take longer to describe. Second, the chapter examines how dispersed tax revenues are across multiple different types of taxes, such as income taxes, consumption taxes, and property taxes, borrowing this measure from the "fiscal illusion" literature in economics which links tax complexity to government growth (Dollery and Worthington 1996). With both measures, the chapter finds that countries with more access points tend to have more complex tax codes. Finally, chapter 8 concludes the book by discussing additional policy areas that Access Point Theory might explain and extensions to the theory such as combining it with Veto Player Theory.

CHAPTER 2

What Are Access Points and What Are Their Effects?

Access Point Theory argues that the number of access points to the policymaking process will influence the degree of policy complexity and, if one side has an inherent lobbying advantage, the degree of policy bias. Increasing the number of access points decreases the costs of lobbying which will increase the amount of lobbying. This increased lobbying leads to additional provisions in the policy benefiting special interests, leading to more complex policy. Further, if those on one side have an inherent lobbying advantage, they will be better able to take advantage of the lower lobbying costs, enabling them to push policy in their desired direction. For example, in the case of trade policy, cheaper lobbying costs will encourage industries to lobby more for their preferred policies: import-competing industries will ask for higher tariffs on their products while industries that import raw materials will ask for lower tariffs on the products they import. This will lead to a more differentiated trade policy with different products having different tariff rates relative to what would occur if lobbying costs were higher and more industries were shut out of lobbying. In addition, because protectionists enjoy a collective action advantage, lower lobbying costs will lead to relatively more lobbying by the protectionist side, pushing overall policy in a protectionist direction.

This chapter explains Access Point Theory in detail by describing what access points are and what effects they have. First, access points are defined, and some general discussion is provided about which types of institutions have more access points than others, though a full discussion of how common institutional features affect the number of access points is postponed until the end of the chapter. Second, the effect of the number of access points on the costs of lobbying is demonstrated using a stylized policymaking process involving majority voting in a unicameral legislature with equally powerful policymakers. Third, the chapter describes how lower lobbying costs lead to more policy complexity. Fourth, the chapter describes what lobbying advantages are and why additional access points lead to more policy bias when one side has such an advantage. Fifth, the chapter demonstrates that the theory is robust to different policy-making processes. Finally, the chapter describes how common institutional features relate to the number of access points and derives testable hypotheses from these. Throughout the chapter, Access Point Theory is presented in general terms that can be applied to multiple different policy areas; however, trade policy is used as a running example to illuminate how the theory works.

WHAT ARE ACCESS POINTS?

An access point is any policymaker who can provide meaningful access to interest groups trying to influence policy, that is, someone whom an interest can lobby in the hopes that lobbying will increase the probability of a preferred policy outcome. In order to provide "meaningful access," and, thus, be counted as an access point, a policymaker must satisfy a number of conditions. First, the policymaker must be *susceptible* to lobbying: a policymaker who is prohibited from listening to or has no incentive to listen to interest groups cannot or does not provide access. As will be described in more detail below, interest groups can provide many goods valued by policymakers, such as campaign contributions, information, and work subsidies, so that any policymaker who is electorally or policy motivated is likely to have an incentive to listen to interest groups. Only policymakers who are not elected, who are pure-rent seekers (i.e., they do not care about policy outcomes), and who are in a system where bribery is effectively prohibited have no incentive to be lobbied. In addition, some policymakers may be effectively forbidden to be lobbied, as may be the case with the judicial branch in some governments. With the exception of these limited cases, all policymakers are susceptible to lobbying.

Second, policymakers must be *relevant*, that is, have power in the policy area interest groups wish to influence. Usually, this power is having a vote in the legislature or having a role in the enforcement of the policy. If a policymaker has no power to influence the creation or enforcement of a policy, then there is no incentive to lobby that policymaker. Frequently, all members of the legislative and executive branch will be relevant, but the number of relevant policymakers can vary within a country based upon issue area. For instance, in the United States, all members of both houses of Congress and the President are relevant on budgetary issues, but only Senators and the President are relevant for treaty signing, and only the President is relevant for certain military and diplomatic policies. Further, in countries with federal institutions, subnational policymakers may be relevant on some issues where power is shared across levels of government but irrelevant on other issues. For example, Germany's constitution divides policymaking authority into three categories: exclusive powers, where only the federal government has power such as in foreign policy, immigration, and currency; concurrent powers, where the federal and state governments share power, such as in consumer protection and public health; and framework powers, where the federal government only sets general principles which state governments are free to implement however they like, such as in media policy and some environmental policy (Solsten 1995). The state governments will only be relevant in the latter two types of policies and not in those covered by exclusive powers.

Not all relevant policymakers are access points, though. In order to count as an access point, a policymaker must, third, be either independent or distinct. *Independence* means the ability to exercise one's power based upon one's own preferences. For instance, if a legislator is allowed to cast her vote however she wants, she is independent. If, on the other hand, a legislator must vote as her party demands, either by rule or because the sanction for not doing so is so great that an opposing vote is impossible, then she is not independent; rather, she is dependent on her party leader. If the policymaker is independent, it may be useful to lobby the policymaker since interest group pressure may be able to influence her vote. If the policymaker is dependent, then the only way to change her vote is to change the instructions that the party leader gives her. This could involve changing how the party as a whole will vote on a bill; or it could involve allowing the legislator to "vote her district" regardless of how the rest of the party will vote; or it could involve changing the bill to make it more favorable to the interest group. Regardless of the form, the power to do this resides with the party leadership and not the individual legislator; therefore, except in the circumstance noted below, there is no value in lobbying the dependent legislator. Instead, only lobbying the party leader-ship will be effective.[1]

However, if a legislator is distinct, this can, in a sense, restore her power to her and, thus, her attractiveness to interest groups. *Distinctiveness* refers to representing a distinct constituency, usually by being elected from separate geographic districts. Although interest groups still may not lobby a dependent but distinct policymaker directly, distinctiveness pro-vides another avenue of access to party leaders: an interest group can lobby for their preferred policy by suggesting it will benefit the party as a whole or by suggesting it will benefit the election chances of the party in a particular district. Further, an interest group can lobby the distinct poli-cymaker directly with the hopes that the policymaker will take such argu-ments to her party leader. The dependent policymaker thereby becomes a conduit for interest group pressure and, since this conduit is an elected official and a party member, a potentially effective conduit. As a result, distinct policymakers become potential targets of lobbying, either directly or indirectly, whether or not they are independent. McGillivray (1997) demonstrates that party leaders in systems with distinct but dependent legislators do tailor policy to affect the electoral chances of their members in marginal districts: in Canada, a country with many single-member dis-tricts and strong party discipline such that each legislator is distinct but typically follows party orders, trade policy is partially designed to protect industries in marginal districts.

A policymaker only needs to be independent or distinct to be an access point; although a policymaker that is both independent and distinct is also an access point, both are not necessary. As just described, a dependent but distinct policymaker still provides meaningful access, if only indi-rectly. Further, independent policymakers are potential lobbying targets whether or not they are distinct since even if two policymakers face the same constituency pressures, they may reach different policy conclusions. One only needs to note how often U.S. Senators from the same state vote differently on the same bill. However, if a policymaker is both dependent

---

1. In practice, while there will be circumstances where a policymaker will be com-pletely dependent on party leaders (for instance, countries where backbenchers *must* vote with their party), legislators will rarely be completely independent. In other words, independence is a continuous variable. For instance, a policymaker can be only somewhat independent if he is able to vote against his party but has to pay high costs for his reelection chances in the future. The more independent a policymaker is, the better a lobbying target he will be. For the sake of clarity, I dis-cuss independence as a binary concept here, though.

and indistinct, then they do not provide meaningful access: they cannot vote how they wish and there is no reason for party leaders to tailor policy to enhance their electoral chances.

In summary, an access point is any relevant policymaker who is susceptible to lobbying and either independent or distinct. Access Point Theory argues that the number of these access points positively influences the level of policy bias and policy complexity because of the effect that the number of access points has on the cost of lobbying, an effect described in the next section.

ACCESS POINTS AND THE COST OF LOBBYING

The number of access points matters because it influences the cost of lobbying which influences the amount of lobbying. This section describes how and why this effect occurs by, first, explaining how the number of access points influences the cost of lobbying each individual policymaker and, second, showing how this influences total lobbying costs faced by interest groups and, thus, the probability of an interest group lobbying. This effect on total costs is shown using a stylized policymaking process that drastically simplifies real-world policymaking processes but that captures the important elements of policymaking. The fifth section of this chapter demonstrates that the results of this section are robust to altering the assumptions underlying the policymaking process.

Access Point Theory views access to policymakers as a "normal good." Normal goods are those that are governed by supply and demand such that increases in price will reduce demand and increase supply; further, increases in income will increase demand for normal goods. As such, there will be a market for access and a price for access determined by supply of access and demand for access. This market exists because policymakers have limited amounts of time and being lobbied consumes some of this time, making access to policymakers a scarce resource.[2] Making policy is more than just casting roll call votes on legislation: the legislation must be written, oftentimes with significant research and time-consuming hearings held; details must be negotiated between policymakers; and policymakers need to determine which way to vote on legislation. Each of these processes is time-consuming but can be aided by interest groups, as

---

2. This view of policymakers attempting to accomplish multiple goals under a time constraint is informed by Kingdon (1989) and Hall (1996).

discussed next. However, the act of listening to an interest group is in itself time-consuming and, thus, cannot be infinite.[3]

While policymakers supply access, interests demand access. Interests here can be formally organized interest groups, an ad hoc group, or an individual with particular interest in passing a specific policy. These interests want access in order to influence policy outcomes. In broad terms, lobbying can influence policy preferences for three different reasons. First, interest groups can provide money to policymakers and, in a sense, buy their votes or their support. This money can take the form of outright corruption or, more likely, campaign contributions that allow the policymaker to remain in office. Either way, the goal is to either get a policymaker to support an interest group's preferred policy or keep in office an already-supportive policymaker (Austen-Smith and Wright 1994). Second, interest groups can provide information to policymakers, either about how popular a policy is or about whether a policy will be effective. Here, the goal is to persuade the policymaker to support a policy, either for political or policy reasons (Milner 1998; Bennedsen and Feldman 2001). Third, interest groups can provide work subsidies to policymakers (Hall 1996). Policymaking is a time-consuming process that involves more than a simple roll call vote: legislation must be written; research must be done about the legislation, and hearings held; colleagues must be convinced if policy is to be passed; and so on. Policymakers do not have the time or resources to do this work for every policy, and interest groups can subsidize this effort for the policies they support by providing already written legislation or amendments, conducting research, doing outreach, or other tasks. The goal here is to "activate" the policymakers: they may be supportive of your policies, but given their time constraints, they cannot make the effort to work on every policy they support, but if an interest group subsidizes the effort on a particular policy, this makes it more likely that the policymaker will extend the effort on that policy.[4]

This book is agnostic about the causal mechanism underlying lobbying; it merely presumes that lobbying is potentially effective in determining the policy preferences of policymakers. Given the focus of the theory on how access is a scarce good, the work subsidy approach is particularly appealing; however, the theory is not incompatible with the money or information

---

3. Delegating the listening to an access point's staff may increase the budget and time constraint, but does not eliminate it.
4. This difference in goals is what separates the information and work subsidy approaches: work subsidies are used to activate already supportive policymakers while information is used to persuade policymakers to support you.

approaches. I often use the language of the money approach because this is the most straightforward and also the most familiar in the political economy literatures, especially in trade where one of the seminal works is Grossman and Helpman's "Protection for Sale" (1994) which argued that policymakers support tariffs on industries that want protection from imports because these industries provide them the money needed to win reelection.

Regardless of the form influence takes, though, an interest must first gain access to attempt this influence. The cheaper this access is, the more of it will be purchased, both because interests may want to use more time to influence policymakers (or influence more policymakers) and because more interests will be willing to attempt influence at lower prices. Access is, thus, a scarce resource, essentially the same as any other normal economic good.

As with any scarce resource, a market will therefore exist for access, and the price for access will be influenced by the market conditions of supply and demand. Figure 2.1 shows this market graphically with basic supply-demand curves. D marks the downward-sloping demand curve: the lower the price of access, the higher the quantity of access demanded as described above. S marks the upward-sloping supply curve: the higher the price of access, the more access is supplied as the more money a policy-maker can get by providing access, the more of their time they will devote to this task. The point where the two curves cross, X, is the equilibrium price and quantity of access. Increasing the number of access points increases the supply of access which shifts the supply curve to the right, now represented by the dashed curve, S'. At this new curve, the same amount of access is provided at a lower price. The new equilibrium, X^*, is where D and S' cross.

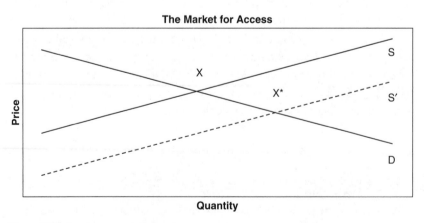

The Market for Access

Figure 2.1
Supply, Demand, and the Price for Access

This new equilibrium price is lower than the original equilibrium price for the same reason that increasing the supply of any good leads to lower prices: competition. With more access points, each one has to compete to attract interest groups, thus driving down the price. Interest groups need to win the votes of a certain number of policymakers and, all else equal, they do not particularly care which subset of policymakers they win votes from. If one policymaker is setting too high of a price for her vote, the interest group can simply bypass that policymaker and lobby a cheaper one. If a policymaker consistently has higher prices, he will be consistently bypassed and, thus, will receive fewer of the goods provided by interest groups. Policymakers will, thus, have to lower their price when they face competition to continue to receive lobbying. The more competition they face, the more they will have to lower their price. In addition to this normal market mechanism, if there are only a handful of access points, these access points may also be able to collude and set oligopolistic rents that drive up the access price even higher than the market level may be. In this scenario, increasing the number of access points makes collusion less likely and thus reduces the price of each unit of access by reducing the chances of oligopoly.

Not only will the cost for each unit of access, that is, lobbying one policymaker, decline with more access points, but so, too, will the total costs of lobbying decline. We can see this with a simple, stylized model of the choice of individuals to contribute to lobbying.[5] First, individuals are assumed to be rational and will only contribute to lobbying if the expected benefits of lobbying, B, outweigh the costs of lobbying, C, or

$$B - C > 0. \tag{1}$$

The expected benefits of lobbying are the value of changing policy multiplied by the marginal increase in the probability of changing policy given your contribution while the costs are the money (or time) spent on lobbying. For the reasons described above, the costs of lobbying each policymaker is a declining function of the number of access points, N, which, for the sake of simplicity, I represent here by setting the costs to lobby each policymaker to equal κ/N where κ represents how efficient a group is at lobbying. The more efficient a group is, the lower κ will be

---

5. This model is similar to Weingast, Shepsle, and Johnsen's (1981) model of distributive politics, which has a similar collective action dynamic as lobbying contributions. See also Franzese et al. (2007) for a different extension of this model of distributive politics, this one based on the idea of "effective constituency size," which combines geographic and partisan constituencies.

and, thus, the lower costs will be. For now, I will assume that the average κ for each group is the same, but the policy bias and complexity sections below will discuss why some individuals have systematically lower κ's than others and what effect this has on lobbying and policy outcomes. I also assume here that individuals are equally efficient at lobbying all policymakers, that is, that they pay the same price to access each policymaker, but this assumption is relaxed in the fifth section of the chapter. Taken together, this means that for every individual, increasing the number of access points reduces the costs of lobbying each individual access point.

Thus, the costs of lobbying any one policymaker declines with an increase in the number of access points, but depending on the policymaking process, the number of policymakers that need to be lobbied might also increase with an increase in the number of access points. However, even in this circumstance, the total costs of lobbying will usually decrease as the number of access points increases. To demonstrate this effect, I employ the following stylized policymaking process: Assume that policy is made in a single legislative chamber where each policymaker has an independent vote (thus, all policymakers are access points) and a majority (or $N/2 + 1$) of votes is needed to pass policy. If we further assume that a policymaker will only vote in the way an interest group desires if she is lobbied by that group, then the total costs of lobbying will be a function of both the number of policymakers and the average cost of lobbying each policymaker. Thus, an interest group will only lobby if

$$B - \left(\frac{N}{2} + 1\right) * \left(\frac{\kappa}{N}\right) > 0. \tag{2a}$$

The first parenthetical term is the number of policymakers needed to lobby to secure a bare majority vote of one-half-plus-one, and the second parenthetical term is the cost of lobbying each policymaker, which is a declining function of the number of access points as described above. By rearranging the terms of this inequality, we can see that the total costs of lobbying are also a declining function of the number of access points, as follows:

$$B - \left(\frac{\kappa}{2} + \frac{\kappa}{N}\right) > 0. \tag{2b}$$

The first part of the parenthetical is constant, but the second part declines with N, so that the total costs decline as the number of access points increases. Loosely speaking, while the cost of buying the "one-half" stays constant as the cheaper individual access points are canceled out by the increasing number that need to be lobbied, the cost of buying the "plus-one" in the "one-half-plus-one" needed to secure a majority vote declines as the number of access points increases. Therefore, increasing the number of access points lowers the total cost of lobbying, which increases the number of individuals who will find that the benefits of lobbying outweigh the costs, which will increase the amount of lobbying.

ACCESS POINTS AND POLICY COMPLEXITY

What effect will this increased amount of lobbying have? First, increased lobbying will increase the complexity of policy because more lobbying is likely to lead to the inclusion of more special provisions within policy benefitting the groups lobbying. In the model described above, it was assumed that all individuals were equally efficient and effective at lobbying; that is, they all had the same κ. This, however, is not going to be true in practice: different individuals will be more or less efficient at lobbying for various reasons and will, thus, have lower or higher κ's as a result. For instance, wealthier individuals might have lower κ's because the financial costs of lobbying are relatively less onerous to them. Well-connected individuals should have lower κ's as well since the access points they are connected to should be predisposed to grant them access (they will be provided a discount price because of prior relationships). In addition, individuals who are part of an established interest group, which has already paid the start-up costs of establishing a lobbying organization and building a network with policymakers, should be more efficient than individuals who are lobbying on an ad hoc basis. But, as will be discussed in more detail below, different interest groups should also vary in their lobbying efficiency based upon a number of factors, including how easy it is to attract members and raise funds from them. From these considerations, it follows that different individuals and interests will have different κ's: those that have the lowest κ's are the most likely to lobby and, therefore, the most likely to influence policy in the direction they want.

There will, therefore, be a distribution of κ's, and increasing N will progressively lead to individuals with a higher κ finding it newly beneficial to lobby. Each individual will ask for policy that benefits him: if policy can be narrowly tailored then this is likely to lead to a higher number of specific provisions being entered into the policy which will lead to increased complexity.[6] Trade policy provides a good illustration of this point as it is easy to narrowly tailor trade policy to benefit specific industries. For instance, one can have a high tariff rate (a tax on imports) on one product, such as automobiles, but have a low tariff rate on another product, such as computers. Import-competing industries will desire higher tariff rates on the products they produce while industries that use imported raw material will desire lower tariff rates on the products they import. The more access points there are, the cheaper lobbying will be, so that an increased number of industries will find it beneficial to lobby for their preferred tariff rate. If these preferred rates differ between industries, then the more industries that are lobbying, the more complicated trade policy will be. If few industries are lobbying, then there will be a simpler, more uniform trade policy where every product receives similar (or even identical) tariff rates.

ACCESS POINTS, LOBBYING ADVANTAGES, AND POLICY BIAS

The second effect of increased lobbying is that it should lead to increased policy bias if one side of the policy debate has a lobbying advantage. As described above, different individuals will have different κ's as they will be more or less efficient at lobbying. If these κ's are randomly distributed across both sides of the policy debate, then policy will be more complex, but the special provisions will cancel out in the aggregate and it will not be more biased. However, if one side of a policy debate has an inherent advantage in lobbying, that is, if one side has systematically lower κ's than the other, than this side will have lower lobbying costs and will lobby more and will be able to move policy in its direction and thereby increase the policy's bias. Under plausible assumptions described below, increasing the number of access points and, thus, lowering the costs of lobbying will magnify this difference in lobbying between the two sides and will serve to increase the bias in policy toward the advantaged side. What might cause one side to have an inherent and systematic lobbying advantage over the other side? As stated above, having an existing and organized interest group would provide an advantage over not having one and having an efficient group able to raise large sums of money would provide an advantage over having an inefficient one. There are a number of reasons

---

6. Not all policies may be able to be narrowly tailored. In these cases, the number of access points will have no effect on policy complexity.

why one side of a policy issue will have a greater probability of being organized and more efficient in their organization.

Collective Action Theory provides one particularly interesting explanation for which groups will have an inherent lobbying advantage, and this theory will be used in this book to determine issue areas where policy bias is likely to increase with the number of access points.[7] Olson (1971) described lobbying as a public good: if lobbying is successful in creating a policy beneficial to a particular group, everyone in that group will benefit from the policy regardless of whether they contribute to the provision of the public good, that is, gave money or time to the lobbying effort. This creates an incentive to free ride on the efforts of others and, therefore, underprovision of the public good or, if everyone is trying to free ride on everyone else, non-provision of the public good. There are ways to overcome this collective action problem, the two most pertinent being that small groups and groups that have concentrated costs or benefits from the policy area are more likely to overcome the collective action problem and form effective lobbies. Small groups can better monitor the behavior of their members to see if they are free riding and, potentially, sanction any member who does so. Concentrated benefits (or costs) are more likely to create situations where some member or subgroup of members is willing to provide the public good even if everyone else free rides, a situation known as a "privileged group." Thus, small groups with concentrated benefits (or costs) will be better able to overcome the collective action problem than large groups with diffused benefits (or costs). When one side of a policy debate is better able than the other side to overcome the collective action problem in this way, I refer to this as one side having a collective action advantage over the other side; that is, they have an inherent lobbying advantage derived from their ability to overcome the collective action problem.

Trade policy serves as a perfect example to briefly illustrate why one side might have such an advantage. Collective Action Theory has been frequently applied to trade policy and is, in fact, one of the most prominent explanations for the existence of trade protection despite the economic efficiency created by free trade. Endogenous Tariff Theory, particularly as described in Magee, Brock, and Young (1989) and Grossman and Helpman (2002), argues that the benefits of protection are increased profits and employment in protected industries while the costs of protection are

---

7. The conclusion will discuss additional potential sources of lobbying advantages, including resource disparities, and discuss additional issue areas to which Access Point Theory could be applied as a result.

higher consumer prices. Since consumers are a very large group and the costs are dispersed across all of them, such that it is unlikely any one or small group of them will be willing to pay the full costs of lobbying, we would expect very little consumer lobbying against protection. Producers, on the other hand, are often small groups, and the benefits of protection are often concentrated quite highly on a small number of firms, thus making it much more likely that producer groups will lobby for protection. Career-minded policymakers will, therefore, craft policy to cater to the interest groups that offer them campaign contributions which will result in protection even though the country as a whole would benefit from free trade. Thus, tariffs emerge endogenously from the political system.[8] As can be seen, Endogenous Tariff Theory postulates that protectionists enjoy a collective action advantage over free traders.

In terms of the model presented above, having a collective action advantage means that an organization is more efficient in lobbying and, therefore, has a lower κ. As a result, at any given benefit of lobbying, more organizations on the advantaged side will lobby than on the disadvantaged side. As costs of lobbying are further lowered by increasing the number of access points, more of the advantaged side will find it newly beneficial to lobby. This can be seen graphically in figure 2.2, which is an illustration of how lobbying costs and number of groups lobbying are related. The vertical axis represents the number of interest groups that find it beneficial to lobby and the horizontal axis represents the number of access points in the system. The two curves represent the distribution of interest groups on the two sides of a given issue; the curve toward the left is the side with the lobbying advantage, as they will lobby more at higher costs, while the curve on the right is the disadvantaged side. The curves here assume a normal distribution of cost-to-benefit ratios within the two sides and assume that there are equal numbers on the two sides. Both of these assumptions are made for ease of presentation and are not crucial to the result as will be discussed below.

The vertical difference between the curves represents the additional lobbying by the advantaged side. As the number of access points increases, and the costs of lobbying go down, the amount of lobbying by both sides will increase but, at least at low numbers of access points, the gap between the two sides also increases. For instance, the left-most vertical line represents a small number of access points: here, very few advantaged groups

---

8. Chapter 3 will describe this theory in more detail, including the fact that there are free-trade interests that can overcome the collective action problem, such as firms that import raw materials.

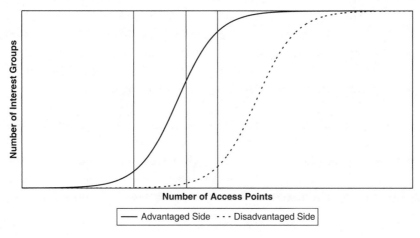

Figure 2.2
The Distribution of Lobbying Costs and Lobbying Activity

lobby, but almost no disadvantaged groups find it beneficial to lobby, giving the advantaged side only slightly more lobbying, which should lead to policy biased slightly in their direction. Increasing the number of access points to a higher number, as depicted in the middle vertical line, does result in more disadvantaged groups finding it beneficial to lobby, but it also results in even more advantaged groups finding it beneficial, thus increasing the gap in lobbying and, therefore, the bias in policy.

At a high enough number of access points, here depicted with the right-most line, the disadvantaged groups will begin to catch up to the advantaged groups and reduce the bias in policy, but this is only after nearly all the advantaged groups are lobbying, and Access Point Theory assumes this point is never reached in practice.

The location of where the disadvantaged size starts to catch up will be influenced by the size and shape of the two curves. If the disadvantaged side, for instance, more quickly reacts to changes in the cost of lobbying (i.e., the slope of their distribution is steeper), then they will start catching up at a lower number of access points as will also be the case if the disadvantaged side is numerically larger. Regardless of the location of this point, increasing the number of access points will lead to more bias as long as we are to the left of this point. How realistic is the assumption that the costs of lobbying are to the left of this point? Systems with a large number of access points, like the United States, still have expensive lobbying, and dispersed interests such as consumers are only loosely organized at best, which suggests that the assumption is plausible. Further, chapter 3 will present direct evidence that demonstrates that a reduction in the number of access points for trade policy in the United States in the 1930s did lead to a reduction in the amount of protectionist lobbying relative to free-trade lobbying, as expected by the theory given this assumption. If this assumption were not met, then we would expect there to be a tipping point at which the number of access points stops increasing the amount of policy bias and instead starts to reduce the amount of policy bias. Since the evidence suggests that the practical institutional environments around the world reside to the left of the third line in figure 2.2, increasing the number of access points thus increases the net amount of lobbying for the advantaged side, which should enable the advantaged side to increase policy bias in their direction.

ACCESS POINT THEORY WITH DIFFERENT POLICYMAKING PROCESSES

The effect of access points on the costs of lobbying developed above depended upon a stylized policymaking process. In practice, policy is not typically set by a pure majority vote among equally powerful policymakers. This section will demonstrate that the results of Access Point Theory do not depend upon the simplifying assumptions about the policymaking process made above. In particular, this section will show that the results are robust to such changes as different voting processes, internal lobbying by policymakers, differences in power between access points, and separation of powers. In fact, some of these modifications actually magnify the effect of access points.

The first assumption that I examine is that of the voting process: the effect of the number of access points is not dependent on a majority vote process. The most straightforward extension is to a supermajority requirement. Instead of needing $N/2 + 1$ policymakers, as would be required in a majority vote, suppose instead that policy needs $2N/3 + 1$, or a two-thirds supermajority, to pass, as is the case, for instance, for treaties in the U.S. Senate and amendments to India's constitution. In that case, individuals will only contribute to lobbying if

$$B - \left(\frac{2*N}{3} + 1\right) * \left(\frac{\kappa}{N}\right) > 0. \tag{3a}$$

The first parenthetical term is the two-thirds-plus-one of the policymakers needed to be lobbied, and the second parenthetical term, as above, is the average cost of lobbying each policymaker. Rearranging terms demonstrates that individuals will contribute to lobbying if

$$B - \left(\frac{2*\kappa}{3} + \frac{\kappa}{N} \right) > 0. \tag{3b}$$

As in the majority vote scenario, the second term declines with N and, thus, so too do the total costs of lobbying, although the amount that the costs decline with each additional access point will be relatively smaller than it is in the majority vote scenario.

Another plausible policymaking scenario is a logroll whereby policymakers trade support for policies they desire for promises to support other policymakers' policies. It is quite common to describe trade policy, particularly U.S. trade policy in the nineteenth and early twentieth centuries as being set by a logroll, going back at least to Schattschneider (1935). Budgetary policy, particularly pork barrel politics, is also often described as a logroll. In a functional logroll arrangement, an individual only needs one policymaker to support their policy in order to get it enacted. In trade policy terms, an industry would only need to find one policymaker willing to support a tariff on their product; that policymaker will then promise other policymakers to vote for their preferred tariff on their products and the tariff will pass. As a result, an individual will contribute to lobbying if

$$B - \left(\frac{\kappa}{N} \right) > 0. \tag{4a}$$

The parenthetical term is the cost of lobbying the single policymaker whom an individual needs to convince to pass policy. Obviously, this cost declines with N; in fact, the effect of access points is much greater in a logroll scenario than in a majority vote scenario, and anytime policy is set by a logroll, then we might expect the effects of access points on complexity and bias to be greatly magnified.

The only plausible voting process where access points will not have an effect is if unanimity is required. In this case, an interest group will need to lobby all N access points, each costing an average of κ/N, to pass policy. Thus, interest groups will only lobby when

$$B - (N) * \left(\frac{\kappa}{N} \right) > 0. \tag{5a}$$

Multiplying out the parenthetical terms yields the following:

$$B - \kappa > 0, \tag{5b}$$

which is invariant to the number of access points; that is, the costs do not decline with the number of access points, although neither do they increase. In a pure unanimity system, the number of access points has no effect on the costs of lobbying. However, if some fixed number of policymakers are likely to support a policy even without lobbying or if one policymaker, once lobbied and convinced, lobbies other policymakers, then even in a unanimity system, increasing the number of access points can reduce the costs of lobbying. This leads us to the second assumption to be relaxed.

The policymaking process described so far has assumed that policymakers will only support a policy if an interest group that wants the policymakers to support the policy lobbies them. This is unlikely to be true in practice, though. First, some policymakers may be predisposed toward a policy and will vote for it regardless, although the converse is also true that some policymakers may be so predisposed against a policy that no amount of lobbying can get them to support a policy. This suggests that κ may not only vary by individual but also vary by access point. Individuals will seek out the cheapest coalition of access points necessary to pass policy by lobbying those who are already most receptive to the individual's preferred policy. However, if a policy is so unpopular that there exists more than $N/2$ (if the voting rule is majority) who will oppose the policy no matter how much they are lobbied, then increasing the number of access points will have no effect on policy bias.

Second, and more important, policymakers can be influenced to vote for a policy not only from outside interest group pressure but also by "inside lobbying," or one policymaker attempting to convince another policymaker to support their preferred policy. Once a policymaker supports a policy enough, it becomes in her own interest to get that policy passed, and she might be willing to persuade her fellow policymakers to also support that policy.[9] Also, on some issues certain policymakers command the respect and attention of their fellows such that other policymakers might show deference to this policymaker and support their preferred policy. Finally, policymakers can make cross-issue linkages and trade support on one policy for support on another to pass desired policy. Any such inside lobbying or deference or linkages would make policymaking begin to resemble a logroll, even if it is not a complete logroll where only one policymaker is needed.[10] As shown above, the effects of the number of access points are

---

9. As discussed above, the literature on U.S. lobbying often focuses on how interest groups lobby to "activate" their supporters rather than to convince fence-sitters. This activation is likely to produce the "inside lobbying" described here.

10. In fact, it is exactly these sorts of processes, if rampant enough, which create and sustain a complete logroll.

magnified in logrolls. Thus, the more inside lobbying, deference, and linkages that exist, the more important the number of access points will be.

The third assumption to be relaxed is that of a policy being set by a single house of a legislature. Although this does describe some institutional systems, many countries have a separation of power system where they have two legislative chambers or a separate legislature and executive or both, and each of these legislative or executive bodies needs to support the policy for it to pass. First, assume that there are two legislative houses, each of which must approve a policy for it to pass and each of which sets policy by majority vote. In this case, an individual will contribute to lobbying if

$$B - \left(\frac{N'}{2} + 1\right) * \left(\frac{\kappa}{N'}\right) - \left(\frac{N''}{2} + 1\right) * \left(\frac{\kappa}{N''}\right) > 0. \tag{6}$$

The first set of parentheticals is the cost of lobbying the first house and the second set the cost of lobbying the second house with N' and N'' the number of legislators in either house. Increasing either N' or N'' will lower the costs of lobbying that house and, thus, the total costs of lobbying.

Second, assume that policy is set by a legislature deciding by majority vote and an executive who can veto the legislature and cannot be overturned. The executive here is a single access point that must be purchased and whose price will be $N*(\kappa_e/N)$ where κ_e is the price the executive would charge that individual for access (determined both by the efficiency of the individual and the receptivity of the executive to that interest) and N equals 1 because there is only one executive. Thus, the price of the executive reduces to κ_e and, in this scenario, an individual will contribute to lobbying if

$$B - \kappa_e - \left(\frac{N}{2} + 1\right) * \left(\frac{\kappa}{N}\right) > 0. \tag{7}$$

The parenthetical terms are, as above, the costs of lobbying the legislature, and κ_e is the cost of lobbying the executive. The cost κ_e does not change as N changes, but the costs of lobbying the legislature still decline with N and, thus, so, too, do the total costs of lobbying. Thus, in both the cases of bicameralism and separation of powers, the total costs of lobbying still decline as the number of access points increases.[11]

---

11. Systems like the United States combine both bicameralism and a separate executive, but combining these two features does not change the results. Allowing for legislative override of an executive veto would increase the importance of access

Finally, I relax the assumption that all access points have equal power. The theory as constructed assumes that a policymaker either has power in an issue area or does not have power. Relevance is, thus, a simple on-off switch. In practice, some policymakers are more powerful than others: their vote matters more. This can be because of institutional rules, like those described above: the President has more power than a single legislator because his vote is essential while any, for instance, 51 out of 100 Senators will do. In addition, organizational structure within the legislature can matter, as party leaders and committee chairs may have the ability to shape the agenda or structure debate that make them more important lobbying targets than a typical backbencher. This can also be because of inside-lobbying or deference situations described above, as someone who can bring along additional votes might be more important than someone who cannot.

These more powerful access points can demand a higher access price than less powerful access points. However, this does not alter the dynamic that increasing the number of access points will decrease the total cost of lobbying. As shown above in the separation of powers example, increasing the number of access points in the legislature may not reduce the price that the (more powerful) executive can charge, but it does reduce the cost of lobbying the legislature and, thus, the total costs of lobbying as there is no reason the executive should be able to increase his price in response to the larger legislature. Further, within the legislature where power may be unequal between legislators, the more powerful legislators can certainly charge more than less powerful legislators, but increasing the number of legislators will still create more competition for interest group dollars which will decrease the average cost of access. Thus, differences in power should not affect the basic access point dynamic.

However, let us examine in more detail one interesting situation that we will be returning to later in the book: the possibility that the relative power between access points can be changed by the access points themselves, in particular by delegating increased power to the executive. Because of the President's power, and because he can set a monopoly price for the crucial executive vote, κ_e will, on average, be higher than κ. For certain interests that the President is especially receptive to, κ_e may, in fact, be lower than κ, but this is the exception as most of the time, the ability of the President to charge a higher price than any one legislator

points by increasing the power of the legislature over the executive. As described below, any increase in power to a body with more access points relative to a body with less access points will lower total costs.

will cause κ_e to be higher than κ. Given this, for any N greater than 2, κ_e will also be higher than $(\kappa/2 + \kappa/N)$, which is the total cost of lobbying a legislature as described in equation (2b) above. Thus, all else equal, successfully lobbying the executive is more expensive than successfully lobbying the legislature.

However, so far I have assumed that the legislature, as a whole, and the executive are equally powerful. This need not be the case. For instance, if the legislature can override the executive veto with a supermajority vote, this will make the executive less important as an interest group can still win passage of its preferred policy with the executive opposed as long as it is willing to spend enough to gain the support of enough legislators. In this circumstance, shifting power back to the legislature will force the executive to reduce his access price if he wishes to receive lobbying dollars and will, thus, reduce the costs of lobbying. On the other hand, the executive can be even more powerful if he can shape policy in the implementation and enforcement stages of policymaking. The legislature can also explicitly delegate powers to the executive as has been done in trade policymaking in the United States in the twentieth century, where the President negotiates tariff rates with other countries and Congress, typically, only has the ability to vote up or down on the final rates without being able to influence them, as will be discussed in greater detail in chapter 3. Anything that increases the power of the executive relative to the legislature will enable the executive to further raise his access price and will, therefore, increase the costs of lobbying. Finally, though, if we fix the relative level of power between the two branches, any increase in the number of access points will continue to lead to a reduction in the total costs of lobbying, though this effect will be greater the more relative power the legislature has.

MEASURING ACCESS POINTS

The two fundamental hypotheses of Access Point Theory that will be tested in the empirical sections of the book are that increasing the number of access points increases the amount of policy bias and policy complexity. In order to test these hypotheses, we need to be able to determine the number of access points in different countries at different points in time. This chapter outlines two different strategies for measuring access points. First, I discuss how different institutional features, such as federalism and the number of parties, map onto the number of access points by describing how they affect the relevance, distinctiveness, or independence of policymakers. Thus, I develop hypotheses about how the number of parties in government and other institutional features affect the number of access points and, therefore, the amount of bias and complexity. This is the preferred measurement technique and, where possible, the empirical chapters that follow will include each of these features as separate independent variables. However, there will be times when the researcher needs one value to summarize the number of access points in a country. For instance, if we only have cross-section and not time-series data, as will be the case in the bank regulation chapter in this book, then the sample size will be too small to include multiple different institutional variables. In addition, if we have conditional hypotheses, that is, if the number of access points interacts with some demand side variable, then we would want a single measure so that we would not have to interact many different variables with the demand-side variable, which would make interpreting the results difficult. Thus, the end of this section describes a simple strategy to summarize the number of access points in a country. The appendix to this chapter describes the datasets used in the empirical chapters and how the access point variables are measured.

As defined above, an access point is any relevant policymaker who is susceptible to lobbying and who is either distinct or independent. This provides four features that can be affected by institutions to determine the number of access points: susceptibility, relevance, distinctiveness, and independence. The empirical investigations in this book focus on variation in the last three features and, thus, the six parts of this section of the chapter discuss six different institutions that affect these features.[12]

Electoral Districts

To start, the more distinctive policymakers there are, the more access points there will likely be, holding constant the number of relevant or independent policymakers. Thus, any institution that increases the number of distinctive policymakers will also increase the number of access points. The most obvious way for a policymaker to be distinct is if she represents a separate geographic constituency from another policymaker. In other words, each legislative district that represents a different geographic area creates another potential access point.

---

12. The hypotheses will provide only brief descriptions of the institutions and the larger literatures that frequently surround these institutions. Lijphart (1999) provides an excellent overview on most of these institutional features.

If we, for instance, have 100 policymakers, 20 of whom are independent and none of whom are distinct from each other (because they are elected from a single national district), then we will have 20 access points. If we create 1 distinct policymaker (perhaps by electing one policymaker from a separate district representing a different part of the country than the other 99), then this will either have no effect on the number of access points, if that policymaker was already independent, or increase the number of access points to 21, if that policymaker was previously dependent. Electing all 100 policymakers from separate geographical districts, on the other hand, increases the number of access points to 100. Therefore, holding constant the number of relevant and independent policymakers, increasing the number of distinct policymakers will usually increase the number of access points although, under some circumstances, it will have no effect on the number of access points. It will never lead to fewer access points. Thus, a country that elects all legislators from a single national district, such as the Netherlands, will, on average, have fewer access points than countries that elect each of their legislators from separate, single-member districts, such as the United States and the United Kingdom. The more of these electoral districts a country has, the more access points there will be, all else equal. Thus,

Hypothesis 1: The more electoral districts in a country, the more access points there will be and the more biased and complex policy will be.

Party Discipline

Another of the dimensions that determines the number of access points is the level of independence or dependence of policymakers. Holding constant the number of policymakers and, specifically, members of the legislature, the more dependent these legislators are on their party leaders, the fewer access points there will be. Thus, the more party discipline there is the fewer access points there will be. In some systems, backbenchers are forced by rule to vote as instructed by their party leader; in these systems, the backbenchers will not be access points unless they are distinct. In other systems, backbenchers are technically free to vote how they wish, but party leaders have strong tools to force compliance. Frequently, this compliance is forced by the ability of party leaders to remove rebel backbenchers from the ballot or otherwise significantly affect their chances for reelection. In these systems, too, backbenchers will not be access points unless they are distinct. In still other systems, while the party may have some ability to encourage discipline, this power is relatively weak and backbenchers are generally free to vote as they wish. Here, backbenchers will count as access points whether or not they are distinct. Thus,

Hypothesis 2: *The less party discipline there is, the more access points there will be and the more biased and complex policy will be.*

Number of Parties

The third dimension that determines the number of access points is the number of relevant policymakers. In many systems, only parties that are in government have any power, meaning that only these governmental parties are relevant. In parliamentary systems with strong party discipline, for instance, parties that are out of the government have no influence on current policy. Even in systems with weaker party discipline or minority governments, parties in the government will have more power and thus be more important lobbying targets than parties out of the government. Each party, therefore, represents another set of relevant actors and, ceteris paribus, more access points. Thus,

Hypothesis 3: *The more parties there are in government, the more access points there will be and the more biased and complex policy will be.*

Federalism

Federal systems also increase the number of relevant policymakers. In a federal system, significant powers are vested at the subnational levels of government. In those policy areas where such powers are granted, this creates additional relevant policymakers. This increase in the number of relevant policymakers occurs for two reasons. First, federalism is often accompanied by bicameralism, where a second legislative house representing states or provinces has significant powers distinct from the popular lower house of government. This bicameralism will create new relevant and distinct policymakers, adding to the number of access points. Second, federalism often directly empowers subnational leaders, such as state governors, although this will typically vary by policy area, where subnational leaders might have significant power in some areas like education and taxation and none in other areas like foreign policy. When federalism is accompanied by bicameralism, it will always increase the number of relevant policy makers; when federalism empowers subnational leaders, it will increase the number of relevant policymakers in those areas where federalism grants power to lower levels of government. Thus,

Hypothesis 4:   Federalism increases the number of access points and the amount of policy bias and complexity.

Presidentialism

Another institutional feature discussed above, Presidentialism, has unclear effects on the number of access points. A presidential system has an executive elected separately from the legislature that possesses policy-making power. The President is, thus, relevant (at least on some policy areas) and independent (and typically distinct.) Therefore, the President is an access point above and beyond the legislative access points in a way that is different from a Prime Minister in a parliamentary system who would likely be an access point as a legislator even if he or she were not the Prime Minister. On its face, presidential systems, therefore, add an additional access point to the system and should, therefore, have more policy bias and complexity. However, presidential systems typically delegate significant power to the President from the legislature. This delegation reduces the relative power of the many-access-point legislature and increases the relative power of the one-access-point executive and, thus, decreases the number of access points. If Presidentialism is accompanied by delegation, then

Hypothesis 5:   Presidentialism reduces the number of access points and the amount of policy bias and complexity.

Proportional Representation

The previous hypotheses have all concerned institutional features frequently discussed in the literatures on democratic institutions. Not all of the institutions that have often preoccupied prior research will affect the number of access points, though. Most prominently, proportional representation (PR) will have no independent effect on the number of access points. A long and rich literature has explored the benefits and drawbacks of PR over plurality systems, as discussed in Lijphart (1999) and Monroe (1994). One of the findings of this literature is that PR tends to be associated with many of the institutional features already described. For instance, PR systems, by design, must have multi-member districts while plurality systems are frequently single-member district systems; as a result, PR systems tend to have fewer electoral districts. In addition, Duverger's Law (Cox 1997) argues that single-member simple plurality districts will tend to lead to two-party systems while other systems, including PR, will tend to lead to multiparty systems. Thus, PR systems will be more likely to have multiparty governments than, at least, a common form of plurality system. Finally, PR systems often have strong party discipline, especially closed list forms as described above. To the extent that PR encourages high party discipline, few electoral districts, and multiparty government, PR will influence the number of access points.

However, none of these features are inherent or exclusive to PR systems. Many plurality systems, such as the Westminster system used in Britain and many former British colonies, have extremely high levels of party discipline. Meanwhile, many of the PR systems in Latin America have low party discipline (Carey 2003). PR systems also do not necessarily have fewer electoral districts than plurality systems. Within the sample used in this book, New Zealand, as a plurality country, had fewer electoral districts than France did when it was a PR country. Finally, it is not uncommon for PR countries to have single-party governments, particularly minority governments. Denmark, Norway, Spain, and Sweden, among others, are frequently single party. Plurality systems also often have more than one party in government: the United States in periods of divided government, the coalition between the Liberal and National parties in Australia, and the (large) multiparty coalitions that frequently form in France when it is governed by the two-ballot majority system.

Thus, one cannot argue that PR systems automatically have these access-point-related features and, therefore, automatically have either more or fewer access points than plurality systems. Once one controls for party discipline, electoral districts, and number of parties, as the empirical sections of this book do, the only remaining feature that distinguishes a PR system from plurality systems is that the latter leads to more disproportional electoral outcomes than the former; that is, the disparity between votes received and seats won will be greater in plurality than in PR systems. Proportionality, though important in many contexts, does not affect any of the dimensions determining the number of access points. Therefore,

Hypothesis 6:   *All else equal, PR and plurality do not have different numbers of access points or different levels of policy bias and complexity.*

As stated above, the preferred testing strategy in the empirical sections of this book is to test each of the hypotheses listed above by simultaneously including variables measuring each of the six institutions described above. Thus, support for the theory is demonstrated by how many of the hypotheses are confirmed in each analysis. This is the preferred strategy over creating a single summary measure of the number of access points for a number of reasons. First, the summary measure could be significant if there is a strong positive relationship between a few of the institutions and bias or complexity and no relationship between the other institutions and bias or complexity. It is stronger evidence for Access Point Theory if all or most of the coefficients are significant in the expected direction than if, for instance, number of parties and Presidentialism are strongly significant in the expected direction and the other institutions insignificant. The summary measure cannot capture this distinction.

Second, there is no straightforward, theoretically based way to combine the different institutional features into a single measure of access points. Delegation to the President, for instance, reduces the effective number of access points, but by exactly how much? On average, increasing the number of electoral districts increases the number of access points, but if party discipline is strong and the additional districts are noncompetitive, then do they provide additional avenues of access to party leaders? Answering questions like these would require detailed knowledge of every case in the dataset, a task beyond the capabilities of large-N quantitative work. Further, variables like number of electoral districts, number of governing parties, and party discipline interact in complicated ways: we know that holding the other two constant, each will have an independent effect on bias or complexity, which is what the regression analyses model, but they actually covary with each other. Creating a single measure combining them based on these theoretical covariations would be exceedingly difficult.

However, there will be times when it is necessary to employ a single measure of access points rather than all six institutional measures. For instance, if one has a sample size that is small, then using multiple institutional variables will use up too many degrees of freedom. In cases like this, insignificant results could be because access points do not matter or because the tests lack sufficient statistical power because of the small sample size. In these cases, a single summary measure will be preferable. This will be true in a number of the empirical tests conducted in this book, in particular when we do not have time-series data for the dependent variable and are simply measuring a single cross section, leading to sample size of fewer than 40 cases.

A second reason, not explored empirically in this book but discussed in more detail in the Conclusion, would be if one wishes to interact the number of access points with other variables. For instance, Access Point Theory predicts that the more access points there are, the more the lobbying advantage of one side will be magnified. If we could precisely measure how much one side of a debate is advantaged over the other side, this would imply an interactive hypothesis: the larger the initial advantage, the more access points will matter.[13] In addition, the number of access points might matter more when the status quo is easy to change and matter less when the status quo is harder to change; thus, one might wish to interact the number of access points and the number of veto players. To test these interactive hypotheses, once could interact every institutional variable with the conditioning variable, but this would yield a cumbersome and difficult-to-interpret model. Instead, it might be preferable to interact a single access point variable, yielding an easier-to-interpret model.

In order to test Access Point Theory in cases of small sample sizes or interactive hypotheses, one needs a summary measure. However, as described above, there is no straightforward, theoretically informed way to create such a measure. As an alternative, I describe here how to construct a simple empirical measure that, while not perfect, is more than sufficient for the purposes at hand. I assume that each of the five institutions expected to affect the number of access points is equally important in determining the total number of access points and, therefore, construct a simple additive index of the number of parties, number of electoral districts, number of seats in the federal house, (lack of) party discipline, and parliamentarism. Because these variables are measured on different scales, though, I standardize each of them first by dividing each observation of each variable by the standard deviation of that variable. This measure, thus, will assign the highest number of access points to countries that score high on all five of the above variables and the lowest number to those that score low on all variables. Scoring extremely high (or low) on any one or two variables can lead to fairly high (or low) levels of the total number of access points. Having moderate scores on all the variables will lead to an average number of total access points.

---

13. See Ehrlich (2009b) for a preliminary analysis of such hypotheses in the context of European Union trade policy.

CONCLUSION

This chapter defined the concept of access points and then demonstrated how increasing the number of access points leads to cheaper lobbying and when and how this cheaper lobbying leads to more complex and more biased policy outcomes using a stylized policymaking process. Then, the chapter relaxed some of the assumptions of the stylized policymaking process and demonstrated that under more realistic policymaking processes, the number of access points still leads to cheaper lobbying. The fundamental hypotheses of Access Point Theory are, thus, as follows:

1. The more access points there are, the cheaper lobbying should be.
2. The more access points there are, the more lobbying there should be.
3. The more access points there are, the more complex policy should be.
4. The more access points there are, the more biased policy should be if one side has a lobbying advantage.

The chapter concluded by discussing how common institutional features influence the number of access points and, thus, derived testable hypotheses. We are now ready to empirically test these hypotheses, starting in part II by examining how the number of access points influences the level of bias in, consecutively, trade policy, environmental policy, and banking regulations. Then, in part III, we will examine how the number of access points influences complexity in both trade and tax policy.

APPENDIX TO CHAPTER 2
Measuring Access Points

This appendix serves two purposes: explaining how each of the hypotheses discussed in chapter 2 can be tested empirically by describing the measurement of the variables and introducing the two datasets—one encompassing the advanced industrial democracies that are members of the Organization for Economic Cooperation and Development (OECD) and one encompassing all democracies—used in the empirical tests. I begin with this second task.

THE DATASETS

The first dataset is the preferred dataset used to test Access Point Theory in this book as there is more temporal coverage and more reliable measurement of both the political and economic variables. This dataset is based upon the data provided in Franzese (2002b) and covers the 21 main members of the OECD[1] and the years 1948 to 1998.[2] This dataset provides

---

1. The 21 countries are Australia, Austria, Belgium, Canada, Denmark, Finland, France, Germany, Greece, Ireland, Italy, Japan, New Zealand, the Netherlands, Norway, Portugal, Spain, Sweden, Switzerland, the United Kingdom, and the United States. Greece, Portugal, and Spain only entered the dataset after they became democracies. The OECD also includes a handful of smaller countries, like Luxembourg, but not all data are available for these countries. Between 1994 and 2000, the OECD expanded to include a number of less-developed or more recently developed countries, like Eastern European countries, South Korea, and Mexico. Because of the temporal limitations on the sample, these countries are not included. Except where noted , all variables used in the OECD analyses are from Franzese (2002b).

2. The Franzese (2002b) dataset ends in 1998. Because of changes in measurement and collection techniques by the sources underlying the economic data used by

Table 2.1 SUMMARY STATISTICS FOR ACCESS POINT VARIABLE

Variable	OECD Dataset				All-Democracy Dataset			
	Mean	Standard Deviation	Minimum	Maximum	Mean	Standard Deviation	Minimum	Maximum
Electoral Districts	107.01	174.9	1	659	43.77	166.365	1	658
Pool	0.648	0.828	0	2	0.868	0.899	0	2
Number of Parties	2.101	1.29	1	8.677	1.936	1.353	1	14
Bicameralism	17.639	34.37	0	105	0.304	0.46	0	1
Presidential	0.127	0.333	0	1	0.255	0.436	0	1
PR	0.723	0.448	0	1	0.665	0.472	0	1
Access Point Index	-0.01	2.225	-4.839	6.532	0.515	2.25	-3.246	6.953

a long time series for most of the developed democracies around the world and is the primary dataset used in the examinations of trade and environmental policy bias. However, in those analyses where the European Union member-states must be dropped (the trade complexity analysis) or where we have only one observation for each country (the banking regulation bias and tax policy complexity analyses), this dataset does not provide a large enough sample size to conduct rigorous analyses. Thus, in these sections, I turn to a second sample that includes all democracies as defined by Przeworski et al. (2000).[3] This dataset provides broader spatial coverage and includes many democracies in Latin America, a handful in Africa and Asia, the newer democracies in Eastern Europe, and some of the smaller European countries not included in the OECD analysis. However, the dataset only covers 1978 to 2000 because of limited availability of many of the political variables. In addition, some of the variables, as described below, are not as precisely measured as in the OECD dataset, and there are more concerns about the reliability of the economic data from the poorer countries in the dataset. Table 2.1 provides summary statistics for each of the institutional variables as well as the summary access point variable. The left side of the table lists the statistics for the OECD dataset and the right side for the all-democracy dataset.

ELECTORAL DISTRICTS

The measurement of the electoral districts variable is relatively straightforward, as all we need to determine is how many different geographic constituencies exist in a country's legislature. However, as will be the case for many of these variables, the measurement differs slightly between the two

Franzese (OECD and IMF sources as well as the Penn World Tables), it is difficult or impossible to update the dataset to include more recent years without losing the earlier years. There is no reason to believe that the relationship between access points and policymaking has changed in the most recent decade, and there is sufficient variation and sample size even with the data ending in 1998, so this should not be a concern for the analyses conducted here.

3. Przeworski et al. (2000) define democracy as follows: any country where both the executive and the legislature are elected, where there are multiple parties competing in the elections, and where there has been alternation in power between parties is coded as a democracy; any country that fails to meet any of these elements is coded as a dictatorship. The dataset used here includes only countries that were democracies for at least three consecutive years. This limitation is used since many of the variables are lagged in the analyses conducted below. Except where noted, all variables used in the all-democracy analyses are from Przeworski et al. (2000).

datasets. In the OECD dataset, electoral districts are measured by the number of electoral districts in the lower, or popular, house of the legislature. Thus, in the United States, where each of the 435 members of the House of Representatives is elected in her own district, there are 435 electoral districts. Conversely, in the Netherlands, where each of 150 members of the House of Representatives is elected from the same district, there is 1 electoral district. In countries, such as Germany, where there is a multilevel electoral system, I use the number of electoral districts at the level from which the final determination of legislative composition is made. For instance, in Germany, there are 299 geographically based single-member electoral districts to determine representatives for each district; however, there is also a single national electoral district where voters choose parties. Except in those cases where a party wins more single-member seats than it would be assigned from the national constituency, the final number of members for each party is determined by this list; that is, if a party wins 20% of the votes in the national district, it will receive 20% of the overall seats in the Bundestag even if it does not win even one single-member district. If the party does not win enough votes in the national district to receive any seats but does win a single-member district, it gets to keep that seat, or if it wins 10% of the votes in the national district but wins enough single-member districts that these seats alone account for more than 10%, it gets to keep the extra seats, although this is exceedingly unlikely for larger parties. Thus, for the major parties, it does not matter if candidate X wins or loses in constituency Y: they maintain the same number of seats as long as they maintain the same vote share at the national level. The major parties, therefore, do not need to target policy to win local elections, and the legislators are not distinct. As a result, in Germany, I consider there to be a single electoral district. This probably undercounts the number of distinct policymakers, as minor parties do gain their seats oftentimes through the single-member districts; however, this undercount is less severe than the overcount would be if I considered there to be 300 electoral districts (the 299 single-member districts plus the one national district) in Germany, and these minor parties rarely have much relevance anyway. Greece also currently has a multitiered electoral structure like this, and I treat Greece in a similar fashion.

The median number of electoral districts in the OECD dataset is 24, with a minimum of 1 (all the countries with a single national district) and a maximum of 658 (the United Kingdom from 1997 to 1999; it was 650 from 1987 to 1996). The mean is 107 with a standard deviation of over 175: clearly the data is skewed, with the handful of single-member simple plurality countries, such as the UK, United States, and Canada leading the mean to be much larger than the median. In these situations, one often takes the logarithm of the variable to eliminate the skew; this is also done when one believes that the marginal effect of a variable declines as the variable increases. However, there is no theoretical reason to do this here as each additional access point increases the supply of access and, once an oligopoly is broken, there is no reason to think the 500th access point is less important than the 50th. However, logging this variable (and bicameralism below) does not materially change most of the results presented in the analyses in the subsequent chapters.

In the all-democracy dataset, I estimate the number of electoral districts by dividing the number of members in the lower house by the average district magnitude, each provided by Przeworski et al. (2000). The median number of electoral districts in the all-democracy dataset is about 21 (Namibia from 1990 to 1993) with the minimum again being 1 and the maximum again being 658 in the United Kingdom. The mean is about 44, so the gap between the mean and the median is not quite as large as in the OECD sample and, thus, this sample is not quite as skewed. Finally, the standard deviation is quite large, at about 166.

PARTY DISCIPLINE

Party discipline is a notoriously difficult concept to measure as there are no comparable behavioral measures across time and space to precisely and accurately measure the amount of discipline in a country's party system in a panel design such as that used in this book.[4] As such, most researchers use electoral laws that encourage party discipline as a proxy measure for the amount of party discipline, an approach followed in this book. This book uses the measures created by Seddon Wallack et al. (2002),[5] which provides a dataset of electoral laws that influence whether elections are candidate-centered or party-centered. If elections are centered around individual candidates, this gives an incentive to legislators to distinguish themselves from the party or the ability to deviate from the party when they disagree. When elections are centered around parties, legislators have little incentive or ability to vote against the party as their voters will not reward them for their votes and their party could punish them for

---

4. See Bowler et al. (1999) for a detailed treatment of this problem.
5. The Seddon Wallack et al. data is a modified version of the Carey and Shugart (1995) data.

their disloyalty. Seddon Wallack et al. provide a number of different institutional variables that influence this distinction. This book uses their "Pool" variable, which measures "the extent to which a candidate can ride his party's reputation to electoral success" (8) by measuring how much votes for one candidate in a party influence the electoral chances of other candidates in the party, that is, how much votes "pool" across candidates. For instance, in systems where voters simply choose a party, as in closed-list PR systems where the party presents a list of candidates and the voter decides which list to support, then there is complete pooling: once the first candidate on the list receives enough votes to gain a seat, the remaining votes spill over to the next candidate on the list. On the other hand, in single-member districts, there is no pooling: votes for candidates in one district have no influence on votes for candidates of the same party in other districts. The more that votes pool across candidates, the less incentive candidates have to deviate from the party agenda and the more incentive they have to remain in the good standing of the party.

Seddon Wallack et al. also provide two additional measures: "Ballot" and "Vote." "Ballot" measures how much the party controls access to the ballot: if the party decides who runs in which district or where a candidate falls on a PR list, then this gives the party a weapon to use against disloyal party members. "Vote" measures whether voters vote for the party, for the candidate, or for both. Previous scholars using these data have also constructed various indexes, usually in an additive fashion, from these three variables,[6] although Seddon Wallack et al. advise against this since there is no theoretically informed way to do this and the correlations between the three measures are not as high as one normally sees when multiple measures all measure the same concept. If the analyses presented in later chapters use these indexes instead of Pool, or use Ballot, Vote, or all three instead of just Pool, the results are mostly the same and exceptions will be noted when the results are presented. The empirical analyses use the Pool variable because it not only captures the spillover effect of voting but also incorporates some of the elements of "Vote," in that party-list systems will also, by definition, have pooling. Thus, if one is to use only one of the variables, the Pool variable seems to capture more elements than the other two variables for institutional rules that could encourage party discipline.

The Pool variable ranges from 0 to 2 and when there is a single electoral method in a country, the variable simply takes a value of 0, 1, or 2. Countries score 0 when there is pooling at the party level, such as in list-PR systems.

---

6. See, for instance, Hallerberg and Marier (2004).

Countries score 1 when there is pooling at the sub-party level, such as the system in Colombia where each party presents multiple lists and votes pool within the lists but not across them; or in transferrable vote systems where voters choose to whom to transfer their vote if there are excess votes. Countries score 2 when there is no pooling, as in single-member districts and single nontransferable vote systems such as in Japan. When there are multiple electoral methods in the same house of the legislature (such as in Italy after 1994), the score is the weighted average of the different methods. In the OECD dataset, only Italy and Switzerland do not have integer values. After 1994 and before 2005, Italy had a mixed system where 475 representatives were elected in single-member districts and the other 155 in regional PR districts. Thus, 475 of 630 had a Pool score of 2 and 155 had a Pool score of 0, yielding an average Pool score of 1.507. In Switzerland, a list PR system is technically used in every district so that there should be a pooling score of 0 everywhere; however, 5 of the 200 members of the parliament are elected in single-member districts so that they have a pooling score of 2.[7] Thus, the weighted average pooling score is 0.05 in Switzerland. In addition to these two systems, about 54% of country-years have a pooling score of 0; about 18% have a pooling score of 1; and about 23% have a pooling score of 2. In the all-democracy sample, many more counties have multiple electoral rules in the same year, though over 90% of the country-years have integer values for pool, with about 45% having a score of 0, 11% having a score of 1, and 33% having a score of 2. The mean is 0.87 with a standard deviation of 0.9.

NUMBER OF PARTIES

The number of parties is measured by the raw number of parties in the government, regardless of the size of that party. Thus, in parliamentary systems, it is the number of parties that have representation as cabinet ministers. In presidential systems, the variable equals one if there is unified government between the President and the legislature and more than one if one or more parties other than the presidential party control a branch of the legislature. In the all-democracy dataset, the measure is the number of parties in government at the beginning of the calendar year. In the OECD dataset, the measure is the average number of parties

---

7. In a single member district, list-PR is functionally equivalent to plurality election: the list that gets the most votes win and, given that only one seat is assigned, each list contains the name of the one candidate who will take office if that list gets the most votes.

over the course of the year. Thus, if the composition of the government changed from 2 parties in the first half the year to 3 parties starting on July 1, then the measure would be 2.5 parties. If the government changed on October 1, it would be 2.25. In the OECD dataset, the minimum number of parties is 1 (for all single-party governments, which represent just over 40% of the sample), the median is 2, and the maximum is 6.5 (France in 1953). The mean is slightly over 2 with a standard deviation of 1.3. In the all-democracy dataset, the minimum and median is 1 (with about 54% of the sample having single-party governments), the maximum is 14 (India in 1996 and 1997), and the mean is just under 2 with a standard deviation of 1.4.

FEDERALISM

As stated in chapter 2, federalism has two different mechanisms by which the number of access points is increased: bicameralism and relevant subnational actors. There is a significant degree of correlation between these two measures, so that including both in the same regression analysis yields difficult-to-interpret results due to multicollinearity. In addition, there is much less data about subnational actors available for the all-democracy dataset.[8] As a result, the analyses below use bicameralism as a proxy for federalism. In the OECD dataset, I use the number of members in the upper house if that house meets the Tsebelis and Money (1997) definition of effective bicameralism: the two houses each must have substantive policy power and must be elected by different means. In the OECD dataset, five countries are bicameral: Australia (with 76 seats); Canada (105);[9] Germany (69); Switzerland (46); and the United States

---

8. For instance, Beck et al. (2001) provides a variable called "Author" which measures if subnational actors have authority in taxing, spending, or legislating, but it is only available for 38% of his sample. Henisz (2010) provides measures of both effective bicameralism and independent subnational governments, but the latter has 20% more missing data than the former.

9. The Senate in Canada is roughly equal in power to the House of Commons on paper (budget-related bills can only be introduced in the House), but in practice typically defers to the House. However, as opposed to the United Kingdom where both law and custom have largely stripped the House of Lords of any power beyond the ability to temporarily delay some legislation, the Canadian Senate still legally retains the ability to block any legislation they oppose and though they rarely exercise this power, they can and, in fact, have on numerous occasions throughout the sample, including votes against the Canadian-U.S. Free Trade Act in 1988 and abortion restrictions in 1990. As a result, while I code the United Kingdom as being unicameral, I code Canada as being bicameral.

(100). In the all-democracy dataset, I use a dummy variable that measures if a country is bicameral or not, using the L2 variable from Henisz's (2010) Political Constraint Database which similarly defines effective bicameralism.[10] In this dataset, 28% of the country-years are bicameral.

PRESIDENTIALISM

The empirical sections of this book use an indicator variable for Presidentialism. A country is coded as being presidential if it has an independently elected executive with policy power. In the all-democracy dataset, I utilize the Przeworski et al. coding of regime type, where they classify all democracies as parliamentary, mixed, or presidential.[11] In this dataset, 26% of the country-years are classified as presidential. In the OECD dataset, the United States, Finland, and France (under some institutional configurations) are classified as presidential, although the classification of the latter two cases is debatable. Finland has a very weak President who may not be relevant in many policy areas while France has a mixed system with both a President and Prime Minister. The results presented in the following chapters are, generally, not sensitive to coding Finland as parliamentary or coding France as either always parliamentary or parliamentary in periods of cohabitation,[12] although exceptions are noted when applicable.

PROPORTIONAL REPRESENTATION

PR is measured with a variable equal to 0 if the country uses a plurality system such as simple plurality or majority with runoff and equal to 1 if the country uses a proportional system. The variable was constructed by

---

10. None of the available sources provides number of seats for the upper house, though multiple sources provide different measures of whether an upper house exists.

11. The results do not depend upon whether mixed systems are classified as a 1 (for presidential) or a 0 (for not presidential) but in the analyses that follow, I code mixed systems as non-presidential.

12. Cohabitation is when the President and Prime Minister are of different parties. Huber (1996) and others have argued that when this is the case, the prime minister has most of the political power but when the President and the Prime Minister are of the same party, the President has most of the power. If this is true, then the President might not be relevant when there is cohabitation but relevant when there is not cohabitation.

the author for the OECD dataset primarily based upon the electoral law list provided by Lijphart (1999) and using national sources for systems updated after Lijphart's list. About 72% of country-years are PR and 28% plurality. The variable for the all-democracy data is taken from Beck et al.'s (2001) Database of Political Institutions: about two-thirds of the country-years are PR and one-third are plurality.

THE ACCESS POINT SUMMARY MEASURE

As described in chapter 2, the summary measure is constructed by stan-dardizing and then adding all of the previous variables (except PR). In the all-democracy sample, the median access point score is 0.192 and the mean is 0.515 with a standard deviation of 2.25. The minimum is -3.25 (Guyana from 1992 to 1996) and the maximum is 6.95 (France from 1993 to 1996). Guyana scores so low because during that period it was a presidential system with a unicameral legislature elected from a single national district with complete pooling and yet only a single gov-erning party. Guyana's score is actually the lowest possible score as these conditions each provide the fewest number of access points. France, on the other hand, scores so high because it had a large number of electoral districts (584 in this period), no pooling, two governing parties, and, according to the coding described above, was bicameral and not presidential. The number of parties is actually relatively low, keeping France's access point score from being even higher. The rest of the variables, though, are toward the maximum number of observed access points. Colombia between 1978 and 1985 had the median number of access points: they had two governing parties and 26 electoral dis-tricts, both of which are near the median, and they had intermediate levels of pooling; in addition, they were bicameral, which raises the number of access points, but also presidential, which lowers the number of access points.

In the OECD dataset, the median number of access points is -0.78 (Austria between 1991 and 1998 and Belgium between 1974 and 1976 and again in 1989 and 1990) while the mean is -0.01 and the standard deviation is 2.22. The minimum is -4.84 (Finland in 1961) and the maximum is 6.53 (France in 1958). Finland scores so low in 1961 because it had complete pooling, a unicameral legislature, and was presidential, giving it the lowest possible scores on these variables while having a relatively low number of electoral districts (15) and averaging only 1.5

governing parties that year.[13] France in 1958 scores so high because it had both a large number of electoral districts (470) and a large average number of parties (6.5) as well as no pooling. Belgium and Austria (after 1970) both have 9 electoral districts, complete pooling, unicameralism, and parliamentarism. The pooling and unicameralism lower the number of access points while the parliamentarism raises them, and 9 electoral districts is below average but more than the numerous countries with a single national district. When these two countries have exactly three governing parties (as they do in the years listed above) they have the median number of access points, as three parties is slightly above average, counteracting the slightly below average number of electoral districts.

---

13. Finland scores slightly higher in every other year because it typically has between two and six parties in government but had a rare single-party minority government for part of 1961 (Nousiainen 2000).

PART II

Policy Bias

CHAPTER 3

Access Points and Bias in Trade Policy

This chapter begins the empirical investigation of the effects of access points by examining bias in trade policy.[1] The core hypothesis tested in this chapter is that more access points lead to more protectionist trade policy. Bias in trade policy is a particularly well-suited starting point for three reasons. First, there have been numerous studies, dating back many decades, in both political science and economics, studying the level of protection in different countries, thus giving us an excellent starting point for building the empirical analyses in this chapter. Second, the collective action advantage of protectionists has been well established both theoretically and empirically, thus giving us strong predictions for the effects of access points on bias in trade policy. Finally, there has been significant previous work on the effects of institutions on trade policy, and Access Point Theory can help to resolve existing debates and evaluate received wisdom in these literatures.

In particular, and as will be discussed in more detail below, two major controversies exist in the institutional literature on trade policy to which Access Point Theory provides answers. First, one of the seminal works in this field, Rogowski (1987), argues that PR systems should have lower levels of protection because they insulate policymakers from protectionist demands. However, this finding has not always been replicable, and more recent work has suggested that PR might actually lead to higher levels of protection. Access Point Theory argues that, once other institutions influencing the number of access points are controlled for, PR should not

---

1. Parts of this chapter draw heavily from and reproduce elements of Ehrlich (2007) and Ehrlich (2008).

matter, a prediction for which this chapters finds support. Second, in the American trade policy literature, scholars have conducted a multi-decade debate about the role delegation to the President has played in the United States' turn toward free trade. Many analyses, starting with Schattschneider (1935) and continuing to the present with Bailey, Goldstein, and Weingast (1997), Gilligan (1997), and Pahre (2004), have suggested that delegation led to free trade. Numerous causal explanations were given for this effect, including breaking the Congressional logroll, providing insulation to interest groups, and creating a system of reciprocity whereby domestic tariff cuts were tied to foreign tariff cuts, which incentivized export interests to lobby for domestic liberalization. Other analyses, most prominently Hiscox (1999), have suggested that delegation had no effect and was, in fact, epiphenomenal to changes in the economy. Access Point Theory predicts that delegation should lead to free trade by reducing the number of access points as more power is shifted to the one-access-point executive from the many-access-point legislature. This chapter finds evidence for lower tariffs during periods of delegation and, through an investigation of Congressional testimony, finds direct evidence for the causal story offered by Access Point Theory rather than the alternative explanations for delegation's effect offered by previous scholars. Thus, this chapter not only provides a strong first test of Access Point Theory but also helps resolve long standing debates in the trade policy literature.

The rest of this chapter will be organized as follows. First, I provide more detail on previous institutional analyses of trade policy, highlighting the potential Access Point Theory has to shed light on unresolved debates. Second, I discuss how Access Point Theory can be applied to trade policy, describing why protectionists have a collective action advantage, and then develop specific testable hypotheses. In particular, three sets of hypotheses are tested in this chapter: those testing cross-national institutional differences; those examining the effects of delegation on U.S. trade policy; and those testing the microfoundations of the theory by examining lobbying on trade policy in the U.S. Congress. Third, I present the data and methods to tests these hypotheses. The fourth and fifth sections describe these results, first for the cross-national data and then for the U.S. data. The final section summarizes the findings of the chapter.

POLITICAL INSTITUTIONS AND TARIFF POLICY

Early literature on trade policy typically ignored the effect of political institutions, relying on the undifferentiated assumption that protectionist interests will lobby more often than free-trade interests. This assumption lies at the heart of the Endogenous Tariff Theory literature[2], one of the first attempts to explain trade policy through political forces. This literature suggests that politicians enact tariffs not because they are beneficial to the economy but because they help politicians maintain power. Specifically, this literature argues that protectionists have an easier time overcoming the collective action problem than free traders and then pressure policymakers to enact barriers to trade. Though this is a simple and convincing answer for why tariffs arise in the first place, it provides less clear answers for why tariff rates vary between countries or over time as it assumes a constant protectionist advantage. This is because the endogenous tariff literature largely ignores institutions that shape the strategic environment in which interest groups operate. More recently, though, scholars have begun to examine the effects of institutions, both cross-nationally and within the United States, providing a rich literature that this chapter builds on but also presenting us with many puzzles that Access Point Theory can help resolve.

Cross-National Institutions

A large literature has developed examining the effects of different institutions and the level of protectionism in a country. One of the earliest and still most influential institutional arguments derives from Rogowski's (1987) claim that PR makes free trade more likely. Rogowski argues that PR improves the chances of free trade by insulating policymakers from protectionist interests due to the small number of large electoral districts and high degrees of party discipline associated with PR. Large electoral districts insulate policymakers from particularistic interests fighting for protection for just their industry, while party discipline ensures that the party leader, who should be concerned with the national interest, controls policy. Mansfield and Busch (1995), Perrson and Tabellini (2000), and Grossman and Helpman (2004) later make similar arguments about PR. As discussed in chapter 2, though, while PR may encourage high party discipline and frequently has a small number of districts, these are not inherent features of PR. Thus, the causal mechanism specified by Rogowski and others predicts, at best, an indirect effect of PR on trade policy.

---

2. See, for instance, Mayer (1984), Magee, Brock, and Young (1989), and Grossman and Helpman (1994, 2002).

In addition, recent work has suggested that PR should have the opposite effect. Goodhart (2008) argues that majoritarian systems will have lower tariffs as there are very few swing districts in majoritarian systems, so national leaders have few incentives to buy off industries with protection. Also, in a recent set of research with a number of coauthors,[3] Rogowski argues that PR systems are likely to have more regulations that increase the price of goods since increasing the number of votes earned in PR systems has less of an effect on the number of seats won in the legislature than in majoritarian systems.[4] As a result, policymakers will be more concerned about increasing vote share by providing general benefits rather than increasing lobbying contributions by providing specific benefits. Since tariffs are an example of a regulation that raises prices, we would expect from this theory that majoritarian systems should have lower tariff levels than PR systems. Neither of these causal stories necessarily conflates PR with those associated institutions that are not essential to PR; thus, if these causal stories are correct, we might see a significant effect for PR even after controlling for access point institutions.

Other scholars have examined the effects of other institutions on cross-national trade policy. For instance, Neilson (2003) examines the influence of Presidentialism on trade policy. Neilson argues that delegation of power to Presidents will lead to free trade because the President represents a national district and should, thus, be less susceptible to special interests' demands for protection. Presidents, and, in particular, powerful Presidents with disciplined parties, should be able to break the legislative logroll that often leads to high tariffs. McGillivray (1997) examines the effect of party discipline on trade policy, arguing that in high party-discipline countries, like Canada, tariffs will be targeted at swing districts while in low party-discipline countries, like the United States, tariffs are targeted at safe districts. This results from the fact that in low party-discipline countries, party leaders cannot count on moderates elected from swing districts voting with them even if they are members of

---

3. See Kayser and Rogowski (2002), Chang, Kayser, and Rogowski (2008), and Chang et al. (Forthcoming).
4. This is actually only true for those votes that occur around the 50–50 mark in two-party competition. Gaining that final vote that puts your party in the majority is supremely important in a majoritarian system. Once you have that vote, no other votes matter. If you do not get that vote, none of your votes matter. Rogowski and coauthors assume that all votes are these "important" votes and, thus, votes are more important in majoritarian systems. Further, Rogowski and coauthors do not consider that politicians can use lobbying dollars to help them win votes through campaigning.

their party. Thus, there is less incentive to try to win these marginal districts by targeting them with particular benefits; rather, there is an incentive to reward themselves with these benefits even if it costs them the swing districts. Finally, Hankla (2006) argues that strong parties are likely to provide less protection than weak parties because a centralized leadership can prevent protectionist logrolls.[5]

The findings in these works are supportive of Access Point Theory; however, each of these works has studied these institutions in isolation and usually posits causal mechanisms different from, though not necessarily incompatible with, those suggested by Access Point Theory. This chapter examines the institutions simultaneously and provides a single causal mechanism to explain the effects of each of them; if the results are all consistent with Access Point Theory, then this suggests that it is the influence of these institutions on the number of access points that explains their relationship to trade policy rather than the mechanisms suggested in previous work. Further, the literature has engaged in a debate about what effect PR has on trade policy; Access Point Theory predicts that PR should have no effect. This chapter, thus, tests Access Point Theory against these preexisting arguments.

U.S. Institutions

A large literature has focused specifically on the effects of institutions on U.S. trade policy with a particular emphasis on the role of delegation to the President.[6] This literature has largely surrounded the potential effects of the Reciprocal Trade Agreement Act (RTAA) of 1934 and fast-track authority that replaced it in the 1970s. Prior to 1934, tariff policy was primarily set by Congress, which passed omnibus trade bills every few years that specified the tariff rates individually for every product. The President had the power to veto the bill but had no direct ability to shape individual tariff rates. The RTAA began to change this structure by delegating to the President the ability to sign trade agreements with other countries that

---

5. These are only the most salient of a voluminous literature on trade and domestic institutions. See Busch and Mansfield (Forthcoming) for a more comprehensive review.

6. There has also been a large and related debate on the effect of divided government, first started by Lohmann and O'Halloran (1994). I do not directly engage this debate here, though I do discuss the role of partisanship and divided government in my discussion of control variables. See Ehrlich (2004) for more on Access Point Theory and divided government.

would set the tariff rates with these countries. Under fast-track authority, Congress only has the ability to approve or disapprove these agreements (which include the overall tariff rates agreed to by the United States during GATT/WTO negotiations as well as free-trade agreements with specific countries) without offering any amendments that could change individual tariff rates. Thus, delegation has flipped the power structure on trade policy. Passage of the RTAA coincided almost perfectly with a drop in tariff rates in the United States, and much of the literature has suggested that the RTAA was responsible for this change in policy outcomes. More recently, though, some research has questioned this link, suggesting that it is spurious to changes in the underlying preferences of policymakers.

The academic debate over the effects of the RTAA dates back practically to the bill's passage in 1934. Contemporary observers of the pre-RTAA system as well as modern academics have typically described Congressional policymaking on trade as creating a system overrun with special interests mostly demanding protection for their industry (Schattschneider 1935; Destler 2005) which helped create a tariff logroll whereby Congressmen traded protection for products created in their district for support for protection on the products in their peers' districts, usually leading to high overall tariff rates.[7] This process culminated in the now-infamous Smoot-Hawley Tariff of 1929, described only a few years later by E. E. Schattschneider as follows: "In tariff making, perhaps more than in any other kind of legislation, Congress writes bills which no one intended" (13) because the procedure by which tariffs are set "makes the way smooth for groups seeking to benefit by the protective system" (99). In 1934, as part of the New Deal, Roosevelt devised a new way to set tariffs: Congress delegated authority to the President to negotiate bilateral, reciprocal trade agreements.

The RTAA combined two institutional features—delegation to the executive and reciprocity—each of which has been credited with the turn toward free trade by breaking the protectionist logroll. Schattschneider, less than one year after the RTAA's passage, noted the importance of both of these changes. First, reciprocal agreements could create "compensatory support" for free trade by "offering inducements to exporting interests who benefit by the reciprocal agreements" (289) which lower foreign trade barriers. Second, "delegat[ing] authority . . . to the executive who is able to

---

7. Democrats during this period usually supported lower tariff rates than their Republican colleagues and would sometimes pass tariff bills that lowered overall tariffs below where the Republicans had previously set them. Even these Democratic tariffs, though, were high by modern standards.

play interests against each other more easily than members of Congress can because his constituency is larger" (289) eliminated the logroll. This assumption that Presidents are less receptive to protectionist interests and, thus, less protectionist has guided much of the subsequent research on why delegation leads to less protection. A large body of literature, which I refer to here as the Presidential Liberalism Thesis and is exemplified by Baldwin (1985), argues that delegation to the President leads to free trade because the President represents the entire country so that he will be more supportive of free trade, which is in the national interest rather than protection, which is only in the interest of particular portions of the country.[8] Also, Lohmann and O'Halloran (1994; hereafter LO) argue that divided government leads to more protectionism by decreasing the chances that Congress will delegate trade power to a naturally less protectionist President.

The argument that the RTAA had fundamentally changed the nature of trade policymaking and had helped usher in free trade in the United States became common in the political science and economics literatures and was an integral part of most economic histories of trade policy.[9] Bailey, Goldstein, and Weingast (1997; hereafter BGW) provided formal underpinnings for the RTAA's effect on trade policy by focusing on the reciprocity element, as does Gilligan (1997). By linking domestic tariff reductions to foreign tariff reductions, the RTAA provided targetable benefits to exporters, which allowed them to overcome the collective action problem more readily and, thus, lobby legislators. These lobbying efforts then made Congress more supportive of free trade, enabling the RTAA to survive the return of Republican majorities after World War II.

The impact of this new system of delegation and reciprocity has been questioned, though, in particular by Hiscox (1999, 2002).[10] He argues that there was no logroll to break through delegation, as trade bills never generated universal support (Hiscox 1999, 676–677).[11] Further, Hiscox

---

8. See Baldwin (1985), Katzenstein (1977), Krasner (1978), Lake (1988), and Milner and Rosendorff (1997) for examples of the Presidential Liberalism Thesis. Karol (2007) and Ehrlich (2009a) demonstrate that the causal logic underpinning this thesis, namely that representing larger constituencies leads to supporting free trade, is not supported by the empirical evidence in the United States.

9. For instance, Destler (2005) and Pastor (1980) assert, without raising the specter of any controversy, that the RTAA had this effect.

10. See, also, Trubowitz (1998) for a similar argument about how regional preferences for trade changed exogenously rather than because of changing institutions.

11. On the other hand, a *partisan* logroll may have been occurring as there was near unanimity among Republicans on protectionist trade bills.

argues that the idea that "any president, by dint of having a larger constituency, must be less protectionist than the median member of Congress, is hopelessly ahistorical" (677) so that delegation would not always lead to liberalization. He also challenges the reciprocity story, arguing that Republican preferences would not shift because they would still be supported by the same protectionist interests as before. Although he acknowledges that exporters may have started lobbying more after the RTAA, he also argues, contra BGW's assumption that free trade would eliminate some import-competing industries, that protectionist industries would lobby harder as they "dug in and fought for exceptions from trade agreements" (678–679). Hiscox claims these two effects would cancel out and preferences would not change, though he provides no evidence to demonstrate this. I will provide evidence below on this point, finding that while both Hiscox and BGW are able to explain some of the lobbying patterns that emerge, Access Point Theory provides a more complete account. Thus, Access Point Theory is able to resolve one of the most long-standing debates in the trade policy literature.

THE PROTECTIONISTS' COLLECTIVE ACTION ADVANTAGE AND BIASED TRADE POLICY

Access Point Theory predicts that the number of access points will influence policy bias when one side of the debate has an inherent lobbying advantage. There are few policy areas where this lobbying advantage is better established than it is in trade policy. As commented on above, Schattschneider (1935) is one of the first to note how protectionist interests dominated trade policy in Congress. Olson (1971) provides theoretical underpinnings for this as he uses trade policy lobbying as one of his paradigmatic cases of Collective Action Theory. As described in chapter 2, groups are better able to overcome the collective action problem when the benefits are concentrated: in trade policy, as Olson suggests, the benefits of protection are often concentrated while the benefits of free trade are often dispersed, providing a clear advantage to protectionists over free traders in overcoming the collective action problem. This insight, in fact, serves as the primary motivation for the existence of protection in Endogenous Tariff Theory.

Protection benefits the protected industry: increasing the tariff rate on automobiles, for instance, will increase the price of foreign cars which should increase the profits for domestic manufacturers who are not subject to the import tax. This will benefit both the owners and the employees of the domestic automobile industry.[12] On the other hand, the primary beneficiaries of free trade are consumers: tariffs raise the prices of goods by taxing them which hurts consumers who see their purchasing power decrease. Consumers, though, are quite dispersed, as each consumer likely only saves a small amount of money from free trade. As such, the benefits and costs of protection are typically asymmetric: a few benefit a lot from protection while many are hurt a little. Thus, protectionists should enjoy a collective action advantage and lobby more.

This is not to say that free traders never lobby. In fact, the benefits of free trade are sometimes somewhat concentrated. For instance, industries that use imported raw materials have an incentive to lobby for free trade on those goods. In addition, Milner (1988) provides evidence that multinational corporations often lobby to lower tariffs on goods that they produce in one country and then transfer to another. Finally, Gilligan (1997) argues that reciprocity, which is one of the foundational principles of the GATT, provides incentives for exporters to lobby for lower tariffs at home in order to encourage foreign countries to open their markets to their products.

However, on average, protectionists should still enjoy a collective action advantage. The link between lower domestic tariffs and lower foreign tariffs is often indirect as there is no guarantee that lower tariffs on automobiles at home will cause lower tariffs on automobiles abroad. This, therefore, weakens the incentive for exporters to lobby. Further, the benefits of tariffs on inputs are concentrated on the domestic industry producing those inputs while the costs may be dispersed across many industries using the imported product. For instance, steel is used in multiple industries, such as construction, automobiles, appliances, and more. The steel industry will have an easier time coordinating and overcoming the collective action problem than these disparate industries that use steel. In addition, finished products should have no free-trade support apart from consumers, whose collective action problems are notorious.[13]

At least in the United States, the empirical evidence bears out this assumption that protectionists enjoy a collective action advantage and, thus, lobby more. Hiscox (2002, 143) documents appearances before Congressional committees by interest groups to lobby on major trade bills. In every post–World War II bill he examines, at least 70% and as many as

---

12. This assumes that factors are at least partially specific in that owners and workers cannot easily move from one industry to another. See Hiscox (2002) for more on factor mobility.

13. In fact, as Ehrlich (2009b) demonstrates for the European Union, it is common in developed countries for tariffs to be higher on finished goods than raw materials and semifinished goods.

90% of the witnesses supported protectionism. On most of the bills, protectionists accounted for about 80% of the witnesses. Drope and Hansen (2004) examine the effect of political contributions on antidumping decisions by the United States' International Trade Commission (ITC). They find that when the ITC rules in favor of antidumping duties, protectionist industries have spent nearly $2 million in PAC and soft money contributions and lobbying expenditures while free-trade industries have spent only about $300,000. Even when the ITC rules against the protectionist industries and finds no dumping, protectionists have spent over $1 million while free traders have spent only about $130,000. Both of these pieces of evidence suggest that even though free traders do lobby, protectionists continue to dominate in lobbying even if they often end up losing the battle.

In summary, both the theoretical arguments and the empirical evidence strongly suggest that protectionists will enjoy a collective action advantage over free traders. As a result, Access Point Theory predicts that increasing the number of access points will lead to increased policy bias in favor of protectionists, that is, more protectionism. Thus, all of the institutions discussed in chapter 2 that increase the number of access points should increase the level of protectionism. The following list summarizes these hypotheses as applied to trade policy:

Hypothesis 3.1: *The more electoral districts a country has, the more protection there will be.*

Hypothesis 3.2: *The less party discipline a country has, the more protection there will be.*

Hypothesis 3.3: *The more parties in government, the more protection there will be.*

Hypothesis 3 4: *Federalism leads to more protection.*

Hypothesis 3.5: *Presidentialism leads to less protection.*

Hypothesis 3.6: *PR and plurality systems should not have significantly different levels of protection.*

Access Point Theory can also be applied to the debate on delegation within the United States, as was discussed for the general issue of delegation to the President in chapter 2. Delegation reduces the relative power of the Congress, which has many access points, and increases the relative power of the President, who is one access point. Thus, delegation reduces the weighted number of access points, which should lead to less lobbying overall, a smaller lobbying advantage for protectionists, and, therefore, lower tariff rates. From this, the following hypotheses can be derived:

Hypothesis 3.7: Delegation leads to less protection.

Hypothesis 3.8: Delegation leads to lower total lobbying.

Hypothesis 3.9: Delegation leads to lower net protectionist lobbying.

DATA AND METHODS

The cross-national analysis is conducted on the OECD dataset using the full list of access point variables described in chapter 2. Because of limitations in the dependent variable described below, the panel runs from 1948 to 1993 and covers all 21 countries. Because of some missing data and because Greece, Portugal, and Spain only enter the dataset once they become democracies, there are 714 observations in the main results presented below. Given this large sample size, we can use the full set of access point variables, all independent variables that may be theoretically relevant or that previous research has indicated are important, and sophisticated methods for dealing with the dynamic properties of the data, all of which will be detailed below.

The dependent variable in this analysis, labeled *Tariff*, is what is known as the trade-weighted average tariff rate, which is calculated by dividing the collected tariff revenue by the total value of imports.[14] The collected tariff revenue and the value of imports are both taken from Mitchell (1995); unfortunately, these data stop in 1993 and more recent updates of *International Historical Statistics* provide collected tariff revenue data for only a handful of countries in the dataset. Rather than have a nonrandomly unbalanced dataset where certain countries contributed many more observations than others, I choose to stop the analysis at 1993. Since the relationship between access points and tariff rates is unlikely to have changed after 1993, this decision should not be seen as problematic.[15]

---

14. This is called the trade-weighted average tariff rate because it could also be calculated by taking the actual tariff rates on every product, dividing these rates by the share of total imports that each product comprised, and adding these results.

15. The trade-weighted average tariff is an imperfect measure of the level of protection. First, countries can use other tools to protect the economy. However, as Trefler (1993) and others have shown, levels of tariffs and nontariff barriers tend to be positively correlated. This suggests that tariffs may be a noisy proxy for overall protection but, as Greene (2000, 376) points out, measurement error in the dependant variable leads to conservative and unbiased estimates. Second, as Trefler (1993) argues, the trade-weighted average tariff can change even without the underlying tariff rates changing if prices change, which will lead to a change in the pattern of trade. Inclusion of the terms of trade variable described below should ameliorate this concern.

As described above, there exists a large literature examining cross-national trade policy that provides us with many variables that need to be controlled, mostly economic variables that influence the demand for protection or free trade.[16] First, exports as a percent of gross domestic product (GDP) are included as countries with more exports are likely to have more demand for free trade. The unemployment rate is included because when unemployment increases, policymakers may have an incentive to protect domestic industries so as to create jobs. Richer countries tend to have lower levels of protection as poorer countries are more likely to try to protect infant industries, so GDP per capita is included. Total GDP is also included because smaller countries that are more trade dependent may be more likely to support free trade (Katzenstein 1985). The terms of trade, which are the price of exports relative to the price of imports, are included because if the price of imports drops, a government may impose tariffs to offset a potential surge in import volume. Finally, inflation is included because high-inflation countries may be less likely to wish to impose further price hikes on consumers through import taxes.

In addition to these economic variables, a number of additional independent variables are also included. First, *Left* is a measure of partisanship that measures the percent of a government made up of leftist politicians and is included because in postwar developed democracies, left-wing governments have tended to be more supportive of protection since leftist parties generally represent lower-skilled workers who tend to be hurt by free trade in advanced economies.[17] Second, *GATT* is a count of the number of GATT Rounds that had been completed in the year in question: all of the countries in the dataset are GATT members who meet regularly to negotiate new tariff reductions. At the completion of each round, we would expect a drop in tariff rates in all countries as a result. *EU* is a dummy variable for membership in the European Union: EU members significantly coordinate their trade policy, and we might expect EU members to have similar trade policies to each other and potentially different ones from other countries.[18]

---

16. See Magee, Brock, and Young (1989) and Mansfield and Busch (1995) for examples of cross-national analyses using many of these variables.

17. This follows from the Stolper-Samuelson Theorem, as discussed in more detail in Hiscox (2002). The data on this variable is from Franzese (2002b) and updated by the author for more recent elections.

18. In fact, since 1968, EU members actually have identical tariff schedules; that is, tariffs on products are the same no matter which country imports them. However, each country imports a different basket of goods and, thus, has a different average tariff. Ehrlich (2009b) demonstrates that this variation is partially intentional: countries know what products they import and, if they want protection, can push for high tariff rates on those products in EU negotiations while if they want free

Finally, a dummy variable is included for the United Kingdom after 1968 because Mitchell (1995) combines tariff and excise revenue in Britain after 1968, thus artificially raising the average tariff rate after this year.[19]

I analyze these data primarily by using pooled Error Correction Mechanisms (ECMs), which model how the dependent variable, in this case tariffs, responds to temporary or permanent changes in the independent variables. An ECM views the dependent variable as being in an equilibrium relationship with the independent variables: when these variables change it produces an "error" in the dependent variable; that is, they fall out of equilibrium, which is corrected over time as either a new equilibrium is reached (if the change in the independent variables was permanent) or as the shock fades away (if the change was temporary.) A pooled ECM analyzes this model by combining the data from all of the countries in the sample into a single dataset and then differencing the dependent variable on the left-hand side and including both levels and differences of the independent variables as well as the lagged level of the dependent variable on the right-hand side. This difference and lag structure sets up the equilibrium relationship of the variables.[20] I use ECMs because they allow for rich dynamic patterns while remaining relatively simple to implement and interpret.[21] By using ECMs, I can examine both long- and short-term dynamic patterns for many of the included variables[22] and look at both

trade, they can push for low tariffs on those products. Thus, average tariff rates in EU countries are partially independent from each other, meriting their inclusion as separate observation. As shown in Ehrlich (2007), though, the following results are not particularly sensitive to the exclusion of EU countries.

19. Dropping these observations entirely leads to similar results, although *Pool* loses significance due to the smaller sample size.

20. See Beck (1991) for an introduction to ECMs and Franzese (2002b) for an application of pooled ECMs to political economy issues. An ECM models the equilibrium relationship between the variables by assuming that short-term changes in the independent variables will lead to corresponding short-term changes in the dependent variable (the error correction as measured by the differenced variables) while permanent changes in the independent variables will change the equilibrium level of the dependent variable (as measured by the level variables).

21. ECMs have traditionally been used when cointegration is present, which exists when two or more variables have unit roots that determine each other. The search for unit roots in tariff data has often preoccupied previous researchers, such as Lohmann and O'Halloran (1994). However, given that tariffs are bounded, unit roots are not technically possible. Instead, tariffs are probably near-integrated. See DeBoef and Granato (1999) and DeBoef (2000). However, as Beck (1991) argues and DeBoef and Keele (2005) prove, ECMs can be used even when unit roots or cointegration are not present.

22. The larger institutional changes, such as Presidentialism, the number of electoral districts, pooling, and bicameralism, are only entered in levels, which means I can only examine long-term dynamics for these variables. This is because these

within-country and cross-national variation simultaneously. In sum, the main model testing the cross-national hypotheses is as follows:

$$\Delta\text{Tariff} = \beta_0 + \beta_1\text{Tariff}_{t-1} + \beta_2\text{Number-of-parties}_{t-1}$$
$$+ \beta_3\Delta\text{Number-of-Parties} + \beta_4\text{Electroal-Districts}_{t-1} + \beta_5\text{Pool}_{t-1}$$
$$+ \beta_6\text{Bicameralism}_{t-1} + \beta_7\text{Presidential}_{t-1} + \beta_8\text{PR}_{t-1}$$
$$+ \beta_9\text{Exports}_{t-1} + \beta_{10}\Delta\text{Exports} + \beta_{11}\text{Unemployment}_{t-1}$$
$$+ \beta_{12}\Delta\text{Unemployment} + \beta_{13}\text{GDP}/\text{Capita}_{t-1} + \beta_{14}\Delta\text{GDP}/\text{Capita}$$
$$+ \beta_{15}\text{GDP}_{t-1} + \beta_{16}\Delta\text{GDP} + \beta_{17}\text{Terms-of-trade}_{t-1}$$
$$+ \beta_{18}\Delta\text{Terms-of-trade} + \beta_{19}\text{Inflation}_{t-1} + \beta_{20}\Delta\text{Inflation}$$
$$+ \beta_{21}\text{Left}_{t-1} + \beta_{22}\Delta\text{Left} + \beta_{23}\text{GATT}_{t-1} + \beta_{24}\text{EU}_{t-1}$$
$$+ \beta_{25}\text{UK}(1968-1993) + \varepsilon. \tag{1}$$

The first independent variable, the lagged level of the dependent variable, combined with the differenced dependent variable, sets up the error correction relationship. The next group of variables (β_2 through β_8) represents the access point variables described in chapter 2 and which test Hypotheses 3.1 through 3.6 above. The rest of the variables are the controls described above. The coefficients on the differenced variables are the short-term effects of these variables. The coefficients on the lagged levels are used to determine the long-term effects by dividing this coefficient by $(-\beta_1)$.[23]

In addition to these pooled ECMs, two different analyses are conducted to test the U.S.-specific hypotheses: the first examines a time series of tariff rates to test Hypothesis 3.7 and the second examines Congressional testimony by interest groups to test Hypotheses 3.8 and 3.9. The tariff analysis builds on the time-series analyses of annual U.S. tariff rates by LO and Magee, Brock, and Young (1989; hereafter MBY), two of the most extensive political economy analyses of tariff rates to date. The variables in the analyses below are mostly chosen and coded to correspond with the models and theories presented by these earlier studies in order to ease comparison with previous work. The dependent variable, *Tariff*, is described

institutions rarely change within countries and, when they do, the political landscape is likely to be undergoing such radical change that policymakers are not focusing on changing trade policy in the immediate aftermath. Inclusion of differenced variables, though, does not change the results presented below.

23. Because the ECMs are analyzed on time-series cross-section data, I also employ panel-corrected standard errors to provide consistent estimates despite the spatial and temporal correlation typically found in panel data (Beck and Katz 1995). Also, see Ehrlich (2007) for numerous robustness tests for different dynamic specifications.

above. This section tests Hypothesis 3.7 that passage of the RTAA led to lower tariff rates. To conduct this test, I include the dummy variable, *RTAA*, which is equal to 1 in periods of delegation and 0 otherwise: within the sample used in the main model, which for data reasons covers 1902 to 1988, this means that *RTAA* is equal to 0 before 1934 and 1 after 1934. In the extended sample, *RTAA* also equals 0 after 1994, as President Clinton lost fast-track authority in this year and, thus, tariff policy was no longer technically delegated to the President until President Bush won it back in 2002.[24] Access Point Theory predicts that the coefficient on this variable will be negative and significant.

In addition to this variable, a number of economic and political variables are included as controls. *UE* is the percent of the civilian workforce that is unemployed. *Inflation* is calculated as the percentage change in the GNP deflator. These two variables appear in the models of both MBY and LO and test if tariffs are increased in periods of poor economic performance. *Terms* are the terms of trade, calculated as the price of U.S. manufacturing exports divided by the price of manufacturing imports. *KL* is the capital-labor ratio, calculated as the ratio of U.S. employees to $100,000 of real capital. Both of these variables are included in MBY and test to see if trade policy is influenced by shifting patterns of trade. *Exports* are the value of U.S. exports divided by GNP and is included to test Hiscox's (1999) hypothesis that it was the exogenous expansion of exports after World War II that changed policymakers' preferences toward free trade and which led to lower tariff rates.

The rest of the variables in the analysis test for the effects of political and international changes. *War* is equal to 1 during the world wars and 0 otherwise, and controls for the fact that trade skews in unusual directions during major wars. *Income* is a dummy variable for the effects of the income tax, coded as 1 after 1917 and 0 before, and is included because before introduction of the income tax, tariffs were an important revenue source for the U.S. government. As above, *GATT* is an ordinal variable that starts at 0 and then increases by 1 at each signing of a GATT round.

To control for the effect of partisanship, I employ a series of dummy variables determining the partisan composition of the government.

---

24. Congress did not take advantage of their tariff authority in the intervening years, allowing the status quo tariff rate set under delegation to continue. One can argue, therefore, that these years should also be coded as 1 instead of 0. Doing so in Model 2 below actually strengthens the predicted effect of the RTAA, both substantively and statistically. Fast-track authority has since expired without being renewed, but this occurred after the end of the data presented in this chapter.

Following the argument in Karol (2002), I label one party the Free-trade party (the Democrats before 1970 and the Republicans after) and one party the Protectionist party (the opposite). If the Protectionist party controls both houses of Congress and the Presidency, they are labeled a PP government; if the free traders have unified control, they are labeled an FF government; if the protectionists control the Presidency but the free traders control at least one House, they are labeled a PF government; and if the free traders control the Presidency while the protectionists control at least one House, they are labeled an FP government. I then create dummy variables for each of these types of government, excluding the FF dummy and using unified free-trade control as a baseline. This coding scheme differs from that used by LO, but replicating the results below with their coding scheme, as well as many others, does not change the results for the RTAA or most of the economic controls.

Except for *KL*, all of the data are obtained from *The Historical Statistics of the United States* for before 1970 and *The Statistical Abstract of the United States* for after 1970. *KL* is obtained directly from MBY (326–328), and it limits the size of the sample: while all of the other series have data for at least 100 years, and often for over 150, MBY only include data on *KL* from 1901 to 1988, thus yielding only 87 observations in the model including this variable. I analyze these time series using ECMs as described above.[25] The main model tested in the U.S. section is as follows:

$$
\begin{aligned}
\Delta \text{Tariff} = {} & \beta_0 + \beta_1 \text{Tariff}_{t-1} + \beta_2 \text{RTAA} + \beta_3 \Delta \text{UE} + \beta_4 \text{UE}_{t-1} \\
& + \beta_5 \Delta \text{Inflation} + \beta_6 \text{Inflation}\beta_{t-1} + \beta_7 \Delta \text{KL} + \beta_8 \text{KL}_{t-1} \\
& + \beta_9 \Delta \text{Terms} + \beta_{10} \text{Terms}_{t-1} + \beta_{11} \Delta \text{Exports} + \beta_{12} \text{Exports}_{t-1} \\
& + \beta_{13} \Delta \text{PP} + \beta_{14} \Delta \text{PF} + \beta_{15} \Delta \text{FP} + \beta_{16} \text{Income} \\
& + \beta_{17} \Delta \text{War} + \beta_{18} \text{GATT} +
\end{aligned}
\tag{2}
$$

The RTAA is entered as a level as most of the effect of the RTAA (and the delegation it ushered in) should be in the long term as treaties are slowly negotiated and renegotiated with individual countries and tariff levels gradually reduce over time. In other words, the RTAA led to a new, lower equilibrium tariff level and should not have had much of an immediate decrease on tariff rates. Including a differenced variable for the RTAA (which amounts to a dummy variable for 1934) does not change the overall

---

25. The ECMs presented in the U.S. section below are estimated using OLS with Newey-West robust standard errors with a maximum of three lags to provide consistent estimates despite the autocorrelation in the data.

results, though this differenced variable is almost always insignificant. The next set of variables—the economic variables—are entered as both levels and differences as they should have both long- and short-term effects on tariff rates; that is, a one-year increase in unemployment is predicted to increase tariff rates in the short term to provide protection to falling industries while a permanent increase in unemployment should cause tariff rates to slowly rise to a new permanent equilibrium level. Partisanship is only entered as differences as party control should only have short-term effects on tariff rates. A new President or Congress of a different party should attempt to raise (or lower) tariff rates to their preferred level as soon as possible, suggesting a short-term effect. *War* is entered as a differenced variable to measure the short-term dislocations world wars have on trade policy. *Income* is entered as a level as the introduction of the income tax should not have had much of a short-term impact on tariff rates although it would reduce the long-term need for them.

The second set of tests in the U.S. section examines interest group testimony before Congress to test the microfoundations of the theory and is based on data presented in Hiscox (2002). Hiscox examines the number of interest groups testifying before the House trade committees on important trade legislation in the nineteenth and twentieth centuries, and categorizes each of these interest groups as either supporting protection or supporting free trade based upon their testimony. Though this measure is not without flaws, it serves as a useful proxy for lobbying activity and is certainly the only measure available for such a long time series.[26] Hiscox includes lobbying on 18 different trade bills, which leads to an extremely small sample. Thus, the tests will, by necessity, be rather simple. However, it should be hard to find significant results with such a small sample, thus providing a conservative test of the argument. Access Point Theory

---

26. Perhaps the most serious flaw is that Congress frequently chooses which interest groups to invite and, thus, can manipulate this measure. Schattschneider (1935) describes how Congress intentionally invited protectionist interest groups to give testimony for the Smoot-Hawley bill in order to justify the tariffs they wished to provide. The 1930 case, therefore, might be an outlier. Replicating the analyses shown below with a dummy variable for this case does not alter the conclusions of the analysis. (With such a small sample size, it is possible that any one outlier is, in fact, unduly influencing the results. Reanalyzing Models 7 and 8 by dropping each observation one at a time does not produce any noticeable changes in the results, suggesting that they are not due to influential outliers.) One might also suspect that when the protectionist party controls the House, they may invite more protectionist lobbyists, but controlling for partisanship of the House has no effect on the results.

predicts that the total amount of lobbying (the number of protectionist groups plus the number of free-trade groups providing testimony) and net protectionist lobbying (the number of protectionist groups minus the number of free-trade groups providing testimony) should both be lower on bills after the RTAA than on bills before the RTAA. Thus, a simple dummy variable denoting whether a bill was pre- or post-RTAA will be used to test Hypotheses 3.8 and 3.9. In addition, a variable measuring factor mobility will be included to test Hiscox's alternative hypothesis, which will be described in the result section below.

CROSS-NATIONAL TARIFF POLICY

The cross-national results are reported in table 3.1, where Model 1 is the main ECM discussed above in equation 1. As can be seen, the results are very supportive of Access Point Theory as, with only one important exception discussed below, the coefficients on the access point variables are all significant in the expected direction. As explained above, the coefficients on the differenced variables are the short-run effects of the variables, that is, the immediate impact of a change in the independent variable that fades away over time, while the coefficients on the lagged variables divided by the inverse of the coefficient on the lagged level of the dependent variable are the long-run effects, that is, the amount that the eventual, new equilibrium will differ from the current equilibrium if the independent variable changes. Thus, for instance, the coefficient on the number of electoral districts is .0029 while the coefficient on the lagged level of tariffs is -.092; therefore, the long-term effect of each additional electoral district is .0029/-(-.092), or 0.0315 higher tariff rates for each additional electoral district. This might seem like a small number, but the number of electoral districts ranges from 1 to 658. Thus, the United Kingdom is estimated to have nearly 21% higher tariffs than countries with a single electoral district. The standard deviation for number of electoral districts is about 173, so a one standard deviation change in the number of electoral districts yields about 5.5% higher tariff rates, a sizable figure especially considering that the average tariff rate in the sample is 6.98% with a standard deviation of 8.26%. Thus, the effect of the number of electoral districts is both statistically and substantively significant, and Hypothesis 3.1 is supported.

Similarly, the level of party discipline also has a statistically and substantively significant effect, confirming Hypothesis 3.2: a one-unit change in the level of pooling leads to a 2.1% increase in tariff rates while moving

Table 3.1 THE EFFECT OF ACCESS POINTS ON CROSS-NATIONAL TARIFF RATES

Variable	Model 1	Model 2
Number of Parties	0.228***	–
	(0.045)	–
Change in Number of Parties	0.226**	–
	(0.089)	–
Electoral Districts	0.003***	–
	(0.001)	–
Pool	0.194**	–
	(0.093)	–
Bicameralism	−0.004***	−0.005***
	(0.001)	(0.001)
Presidential	−0.842***	−0.270**
	(0.141)	(0.112)
PR	0.088	−0.502***
	(0.234)	(0.163)
Exports	0.263	0.020
	(0.401)	(0.428)
Change in Exports	−0.656**	−0.802***
	(0.302)	(0.307)
Unemployment	0.014	0.021
	(0.015)	(0.014)
Change in Unemployment	0.208***	0.227***
	(0.064)	(0.064)
GDP per capita	−3.90E−05	1.35E−05
	(3.33E−05)	(3.37E−05)
Change in GDP per capita	−4.42E−04**	−3.93E−04*
	(2.12E−04)	(2.12E−04)
GDP	−2.00E−11	3.97E−11
	(6.56E−11)	(5.61E−11)
Change in GDP	1.82E−09*	1.65E−09
	(1.07E−09)	(1.03E−09)
Terms of Trade	0.118	−0.171
	(0.299)	(0.300)
Change in Terms of Trade	2.65***	2.71***
	(0.722)	(0.679)
Inflation	−0.036***	−0.037***
	(0.013)	(0.013)
Change in Inflation	−0.001	0.001
	(0.019)	(0.019)

(*continued*)

Table 3.1 CONTINUED

Variable	Model 1	Model 2
Left	0.266*	0.037
	(0.156)	(0.154)
Change in Left	0.867***	0.694***
	(0.254)	(0.244)
GATT	−0.196*	−0.293***
	(0.102)	(0.106)
EU	−0.531***	−0.238**
	(0.133)	(0.117)
Number of Observations	714	714
R–squared	0.102	0.0822

Notes: Dependent Variable = Change in Tariff Rate
Panel–Corrected Standard Errors in Parentheses
***p<.01; **p<.05; *<p<.1
Constant, lagged tariff rate, and other controls not reported

from complete pooling (0 on the scale) to no pooling (2 on the scale) leads to a 4.2% increase in tariff rates. Hypothesis 3.3 is confirmed in both the short- and long run. Each additional party in government leads to an immediate 0.22% increase in the tariff rate, a small but not meaningless effect. In the long run, though, the effect is even larger, as each additional party adds about 2.5% to the tariff rate. A one standard deviation change in the number of parties leads to a nearly 3% increase in the tariff rate.

Presidentialism has an even larger substantive effect as presidential systems have over 9% lower tariffs in the long run than parliamentary systems.[27] Finally, Hypothesis 3.6 is also confirmed as, once one controls for the other institutional variables, PR is not significant. As Model 2 shows, though, when one does not control for number of parties, number of electoral districts, and party discipline, PR is statistically significant, with PR countries having over 7% lower tariff rates than plurality countries.[28] This explains why some previous analyses, which only looked at PR

---

27. This result is not particularly sensitive to the coding of Presidentialism. If we only consider the United States and France to be presidential systems, not only does this coefficient remain significant, but also no other coefficients change appreciably. If we only consider the United States and France under periods of cohabitation as presidential systems, then this coefficient remains significant, though the long-run coefficient on *Left* becomes insignificant. If we only consider the United States a presidential system, then the coefficient on Presidentialism becomes marginally insignificant.

28. For the most part, Models 1 and 2 are similar in all other respects. The only variable that loses statistical significance in Model 2 is the lagged level of partisanship.

in isolation, found that PR countries had lower tariff rates. As can be seen here, though, this effect is only indirect and depends on the extent to which PR systems have high party discipline and few electoral districts.

Only one hypothesis was not confirmed: contrary to Hypothesis 3.5, federalism is significantly associated with lower tariff rates. Each additional member of an upper house leads to 0.046 lower tariff rates; a one standard deviation change in the number of seats (about 175 seats) is associated with nearly 8% lower tariffs, a very meaningful amount. Why does bicameralism lead to lower tariff rates when it introduces more access points? It is possible that these additional access points are particularly hostile to protectionism and friendly to free trade such that including these access points actually benefits free traders. Research in American politics has long found that the Senate is more supportive of free trade than the House of Representatives: typically, it is argued that larger constituencies lead to more support for free trade because policymakers from larger and more heterogeneous districts are less likely to be captured by individual industries pushing for protection on products they make. However, recent research (Karol 2007; Ehrlich 2009a) has found that whatever difference exists between the houses of Congress, it is not driven by the differences in constituency size between Senators and Representatives. Thus, it is unknown why this difference exists and whether it is generalizable to other bicameral countries. Future research should continue to explore this possibility, and it does raise the issue that only on average does increasing the number of access points increase policy bias: if there is a systematic reason why the additional access points are unreceptive to the side with the lobbying advantage than we might actually observe access points leading to less bias, as may be occurring here.

Briefly looking at the control variables, all of the economic control variables are in the direction expected from previous studies. For instance, the more exports grow within a country, the lower tariff rates will be, as predicted by Hiscox (1999), and the more unemployment grows, the higher tariff rates will be, perhaps as countries implement protection to help declining industries. Larger countries have slightly higher tariffs, perhaps because they are able to implement optimal tariffs that change the terms of trade in their direction, while poorer countries also have higher tariffs, perhaps to protect their developing industries. Terms of trade are also significant: as the price of imports declines, tariffs increase, potentially to offset these cheaper prices. These variables, and all but one of the other economic variables, are only significant in the short run. Only inflation is significant in the long run, perhaps because high-inflation countries may not wish to further raise domestic prices by taxing imported goods.

The political controls also behave as expected. Partisanship is significant in both the short- and long run. If a completely left-wing government replaces a completely right-wing government, this will lead to an immediate 0.87% increase in tariff rates. In addition, a country that always has left-wing governments will have 2.9% higher tariffs in the long run than a country that always has right-wing governments. GATT signings are associated with lower tariff rates, as we would expect: each new GATT round led to a long-run decrease in tariff rates of 2.14% on average. Finally, the EU has, on average, about 5.8% lower average tariff rates than non-EU countries.

In summary, the results of this section demonstrate that the number of access points increases the amount of bias in trade policy. The model performs well in predicting tariff rates, with the control variables behaving largely as expected, which should increase our confidence in these results. Overall, with the exception of the anomalous finding on federalism, increasing the number of access points is associated with both statistically and substantively higher tariff rates.

U.S. TARIFF POLICY

Access Point Theory not only does a good job explaining cross-national differences in trade policy, but it also explains how and why a major change in the institutional structure of trade policymaking in the United States influenced tariffs rates domestically. First, as can be seen in table 3.2, the RTAA was associated with a significant drop in tariff rates in the United States. In both Model 3, which includes KL and, thus, covers 1901–1988, and in Model 4, which excludes KL and, thus, covers 1891–1996, the coefficient on RTAA is both negative and statistically significant. In Model 3, the RTAA is predicted to have led to over 33% lower tariff rates in the long term, which is quite meaningful substantively.[29] The maximum tariff rate in this sample is the 28% rate (in 1902) while the minimum tariff rate is 3% (in 1980); the effect attributed to the RTAA is, therefore, larger than difference in the sample range. What this model is predicting, therefore, is that without the RTAA, tariffs would have increased even higher given economic and political conditions during the Great Depression and after World War II. In Model 4, the predicted effect of the RTAA is weaker but still significant

---

29. As above, this effect can be calculated by dividing the coefficient on the RTAA by the coefficient on the lagged tariff level and then multiplying by negative one.

Table 3.2 THE EFFECT OF DELEGATION ON U.S. TARIFF RATES

Variable	Model 3	Model 4
Tariff t–1	−0.048	−0.067
	(0.061)	(0.068)
RTAA	−1.618***	−0.952**
	(0.584)	(0.467)
Change in UE	0.091*	0.027
	(0.046)	(0.071)
UE t–1	−0.015	0.059
	(0.032)	(0.041)
Change in Inflation	−0.704	−0.948
	(2.036)	(1.916)
Inflation t–1	−0.795	−1.645
	(3.019)	(2.864)
Change in KL	−0.0001*	–
	(0.00006)	–
KL t–1	−0.00015	–
	(0.0001)	–
Change in Terms	0.011	0.015
	(0.021)	(0.026)
Terms t–1	0.011	−0.019
	(0.013)	(0.022)
Change in Exports	−0.446***	−0.652***
	(0.145)	(0.202)
Exports t–1	−0.183	−0.059
	(0.13)	(0.198)
PF	0.244	−0.245
	(0.327)	(0.502)
FP	−0.932**	−0.786*
	(0.439)	(0.462)
PP	−0.215	−0.026
	(0.502)	(0.452)
Income Tax	1.338*	−0.123
	(0.717)	(0.777)
War	−0.556	−1.122
	(1.064)	(1.146)
GATT	0.243**	−0.008
	(0.118)	(0.081)
Constant	0.422	3.026
	(1.382)	(1.855)
Number of Observations	87	106
F–stat	8.27	2.10

Notes: Newey–West Robust Standard Errors in Parentheses
***p<.01; **p<.05; *<p<.1

both statistically and substantively: here, the RTAA is predicted to lead to a 14% long-term drop in tariffs, or about 85% of the actual drop in tariffs after Smoot-Hawley, which was a 20% tariff, to the postwar low of 3%. In other words, contrary to Hiscox's (1999) hypothesis, delegation had a significant negative effect on tariff rates even after controlling for the increase in exports and other economic changes after World War II.

Hiscox (1999) is correct, though, that changing export patterns do have an effect on tariff rates as the short-term effect of exports is statistically significant in both models. In Model 3, a temporary 1% increase in exports leads to a 0.45% decrease in tariffs while this effect is even stronger in Model 4. UE and KL are the only other economic variables significant in Model 3 as a one standard deviation change in unemployment, about 2.5%, is estimated to produce about at 0.25% increase in tariffs. A one standard deviation change in the capital-labor ratio (about 2,500), leads to a similarly sized effect in the other direction: tariffs are predicted to drop by just over 0.25%. None of the other economic controls are significant, and none of them are significant in the long term. Partisanship also has little effect on tariff rates: only when there is a free-trade President with a protectionist Congress do tariff rates significantly differ. Further, the coefficients on the introduction of the income tax and the passage of GATT rounds are positive and significant, which is the exact opposite of what one would expect. However, neither of these coefficients is particularly robust to changes to specification. Most prominently, for instance, neither coefficient is significant in Model 4. Other than the loss of significance of these variables, Model 4 does not produce any other meaningfully different results, although the coefficient for unemployment also becomes insignificant in this specification.

While these results demonstrate that, even after controlling for changing political and economic circumstances, tariffs were lower after passage of the RTAA than they were before, they are not able to demonstrate why they are lower, a particularly important question to answer given that multiple theories all predict that tariff rates should have declined. Micro-level evidence about lobbying behavior provides a direct test of the causal logic underlying Access Point Theory and is able to discriminate between the different theories predicting the effect of the RTAA, in particular the reciprocity theory offered by BGW and Gilligan (1997).

As noted in Hypotheses 3.8 and 3.9 above, Access Point Theory predicts that both total and net protectionist lobbying should decline after the RTAA as delegation to the President increases the costs of lobbying, which reduces the total number of groups who find it beneficial to lobby and particularly reduces the number of protectionist groups. The reciprocity theory also predicts that net protectionist lobbying should decline but predicts that total lobbying should increase, which provides a crucial distinction between the two theories. The reciprocity theory argues that by linking domestic tariff reduction to foreign tariff reductions, exporters have a greater incentive to lobby for free trade domestically. Thus, the amount of free-trade lobbying should increase. However, the amount of protectionist lobbying by import competitors should be constant, as they still have an incentive to oppose domestic free trade and support domestic tariffs.[30] Because the amount of protectionist lobbying stays the same while the amount of free-trade lobbying increases, net protectionist lobbying is predicted to decline while total lobbying should increase. These contradictory predictions between Access Point Theory and reciprocity theory enable us to test to see which one is better supported.

Figure 3.1 summarizes the amount of lobbying on U.S. trade policy, showing the total number of interest groups presenting testimony in Congress on trade bills as well as the amount of net protectionist lobbying.[31] Hiscox (2002) argues that these data suggest that the RTAA had no effect on lobbying; this figure seems to support that contention as, after a precipitous drop in lobbying on the RTAA and the first two extensions of it, the amount of lobbying quickly rebounded back to levels seen before the Smoot-Hawley Tariff of 1929, which seems to be a slight outlier. However, this analysis ignores the possibility that other factors also affect the amount of lobbying. In particular, it ignores factor mobility, which Hiscox focuses on to explain trade policy outcomes. Hiscox argues that when factors are immobile, groups should lobby "intensely" while when factors are mobile, groups should be "inactive" (39). Thus, the number of lobbyists should increase as factor mobility decreases. According to Hiscox's measures, factor mobility was low after World War II and high or intermediate before. In other words, factor mobility was lower after the RTAA than before and, thus, we should expect more lobbying after the RTAA than before.

---

30. The BGW theory provides only one explanation for why protectionists should lobby less: import-competing industries disappear under increased external competition (327–328). The available evidence, though, suggests that industries, at least in the short term, did not disappear outright. See Destler (2005) and Hiscox (1999).

31. These data are collected from tables 4.4, 4.7, and 4.9 in Hiscox (2002, 53–66). I do not include data from table 4.2 (47) which examine lobbying from 1824 to 1842 because lobbying in this period is in the form of memorials, or letters written to the Congressional committee, which is quite different from appearing in person as a witness, which is the measure for lobbying in all the other time periods. Comparing the number of memorials written to the numbers of witnesses attending may be misleading.

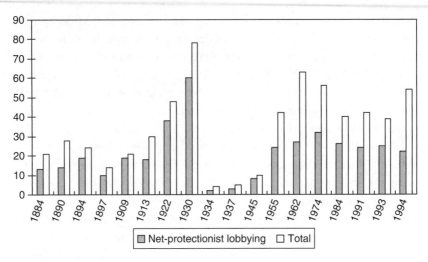

Figure 3.1
Lobbying on Trade Policy in the United States

Looking at the effects of the RTAA alone makes it seem that delegation has no significant effect on the amount or composition of lobbying; controlling for the anticipated effects of factor mobility tells a different story,[32] as shown in table 3.3, which reports regression results on the total number of lobbyists and the amount of net protectionist lobbying discussed above. Models 5 and 6 confirm that the effect of the RTAA is insignificant when considered in isolation: on average 2.5 more interest groups lobbied and 4.5 fewer net protectionist groups lobbied each bill after passage of the RTAA, although both of these effects are far from significant. Models 7 and 8 show what happens when one controls for factor mobility by including an ordinal variable equal to 1 in periods of low factor mobility, 2 in periods of intermediate factor mobility, and 3 in periods of high factor

---

32. Many other factors should also affect the amount of lobbying, but as there are only 18 trade bills in the dataset, it is impossible to include all of these variables. One obvious variable, though, is the size of the economy: the more economic activity that is occurring in the economy, the more lobbying may occur. Controlling for GDP does not alter the results measurably except that the RTAA has a marginally significant negative effect on net protectionist lobbying even without controlling for factor mobility. In addition, as stated above, partisanship has no effect. Nor does including a number of economic variables (one at a time) that might change the demand for protection, such as amount of imports or exports; changes in imports or exports; inflation; the terms of trade; or unemployment. While it is impossible to include in the model all of these variables at the same time, that none of them on their own change the overall result that the RTAA decreased both the amount of total lobbying and net protectionist lobbying should increase confidence in the results.

Table 3.3 EFFECT OF RTAA ON AMOUNT OF LOBBYING

Variable	Model 5	Model 6	Model 7	Model 8	Model 9
RTAA	2.5	−4.58	−58.5***	−46.5***	−
	(10.08)	(6.54)	(12.70)	(7.16)	−
Factor Mobility	−	−	−39.35***	−27.05***	−10.11*
	−	−	(7.22)	(4.07)	(5.15)
Constant	33***	23.88***	101.87***	71.21***	43.37***
	(7.51)	(4.87)	(7.60)	(7.55)	(6.42)
Number of Observations	18	18	18	18	18
Adjusted R-Squared	−0.058	−0.031	0.622	0.722	0.144
F-stat	0.06	0.49	14.96	23.03	3.85

Notes: Dependent Variable = Total Lobbying (Model 1, Model 3 and Model 5) or Net Protectionist Lobbying (Model 2 and Model 4)
***p<.01; **p<.05; *<p<.1

mobility, as determined by Hiscox. The RTAA leads to 58.5 fewer interest groups lobbying and 46.5 fewer net protectionist lobbyists, both quite large effects that are statistically significant at the 0.01 level. Interestingly, Hiscox's own theory receives better support when one controls for the RTAA than when one does not, as illustrated in Model 9. When factor mobility is entered by itself, there are 20 fewer lobbyists in periods of high factor mobility compared to periods of low factor mobility, an effect that is only marginally significant. However, as Model 7 reveals, when the RTAA is also controlled for, the substantive size of the effect increases almost four-fold, to nearly 80 fewer lobbyists when factor mobility is high, and the effect becomes statistically significant at the 0.01 level. This evidence suggests that the RTAA did have the predicted impact on lobbyist behavior, providing support for the causal foundations of Access Point Theory and providing evidence in favor of this theory over the reciprocity-based theory offered by BGW and Gilligan.

CONCLUSION

This chapter conducted the first tests of Access Point Theory and found strong support for the theory. First, countries that have more access points were found to be more protectionist: more parties in government, more electoral districts, less party discipline, and parliamentarism were all associated with higher tariff levels. Only federalism presented an anomalous finding. Second, tariff levels decreased in the United States after significant trade policy power was delegated to the President in 1934 as part of the RTAA, as predicted by the theory. Third, this chapter presents a test of the microfoundations of the theory by examining lobbying behavior on trade policy before the U.S. Congress. After the RTAA's passage, once one controls for the structure of the economy, both total lobbying and the size of the protectionists' lobbying advantage decreased, as expected by the theory.

In addition to this support for Access Point Theory, the chapter also addressed a number of debates within the trade policy literature. First, despite numerous existing research suggesting that PR should lead to either higher or lower tariff levels, this chapter found that once one controls for institutions associated with but not necessary for PR, like party discipline, coalition governments, and a small number of electoral districts, one finds that PR does not affect trade policy. In other words, it is not the proportionality of the electoral rule that matters, but the potential effect the implementation of this rule has on other institutions. Second, this chapter demonstrates that the RTAA had a significant influence on trade policy, despite skepticism from Hiscox and others, and that the delegation aspect of the RTAA, and not the reciprocity aspect as BGW and Gilligan suggest, is responsible for this reduction in tariffs.

CHAPTER 4

How Much Environmental Regulation Will a Country Have?

E nvironmental policy has become increasingly important both to policymakers and to political scientists. In the policy arena, the U.S. Congress has debated cap-and-trade legislation for a number of years; the European Union increased the community's competence over environmental policy in the Treaty of Lisbon to respond to increasing environmental threats; and the international community has met in a number of high-profile summits, such as at Copenhagen, to discuss global warming. In scholarly circles, increasing attention has been paid not only to the politics of environmental policy in general but also to the specific question of the domestic determinants of cross-national differences in the level of environmental regulation. For instance, in both economics and political science, significant attention has been paid to the relationships between economic growth and environmental regulation (Panayotou 2000) and trade and environmental regulation (Antweiler et al. 2001). Within political science, a large and robust literature has explored the differences between democracies and dictatorships in their environmental policymaking (Li and Reuveny 2006).

Yet despite the importance of environmental policy and the growing attention scholars have paid to it, we do not have much information about the political determinants of variation in environmental policy between democracies. A handful of studies have examined the effects of partisanship and corporatism on environmentalism while a few isolated studies have looked at such institutions as Presidentialism and federalism. However, we do not have a comprehensive picture of how institutional differences among democracies influence environmental regulations.

Access Point Theory is well positioned to paint this picture given the underlying dynamics of environmental policymaking.

Regulations in general concentrate costs on those who are being regulated; if the benefits of the regulation are dispersed across a wide swath of the population, as we might expect for such obvious environmental policies as clean air and clean water regulations, then this sets up a classic collective action advantage for the side opposing regulation. In the environmental sphere, as will be discussed in more detail below, we would generally expect industries that will be regulated to oppose regulation since these regulations add to their production costs and, thus, reduce their profits. For instance, if a clean air regulation requires factories to reduce their emissions, industries will have to change their production process or install scrubbers in their smokestacks or engage in other costly behavior to comply with this regulation. On the other hand, everyone who breathes the air benefits from this regulation. Thus, the costs of the regulation are more concentrated than the benefits so that opponents will have a lobbying advantage. If this sort of logic generalizes to most types of environmental regulations, as I will argue below, then we would expect additional access points to magnify the lobbying advantage of industry such that more access points will be associated with fewer environmental regulations.

To demonstrate this relationship, this chapter is organized as follows. First, I briefly review the existing literature on institutional influences on environmental policy, highlighting findings in the existing literature that already support Access Point Theory and debates in the literature that Access Point Theory can resolve. Second, I establish that industries opposed to environmental regulation have a collective action advantage over proponents of regulation and, thus, derive specific hypotheses about how access points affect environmental policymaking. Third, I discuss the data and methods to test these hypotheses, describing how I use environmental treaties as a proxy for environmental regulations as well as describing more direct measures of regulation that are used to test the robustness of the treaty results. Fourth, I present the results of these analyses which strongly support Access Point Theory and provide a more detailed understanding of the cross-national variation in environmental policy. Finally, I summarize the chapter and highlight additional research avenues in environmental policy that the chapter has opened.

DEMOCRATIC INSTITUTIONS AND ENVIRONMENTAL POLICYMAKING

Less scholarly attention has been paid to the domestic institutional determinants of environmental policymaking than to trade policymaking.

Thus, we have fewer studies upon which to build the analyses in this chapter than in the last chapter and fewer unresolved puzzles or debates to resolve beyond the general puzzle of, What are the domestic institutional determinants of environmental policymaking? A relatively large literature dating back over a decade has examined whether democracies lead to better or worse environmental outcomes or policies than dictatorships. Scholars have posited a number of different causal mechanisms for why democracy may affect the environment. On the positive side, for instance, Congleston (1992) suggests that the elite, who rule in autocracies, should be more opposed to environmental protection than the masses, who rule in democracies, since the elite control production facilities that may be hurt by environmental regulation. Further, Congleston suggests that autocracies might have shorter time horizons than democracies and therefore may discount the long-term costs of environmental degradation. Also, Payne (1995) suggests that the political rights associated with democracy enable environmental interest groups to flourish. On the negative side, Midlarsky (1998) argues that competing demands of interest groups in democracies can lead to a policy standstill which can prevent democracies from initiating necessary environmental protections, and Gleditsch and Sverdrup (2002) suggest that the political freedoms associated with democracy may exacerbate the tragedy of the commons as the government cannot stop individuals from overconsuming common resources.

Empirical studies have also been mixed, with each of the above authors finding empirical support for their claims by examining different measures of environmental conditions. However, the two most comprehensive and methodologically sophisticated recent examinations of democracy and environmentalism find that democracies tend to be superior to autocracies over a wide range of environmental measures, although the causal mechanism behind this remains unclear. Li and Reuveny (2006) find that democracies tend to have lower levels of numerous types of pollution as well as better performance in other areas of environmental outcomes. Neumayer (2002), using an empirical strategy most similar to the one employed here, finds that democracies are more likely to commit to environmental policies by, for instance, signing environmental treaties, joining environmental organizations, and making environmental information available.

Thus, despite ongoing debate, evidence seems to be emerging that, on average, democracies will have more environmentally friendly policies and better environmental outcomes than autocracies. But not all democracies are likely to be the same, and there have been only a handful of studies exploring the differences between democracies. A number of studies have investigated the relationship between corporatism and environmental performance and policy. Corporatism is a system of interest group representation where business and labor groups negotiate with each other to form economic, social, and labor policy for a country with the government serving as a mediator for these negotiations. One of the classic expressions of corporatism is coordinated wage bargaining, where a peak organization representing employers in the country negotiates with a national labor union to determine wages in a single contract, as opposed to a more decentralized negotiation process where each employer negotiates a separate contract with each group of workers (Siaroff 1999).

Scruggs (1999, 2001) has examined the relationship between corporatism and environmental quality, providing reasons why one might expect corporatism to lead to both good or bad environmental outcomes. For instance, the privileged position of labor and business interests in the typical corporatist system might shut out pro-environmental voices in favor of pro-growth voices without regard to the environmental impact of that growth. On the other hand, environmental policy passed through a corporatist system might be more effective as businesses and labor groups that were part of the negotiations over the regulations might view them as more legitimate and, therefore, be more likely to comply with them. Thus, corporatist systems might have fewer regulations but better outcomes. In addition, by enshrining peak organizations that represent all of labor or business, corporatism might lead interest groups to internalize the negative externalities of, for instance, pollution such that a peak labor organization might be more willing to support pollution controls than each individual labor union in a separate factory. Thus, corporatism might also lead to more environmental regulations. Despite offering expectation for both positive and negative influences of corporatism, Scruggs (1999, 2001) found, in two different cross sections of environmental performance in Europe, that corporatism is associated with better environmental performance although, given that he provided multiple possible reasons why this might be the case, he is unable to explain the causal mechanism behind this. On the other hand, Neumayer (2003) examines time-series results of environmental performance and finds less consistent results for the effect of corporatism, although his results do not contradict those of Scruggs.[1]

---

1. Neumayer (2003) also examines the effects of partisanship and finds that green and left party strength in the legislature are both associated with lower levels of pollution, the former association a strong one and the latter a weak one.

In addition to this series of articles, a few isolated studies have examined other democratic institutions. For instance, Lijphart (1999) finds that consensus democracies are better for the environment than majoritarian democracies as environmental performance is one of the hallmarks of "kinder, gentler" policy that Lijphart claims distinguished consensus democracies from majoritarian democracies. Poloni-Staudinger (2008) argues, though, that this finding is more complicated than Lijphart suggests in that consensus democracies are only better at "mundane environmentalism," and are, in fact, worse on conservation issues, and are no different from majoritarian democracies on environmental taxation and nuclear energy issues.[2] Walti (2004) examines how federalism affects environmental performance and finds that though federalism conditions the influence of development and corporatism, it does not have a simple and direct influence on pollution levels. Finally, Bernauer and Koubi (2009) conceptualize environmental policy as a public good and, building on Bueno de Mesquita et al.'s Selectorate Theory (2003), suggest that presidential systems will have larger winning coalitions and will, thus, provide more public goods, including better air quality. On the other hand, though they find that air quality is better, on average, in presidential systems, Bernauer and Koubi (2009) highlight that the more general results from Bueno de Mesquita et al. (2003) are weak: presidential systems provide more of some public goods, like peace and prosperity, but not of other public goods, like education and health care.

This existing literature, thus, provides something of a starting point for the analyses that follow. In particular, it highlights the potential importance of corporatism and that there is ongoing debate about whether and why corporatism affects environmentalism. In the next section, I will discuss how Access Point Theory can be extended to provide a prediction for the effects of corporatism, arguing that it should lead to fewer environmental regulations. The existing literature also includes one finding that is in accord with Access Point Theory's predictions—Bernauer and Koubi's (2009) finding that Presidentialism is associated with better environmental outcomes—and one finding that is at odds with Access Point Theory's predictions—Walti's (2004) finding that federalism has no direct

---

2. Poloni-Staudinger (2008) conducts factor analysis on a wide range of environmental indicators, including both outcome and policy variables, and uncovers the four factors listed above. Mundane environmentalism includes measures such as recycling and clean water. Conservation includes endangered species protection and land conservation. Environmental taxation includes taxes on water or energy usage and on nitrous oxide emissions. Nuclear energy includes percent of energy produced by nuclear power.

effect. This chapter, though, provides a more comprehensive test of the role of democratic institutions like Presidentialism and federalism on environmental policy and, thus, provides a richer picture of the domestic institutional determinants of environmentalism.

ACCESS POINTS AND ENVIRONMENTAL POLICY

In order for the number of access points to influence the level of bias in environmental policy, one side of the debate must have a lobbying advantage. I argue that, on average, the antienvironmental side will have this advantage since it will be better able to overcome the collective action problem. As such, increasing the number of access points should lead to lower levels of environmental policy. This collective action advantage for the antienvironmental side exists because environmental policy is a form of regulatory politics, and regulations frequently result in a collective action advantage for the regulated side given the typically concentrated costs of regulation. In a typical regulatory situation, the regulated group faces high costs to comply with the regulation while the benefits of this regulation are dispersed among all the users of the regulated products or all those who suffer fewer negative externalities because of the regulations. Consumer regulations are an example of the costs dispersed among users: for instance, consumer safety regulations concentrate costs on those making the product while dispersing benefits across all consumers of this product. Except in the rare cases where there are fewer purchasers than suppliers of a product, consumers will be more dispersed than producers and, hence, will suffer a collective action disadvantage against them. The next chapter explores bias in banking regulations, which can be viewed as a sort of consumer regulation in that they provide protection for the consumers of banking services.

Environmental regulations, for the most part, are an example of the benefits being dispersed among those who face negative externalities, as the benefits of these regulations are an elimination or reduction of these externalities. For instance, regulations limiting the amount of air pollution emitted by factories improve the quality of the air in surrounding regions (and perhaps around the world), which reduces negative health externalities that poor air quality can lead to. Water pollution regulations are similarly designed to reduce negative health externalities. Regulations to limit carbon are designed to limit the effects of global climate change on everyone on the planet. As can be seen in these examples, the benefits of environmental regulations are often so dispersed that they take on the character of a public good. In other words, not only is lobbying for or against the regulation a public good (as in the case of trade policy and tariffs), but also the policy itself is a public good.[3]

Thus, regulatory politics, and environmental regulations in particular, have the exact opposite pattern as trade policy: the opponents of regulations have the collective action advantage rather than the proponents of tariffs. We would, therefore, expect antienvironmental forces to lobby more than pro-environmental forces. This is clearly a simplifying assumption and will not always be true. For instance, as discussed above, some environmental regulations may not be a public good. Second, some industries support improved regulations, such as multinational corporations supporting improved regulations in developing countries to give them an advantage over domestic companies that do not yet have the capability to compete under these regulations (Prakash and Potoski 2006). However, given that this chapter examines developed countries and that most important environmental regulations, like clean air and water, are public goods (or, at least, common-pool goods), this assumption should be correct on average. Nor should this be taken as an argument that there are no pro-environmental lobbies: obviously, there are many large and powerful environmental interest groups, such as Greenpeace and the World Wildlife Foundation. Environmentalists can and do overcome the collective action problem (just as we saw that free traders can and do in chapter 3); they are merely at a disadvantage on most environmental policies because the costs of regulations are so concentrated on the regulated industry.

Given the collective action advantage of the antienvironmental side, we would expect additional access points to further magnify this advantage and, therefore, reduce the amount of environmental regulation in a country. Thus, following the general hypotheses discussed in chapter 2, the specific hypotheses tested in this chapter are as follows:

Hypothesis 4.1: The more electoral districts a country has, the fewer environmental regulations it will have.

---

3. Although not all environmental regulations may be public goods, there is a long history in political science of analyzing environmental politics as having a public goods component. For instance, Taylor and Ward (1982) argue that many environmental outcomes are "lumpy" public goods which are not continuously divisible; that is, some minimum amount of the good (some lump of it) must be provided for anyone to enjoy it. On the other hand, Ostrom (2003) suggests that environmental outcomes are common-pool goods rather than public goods. Both types of goods, though, exhibit the collective action behavior suggested by Olson (1972) that is necessary to drive bias in Access Point Theory.

Hypothesis 4.2: The less party discipline a country has, the fewer environmental regulations it will have.

Hypothesis 4.3: The more parties in government, the fewer environmental regulations there will be.

Hypothesis 4.4: Federalism leads to fewer environmental regulations.

Hypothesis 4.5: Presidentialism leads to more environmental regulations.

Hypothesis 4.6: PR and plurality systems should not have a significantly different amount of environmental regulations.

In addition to these hypotheses, the focus on corporatism in the existing literature calls our attention to the possibility that Access Point Theory might have predictions for the effects of corporatism as well. Corporatism does not change the number of access points in the system as the number of relevant, distinct, and independent policymakers is not influenced by corporatism. However, what corporatism does is institutionalize the relationship between a particular set of interest groups and the already existing access points. This should make lobbying cheaper for these privileged interest groups relative to other interest groups as existing access points might be more receptive to their concerns given their established relationship with these groups and because this existing relationship might lower the transaction costs of lobbying for the privileged groups. This should make the privileged interest groups even more likely to lobby on other issues than non-privileged interest groups. Thus, if a majority of interest groups privileged under corporatism have similar policy preferences, then we would expect corporatist systems to be more biased in that direction than pluralist systems. As argued above, business groups—one of the privileged actors—should be expected, ceteris paribus, to oppose environmental regulations. Labor unions—the other typically privileged actor—should also be expected to oppose environmental regulations, particularly in developed countries where environmental regulations are often viewed as placing labor at a competitive disadvantage with developing countries which do not have stringent regulations and, therefore, might have cheaper production costs. Thus, the groups privileged by corporatism will, on average, oppose environmental regulation, and so we should expect that corporatism should further bias policy in that direction.[4] As a result,

Hypothesis 4.7: Corporatism is associated with fewer environmental regulations.

---

4. Corporatism should also lead to increased bias in other policy areas if business and labor are united in their policy preferences in these areas as well. In the two other policy areas examined in this book, trade policy and banking regulations, we should not expect such a unity of preferences, so corporatism should have no effect on bias in these policies. Corporatism should also have no effect on complexity.

DATA AND METHODS

Access Point Theory makes predictions about policy instruments and not the outcomes of those policies. While policymakers may care about outcomes, their tool to influence those outcomes is policies. Moreover, many of the interest groups involved in politics care directly about the policy instruments, such as in the environmental case where industries are not opposed to a clean environment but only opposed to regulations that make it costlier for them to do business. While one expects that stronger environmental regulations will lead to better environmental outcomes, much else will also influence outcomes. For these reasons, the above hypotheses are couched in terms of environmental regulations and not environmental outcomes like pollution levels despite most existing work on the institutional effects focuses on environmental outcomes.

Unfortunately, while reasonably good cross-national data on environmental outcomes exist over long time periods, there is much less data on environmental policies. What does exist covers only a handful of countries or a limited number of years. Thus, the primary analyses in this chapter use a proxy variable for environmental policy: the number of environmental treaties to which a country becomes a party.[5] Though not a perfect measure of domestic environmental regulations, environmental treaties serves as a useful proxy since it should be positively correlated with the underlying concept of interest. In other words, the more environmental treaties to which a country is a party, the more domestic regulations they are likely to have. There are two reasons for this relationship. First, committing to environmental treaties often commits a country to enact certain regulations. Although there is debate in the literature about how effective international environmental commitments are in securing better environmental standards, research does suggest that those with more treaty commitments are more likely to have better environmental outcomes (Ward 2006). Second, even if treaties are not enforceable, countries with a strong commitment to environmental policy should be more likely to commit to environmental treaties (Ringquist and Kostadinova 2005; Von Stein 2008). Thus, we would expect treaty commitments to be strongly enough related to level of environmental regulation that they can serve as a useful proxy, though one that certainly contains a degree of measurement error.[6]

---

5. This is an increasingly common proxy measure. See, for instance, Neumayer (2002) and Bernauer et al. (2008).

6. As in the case of tariffs and trade, as long as the measure is positively correlated with the underlying concept, measurement error in the dependent variable yields conservative but unbiased estimates.

In addition to environmental treaties, the chapter also presents results using a more direct measure of environmental policy: levels of environment-related taxation. This measure has its own limitations, though. First, it only measures limited elements of environmental policy. Second, and more important, it is only available for a limited time series. Environmental tax data are available starting in about 1995 for most of the OECD countries, including a number of the newer members in Eastern Europe and elsewhere admitted in the OECD's expansion in the 1990s. This limited temporal sample will necessitate the use of less sophisticated statistical techniques and the use of the summary measure of access points and the all-democracy sample, but combined with the environmental treaty measure, it should provide confidence in the effect of access points on environmental regulations.

The environmental tax data are taken from the *OECD Environmental Data Compendium* (2004). The OECD defines environmental taxes as "those levied on tax bases deemed to be of particular environmental relevance" (286). These include waste management fees and taxes, taxes on the production of pollutants, such as ozone-depleting chlorofluorocarbons, as well as taxes on energy and transportation usage. In order to provide a basis for comparison, total revenue from all of these sources is divided by either total government revenue, to measure how important environmental taxation is relative to the size of government, or by GDP, to measure how much revenue is collected relative to the size of the economy. Thus, there will be two analyses on environmental taxation, one for each of these variables. The data on environmental treaties is taken from the Environmental Treaties and Resource Indicators (ENTRI),[7] which records the environmental treaties that every country signs or becomes a party to. The dependent variable in this study is the current number of treaties to which a country is a party. To create this variable, I compute for each country-year the number of treaties a country is a party to minus the number of treaties previously renounced. I use treaties a country is a party to rather than treaties signed for two reasons: first, treaties that are signed but not ratified (like Kyoto for the United States) do not create regulatory requirements for the signing country; and, second, countries do add regulatory requirements when they accede to a treaty even when they do not sign it. In fact, for all countries in the dataset, the number of treaties to which a country is a party is much larger than the number they have signed. The average number of treaties a country is a party to in any given year is about

---

7. ENTRI is compiled by the Center for International Earth Science Information Network (CIESIN) at Columbia University. The data used to code the dependent variable are available at http://sedac.ciesin.columbia.edu/entri/.

95, with a standard deviation of about 52. The lowest number of treaties in any country-year is 18, which Canada had in 1954 and 1955; the highest is 236, which France had in 1997. The countries with the fewest average number of treaties are Japan, Canada, and New Zealand, each with about 59; the countries which were democratic across the entire sample range with the highest are France with about 132 and Germany with about 124.[8]

For the treaty data, I test Access Point Theory with the disaggregated access point variables in the OECD sample discussed in chapter 2; for the taxation data, I use the summary measure in the full-democracy sample. Given that Access Point Theory also makes predictions about corporatism, I include this measure separately in the treaty analysis. Numerous debates exist about how to measure corporatism as different scholars have focused, theoretically, on different aspects of corporatism, which leads them to measure the concept in different ways, sometimes, for instance, emphasizing how interest groups are represented and sometimes focusing more specifically on the nature of wage bargaining. In addition to this proliferation of competing measures, most of these measures suffer from the problem of being collected for only one year, thus providing a static measure of what has surely been a dynamic concept. As a result, this chapter uses the data from Siaroff (1999), which measures corporatism as how "integrated" the economy and society are, with integration defined as "a long-term co-operative pattern of shared economic management involving the social partners" of business and labor (189). This concept subsumes most of the previous measures of corporatism: for instance, countries that strongly coordinate their wage bargaining and countries which have encompassing interest group structure will have high levels of integration. The data also contain measures for each country at four different time periods (late '60s, late '70s, late '80s, and mid-'90s) rather than a single data point for each country. While this is less than ideal for the annual data used here, it is a vast improvement over previous measures which often provided only one observation for each country. The analyses below assume that the corporatism scores are

---

8. An alternative dataset compiling environmental treaty data is Mitchell (2008). This dataset provides less temporal coverage than ENTRI as well as an overly expansive definition of environmental treaty. For instance, nuclear arms reduction treaties are considered environmental treaties; while it is true that these treaties have an environmental impact (and having an environmental impact is the criteria for inclusion in this dataset), it is likely that these treaties are governed by different political processes than, for instance, pollution control treaties. As a result of these two considerations, the Mitchell data likely have more measurement error than the ENTRI data for the purposes of this study. Replicating the analyses described below with the Mitchell data, though, is broadly supportive of access point theory, though the results are less robust with these data.

constant across the years in the measured decade, so that each country has the same score for every year in the '70s, for instance. Further, it uses the late '60s score for the 1940s and 1950s as well.

A number of control variables building on previous work on the cross-national determinants of environmental policy are also included. For instance, Neumayer (2003) investigated the role of partisanship on environmental policy, arguing that, traditionally, left parties were seen as hostile to the environment as increased regulation may harm the competitiveness of labor, but that left parties have increasingly begun to represent pro-environmental interests as well, especially in countries without a variable Green party. To explore this question, I include the variable *Left*, as in the previous chapter, measuring the percent of the cabinet made up of left-leaning ministers and adapted from Franzese (2002b).

Much attention in the cross-national environmental outcomes literature investigates the Environmental Kuznets Curve (EKC) (Dinda 2004; Panoyatou 2000),[9] which describes a possibly curvilinear relationship between economic growth and environmental outcomes. Economic growth might be expected to lead to degradations in the environment as growth is usually accompanied (or caused) by increased industrialization that leads to increased pollution or other negative environmental effects. However, economic growth also might lead to technological developments such as greener industrial techniques and increased demands by the population for better environmental policies. Combining these two considerations, the EKC suggests that there is an inverted-U relationship between wealth, as measured by GDP per capita, and environmental outcomes: growth initially leads to poorer environmental outcomes but, at a certain point, starts to lead to better environmental conditions.

To test for this, research on the topic usually includes both GDP per capita and its squared term: if the EKC exists, then we would expect, if the dependent variable is environmental quality, the coefficient on GDP per capita to be negative, the coefficient on the squared term to be positive, and the absolute value of the coefficient on the squared term to be smaller than the absolute value of the coefficient on GDP per capita. While the EKC seems to exist for environmental outcomes, it is less clear why it should exist for environmental policy. Indeed, we might simply expect that wealthier countries, which can afford better regulations and which tend to have a higher demand for regulations, to have more regulation.

---

9. See also Li and Reuveny (2006) for a brief application to the environment and democracy literature.

However, to test for the possibility of an EKC in policy, I include both per capita GDP and squared per capita GDP as measures of income.

In addition, I include GDP as a control variable: first, larger countries tend to have economies that are more complex and might, as a result, find more environmental treaties relevant; and, second, larger countries might have more power in shaping environmental treaties and, thus, find the finished product more acceptable to them. A final economic control is the level of trade openness. A large literature exists exploring the relationship between trade and the environment with arguments and evidence provided both that trade should improve the environment—by diffusing pro-environmental norms from rich countries to poor—and that trade should harm the environment—by creating a race to the bottom in environmental policies (Antweiler et al. 2001; Prakash and Potoski 2006). Thus, the analyses below include trade openness, or exports plus imports divided by GDP, as a control.

When a country enters into an agreement, it tends to stay a party to that agreement: although it can renounce the agreement, this is extremely rare. Thus, the number of agreements to which a country is a party in year t is influenced by the number to which it was a party in year t-1. Therefore, I include the lagged number of agreements as an independent variable. In addition, the rate of growth in the number of environmental treaties may have increased over time as environmentalism has become a more prominent issue. Thus, I include an annual trend term, *Year*, in the analyses below. Finally, some of the agreements in the database are European Union treaties which only EU members can join. Thus, I include a dummy variable for EU membership, though excluding this variable does not affect the substantive results in important ways.

Because the treaty variable is a count of the number of treaties, the results presented below are estimated with a Poisson regression, a standard maximum likelihood estimator for such variables.[10] The main model estimated is as follows:

$$
\begin{aligned}
\text{Treaties} = {} & \beta_0 + \beta_1 \text{Treaties}_{t-1} + \beta_2 \text{Electoral-Districts}_{t-1} + \beta_3 \text{Pool}_{t-1} \\
& + \beta_4 \text{Number-of-parties}_{t-1} + \beta_5 \text{Bicameralism}_{t-1} \\
& + \beta_6 \text{Presidential}_{t-1} + \beta_7 \text{PR}_{t-1} + \beta_8 \text{Corporatism}_{t-1} \\
& + \beta_9 \text{GDP/Capita}_{t-1} + \beta_{10} \text{GDP/Capita}^2_{t-1} + \beta_{11} \text{GDP}_{t-1} \\
& + \beta_{12} \text{Openness}_{t-1} + \beta_{13} \text{Left}_{t-1} + \beta_{14} \text{EU}_{-1} + \beta_{15} \text{Year} + \varepsilon.
\end{aligned}
\tag{1}
$$

10. In addition, the main model includes fixed-effects by country to control for any unmeasured heterogeneity, and all of the independent variables are lagged one year to avoid temporal correlation concerns. Poisson models are used for the treaty data because tests demonstrate that they do not suffer from over-dispersion; that is, the assumption that the mean and variance of the distribution are equal is not violated.

The environmental tax models use Ordinary Least Squares (OLS) with robust standard errors, partly because the relatively small sample size makes panel analysis difficult but also because the dependent variable here is continuous, making the simpler OLS estimation appropriate. Because of the switch to the all-democracy dataset, not all of the independent variables listed above are included, though measures of the business cycle are included—unemployment and inflation—as the state of the overall economy is likely to influence a country's taxation decisions.[11] The tax models estimated below are as follows:

$$\text{Tax} = \beta_0 + \beta_1 \text{Access Points}_{t-1} + \beta_2 \text{PR}_{t-1} + \beta_3 \text{GDP/Capita}_{t-1}$$
$$+ \beta_4 \text{GDP/Capita}^2_{t-1} + \beta_5 \text{GDP}_{t-1} + \beta_6 \text{Openness}_{t-1} + \beta_7 \text{EU}_{t-1}$$
$$+ \beta_8 \text{Unemployment}_{t-1} + \beta_9 \text{Inflation}_{t-1} + \varepsilon. \qquad (2)$$

RESULTS

The results of the analyses, shown in table 4.1, provide strong support for the argument that countries with more access points tend to have fewer environmental regulations. Model 1 shows the results of the main model and, as can be seen, all of the access point variables are statistically significant in the expected direction. The only hypothesis that does not receive empirical support is Hypothesis 4.6, as PR is negative and significant rather than insignificant as predicted.[12] The other hypotheses are all supported, though, suggesting that the number of access points is a key predictor of environmental regulations. The more government parties or electoral districts there are, the less regulation there will be; federalism is also associated with less regulation while party discipline and Presidentialism are associated with more regulation. Finally, corporatism is associated with lower levels of regulation, as predicted.[13]

---

11. Because of the smaller sample size in these regressions, the country dummies are dropped as is the lagged dependent variable since there are few time periods in the panel data. The *Corporatism* variable is dropped because Siaroff (1999) does not provide measures for the newer countries that joined the OECD in the 1990s. The *Left* variable is also dropped as the full-democracy sample does not have a good measure of partisanship.

12. This finding suggests that Lijphart (1999) might be correct that PR systems (instead of the winner-take-all nature of plurality systems) encourage "kinder" and "gentler" policy. We would need to examine further areas where Access Point Theory predicts bias in "kinder, gentler" policies to see how generalizable this finding for PR is.

13. The results presented here are robust to numerous alternative specifications. For instance, dropping the lagged dependent variable, to account for the possible concerns raised in Achen (2000) about lagged dependent variables "stealing"

Table 4.1 THE EFFECT OF ACCESS POINTS ON NUMBER
OF ENVIRONMENTAL TREATIES

Treaties (t–1)	0.0009***
	(0.0003)
Electoral Districts	−0.0006***
	(0.0002)
Pool	−0.111***
	(0.03)
Number of Parties	−0.018***
	(0.004)
Bicameralism	−0.005***
	(0.001)
Presidential	0.153**
	(0.066)
PR	−0.243
	(0.076)
Corporatism	−0.059***
	(0.021)
GDP per capita	0.0001***
	(8.67E-06)
GDP per capita (squared)	−4.25E-09***
	(3.54E-10)
GDP	8.27E-11***
	(1.79E-11)
Openness	−0.137***
	(0.047)
Left	−0.011
	(0.012)
EU	−0.017
	(0.016)
Year	0.030***
	(0.002)
Number of Observations	903
Psuedo R-squared	.799

Notes: Dependent Variable = Number of Environmental Treaties
Standard Errors in Parentheses
***p<.01; **p<.05; *p<.1
Constant and fixed-effects coefficients not reported

explanatory power from other variable, does not change the results. Dropping the country dummies only marginally changes the results: number of parties is no longer significant, but all the other access point variables are. Changing the coding of Presidentialism to not include Finland or France does influence whether or not Presidentialism is significant, but none of the other variables see their significance change.

Because Model 1 is a Poisson estimation, table 4.1 is only able to show the statistical significance of the variables and not the substantive size of the effects, as these are not directly interpretable from the individual coefficients. Table 4.2, therefore, shows the change in predicted number of environmental treaties resulting from specified changes in institutions using the Clarify program as described in King, Tomz, and Wittenberg (2000). Clarify simulates the results of the model an arbitrary but large number of times (in this case 1,000) and provides both an estimated effect of changing the value of one of the variables and a standard error around that effect. Table 4.2 reports the change in the number of predicted treaties if a particular variable is changed from its mean (or median) to its minimum, maximum, and one standard deviation above or below the mean (or median) as well as the 95% confidence interval around that predicted change. All other variables are held at their means (for continuous variables), medians (for ordinal variables), or modes (for categorical variables.)

As can be seen, the substantive size of the effects range from modest to large, but none are trivially small in a substantive sense. For instance, a one standard deviation increase in the number of electoral districts is predicted to lead to over 15 fewer treaties. Moving from the minimum number of electoral districts (the Netherlands and other countries with one national district) to the largest number of electoral districts (the UK, with over 600) is predicted to lead to nearly 35 fewer treaties (by summing the change from moving from the minimum to the mean and the mean to the maximum). Compare these figures to the overall statistics on number of treaties signed: the average is about 94 with a standard deviation of about 50 and a range from 18 to 236. Thus, while 15 fewer treaties from a one standard deviation change in number of electoral does not represent a shift from having among the most treaties to having among the fewest, it does represent a sizable change, roughly akin to the difference between France, which has the most treaties among countries that were democratic throughout the sample, and Belgium, which had the sixth most treaties.

Coalition government has a somewhat smaller effect with single-party governments predicted to have about 9 more treaties than the largest coalition governments. Party discipline produces a substantive effect in between number of districts and number of parties: a one standard deviation increase in pooling leads to about 8 more treaties and the difference in the minimum and the maximum is about 21 more treaties. Corporatism has a similarly large effect, while bicameralism has an extremely large effect: unicameral countries are predicted to have nearly 80 more treaties than the bicameral country with the most members in

Table 4.2 SIMULATED SUBSTANTIVE EFFECTS OF INSTITUTIONS

Variable	Minimum	1 S.D. Below	1 S.D. Above	Maximum
Electoral Districts	7.442	7.442	-15.57	-27.15
	(2.434, 13.05)	(2.434, 13.05)	(-25.83, -5.571)	(-43.93, -10.24)
Pool	8.286	8.286	-8.33	-12.595
	(3.291, 13.799)	(3.291, 13.799)	(-13.426, -3.493)	(-20.112, -5.362)
Number of Parties	2.006	2.006	-2.215	-7.474
	(0.964, 3.094)	(0.964, 3.094)	(-3.388, -1.077)	(-11.32, -3.688)
Bicameralism	22.7	22.7	-30.36	-56.91
	(-16.36, 30.0)	(-16.36, 30.0)	(-38.55, -23.02)	(-70379, -44.55)
Presidential	17.33	–	–	–
	(2.748, 35.047)	–	–	–
PR	-27.59	–	–	–
	(-49.319, -9.495)	–	–	–
Corporatism	9.909	6.868	-6.301	-8.82
	(2.565, 16.78)	(1.8, 11.534)	(-10.23, -1.749)	(-14.2, -2.476)

Notes: Effect of moving specified variable from mean or median to specified value listed on first line 95% Confidence Interval listed in parentheses on second line
Effect for Presidentialism and PR is the effect of moving from 0 to 1
When 1 S.D. Below Mean is below the minimum value, effect of moving from minimum to mean is substituted

the upper house (Canada, with 105). Presidential countries are predicted to have roughly 17 more treaties than parliamentary countries. On the whole, these results are strongly significant both statistically and substantively, and suggest that the more access points there are, the fewer environmental treaties to which a country will be a party.

Before moving on to the control variables, I will discuss in more detail the implications of the corporatism results. Previous work by Scruggs (1999, 2001) has found that corporatism is associated with better environmental outcomes, such as lower levels of pollution. The results presented here find, on the other hand, that corporatism is associated with fewer environmental regulations. Rather than being seen as conflicting findings, though, these two sets of results might actually help us to better understand the causal pathway by which corporatism affects the environment. In particular, Scruggs offers a number of different possible causal mechanisms by which corporatism affects environmental outcomes but, as he acknowledges, his results do not provide a test between these possible mechanisms. The two main causal mechanisms Scruggs discusses are, first, that the peak associations that comprise corporatism allow interest groups to internalize the externalities often associated with pollution and, thus, make them more likely to lobby for environmental regulations than interest groups that are fragmented based on industry and less sensitive to the negative externalities from their production activities; and, second, that there might be better monitoring and enforcement of regulations under corporatism because industries and unions find them more legitimate given that they took part in negotiations over them. The first causal story implies that corporatism should be associated with more regulations while the second causal story has no implications for amount of regulations, just how well those regulations are enforced. Since the results in this chapter show that corporatism is associated with fewer regulations, it is likely the latter, enforcement-based causal story that explains corporatism's association with better environmental outcomes instead of the lobbying story. To further test this argument, though, we would want to examine data on enforcement of treaties and other regulations.

Briefly looking at the control variables in Model 1, we see some interesting results as well. First, partisanship is not significant, which is mildly surprising: neither left nor right governments are more likely to become parties to environmental treaties. This might be because the measure of partisanship conflates traditional left parties, which tend to represent workers who might be opposed to regulations for job-related reasons, and new left parties, which tend to be more environmentally oriented. Second, EU countries are also not statistically different from non-EU countries. Third, trade openness leads to fewer environmental treaties, suggesting that there may be a race to the bottom or, at least, some regulatory chill as discussed above. Fourth, larger countries are party to more agreements, possibly because they have more complex economies and societies and, therefore, might find that more agreements are relevant to them or because they have more power internationally and are able to shape agreements and, thus, find more of them preferable. Finally, there is no evidence of an EKC in policy as there is in outcomes. In fact, increasing wealth leads to increasing amounts of treaties, although the negative coefficient on the squared term suggests that this effect tapers off at high levels of wealth.

Table 4.3 presents the analysis of environmental taxation, with Model 2 using environmental taxation as a share of GDP as the dependent variable and Model 3 using environmental taxation as a share of total government revenue. Most important, the summary access point measure is negative and significant in both models: the more access points a country has the

Table 4.3 THE EFFECT OF ACCESS POINTS ON ENVIRONMENTAL TAXATION

Variable	Model 2	Model 3
Access Points	−0.108***	−0.336***
	(0.035)	(0.122)
PR	−0.293	−0.614
	(0.195)	(0.668)
GDP per capita	−5.26E−06	−4.88E−05
	(2.17E−05)	(7.91E−05)
GDP per capita (squared)	3.31E−10	−2.27E−10
	(4.70E−10)	(1.81E−09)
GDP	−2.34E−11***	−3.37E−13***
	(2.67E−14)	(7.35E−14)
Openness	−0.005***	−0.010**
	(0.001)	(0.005)
EU	0.982***	1.468***
	(0.125)	(0.414)
Unemployment	−0.061***	−0.240***
	(0.012)	(0.047)
Inflation	0.008**	0.030**
	(0.004)	(0.009)
Number of Observations	163	163
R−squared	.567	.430

Notes: Dependent Variable = Environmental Taxation as a share of GDP (Model 1)
Environmental Taxation as a share of total taxation (Model 2)
Robust Standard Errors in Parentheses
***p<.01; **p<.05; *<p<.1

lower their levels of environmental taxation. A one standard deviation change in the access point variable leads to about 0.25% lower taxes relative to GDP and about 0.75% lower taxes relative to overall revenue. Each of these effects is substantial in substantive terms: the means for the two dependant variables are 2.7% for the GDP measure and 7.4% for the revenue measure with standard deviations of 0.8 and 2.2 respectively. PR is negative but is insignificant in both models.

The coefficients on the control variables are all in the same direction in the two models except for the squared term on GDP per capita. In both models, larger countries have lower levels of taxation, which is at odds with the finding above that larger countries agree to more treaties, suggesting that the finding from Model 1 may be an artifact of power or economic complexity rather than a true preference for larger countries to have more environmental regulation. Similar to the above results, though, the more a country trades, the lower the tax rates, reinforcing the concerns about a race to the bottom suggested above. Further, economic conditions have a mixed effect on environmental taxation: high unemployment leads to lower taxes, while high inflation leads to higher taxes.[14] European Union countries have higher tax levels than non-EU countries in this sample. Finally, richer countries are not predicted to have different levels of environmental taxation than poorer countries, which is at odds with the treaty results above that found that richer countries had stronger environmental regulations.

CONCLUSION

This chapter continues to find strong support for Access Point Theory. All of the institutions associated with more access points influence the number of environmental treaties a country signs in the expected direction: the more parties in government, the more electoral districts, the less party discipline, and the presence of bicameralism and parliamentarism all lead to fewer treaties. Further, the more access points a country has, the lower its level of environmental taxation. Thus, the more access points there are, the more biased policy is toward industry and away from environmental protection or improvement.

---

14. This is actually in keeping with standard Keynesian macroeconomic advice: during recessions, one can stimulate the economy by cutting taxes, and one can reign in inflation by raising taxes.

In addition to this support for Access Point Theory, the results of this chapter have interesting implications for the literature on environmental policy. As stated at the start of the chapter, while a lot of research has investigated the differences between democracies and autocracies on environmental policy and outcomes, significantly less research has addressed the question of what causes variation within democracies. The results of this chapter suggest that, at least within democracies, traditional interest group politics can explain a lot of the variation in environmental policy: industries oppose regulations because they add costs to the production process and where interest groups have power, these industries can lobby the government to reduce the amount of regulations or prevent regulations from being created.

Thus, while this chapter investigated conditions that lead to interest groups having more power, it largely ignored the possible interest groups themselves. In other words, the balance between industry and environmentalists is likely to vary between countries and over time. As environmentalism has grown more popular, the collective action advantage of industry has possibly shrunk while countries with more heavy industry likely have stronger demands for low regulations than countries with a larger service sector. Future- research on environmental policy should explore these demand factors more while keeping in mind that the importance of the different levels of demands for and against regulations will depend upon how much access is given to the different sides of the debate.

CHAPTER 5

Regulating Banks

Capital-Friendly or Consumer-Friendly Rules?

There are many reasons for the global recession and financial crisis that began in 2008, but given that a major component of the crisis was the collapse of banks and investment firms, a lot of attention has been paid to the role of banking regulations. Banks were engaging in ever riskier investment practices and new, complicated financial instruments were created, such as collateralized debt obligations and credit default swaps. When the U.S. housing market began to crumble, it became clear that the success of all these investment instruments across the world was predicated on continued high levels of growth in housing prices. When this failed to occur, venerable investment firms like Merrill Lynch, insurance firms like AIG, and banks like Citigroup all collapsed, and the U.S. government stepped in to bail out many of these companies in fear that panic would spread, bringing down the entire global financial system. American banks and the U.S. government were not alone in this process: for instance, the British government had to nationalize Northern Rock bank in 2007 and virtually the entire Icelandic banking and financial sectors collapsed starting in 2008.

How did this happen? While it is beyond the scope of this book to provide a detailed examination of the causes of the global recession, many have suggested that lax banking and financial regulations played a crucial role. For instance, many of these new financial instruments were unregulated (and were created because they were unregulated), meaning that consumers had poor levels of information about them, and there were no clear rules about how companies were supposed to account for these investments on their balance sheets. Thus, no one knew how financially sound banks and investment firms really were. Others have suggested that the 1999 repeal of the Glass-Steagall Act of 1933, which had prevented banks in the United States from engaging in many investment activities, allowed banks to engage in overly risky behavior. Still others have suggested that international agreements which require banks to keep a certain amount of capital on hand to prevent bank runs and to pay off bad investments— namely the Basel Accords—were not strong enough nor able to cope with the different types of risks that new investment vehicles created.

There is vast variation in both how much regulation different countries have and in the form of these regulations. While large literatures in economics and finance, both before and after the crisis, have investigated the effect of different levels and types of regulation on bank solvency, bank competitiveness, economic growth, and other financial outcomes, less attention has been paid to why this variation exists at all. Given how important these regulations might be, the causes of this variation take on added importance. Why, for instance, did the United States abandon the strong Glass-Steagall Act and Japan abandon its own version of the Glass-Steagall Act (Lindner 1993), while other countries, such as Israel and Indonesia, maintain restrictions on bank investment activity and still other countries, such as Germany, never had these restrictions? Why have some countries complied with the Basel Accords and others have not? Why do some countries have stronger deposit insurance schemes than others?

Access Point Theory can provide answers to these sorts of questions. As discussed in the previous chapter, regulations tend to concentrate costs on the regulated industry but disperse the benefits across the entire population or all consumers of a product. Thus, opponents of regulations should have a collective action advantage and countries with more access points should have fewer regulations. This should be especially true in the case of banking regulations as regulations are designed to prevent not only the collapse of individual banks, which would hurt all depositors at that bank, but also account for "systemic risk," the idea that the collapse of one bank could spread to bring down the entire financial system. In other words, regulations benefit everyone in the country and, for large and integrated economies, everyone in the world.[1] On the other hand, the

---

1. This is actually a more contentious point than one might imagine. As will be described in more detail in the next section, some scholarly analyses suggest that many bank regulations actually increase the risk-taking behavior of banks.

effect of access points on banking regulations is complicated by the fact that not all regulations are opposed by all banks: banks actually like certain regulations as will be discussed in the next two sections. Thus, Access Point Theory predicts that more access points will lead to fewer regulations that banks oppose but more regulations that banks support.[2]

To demonstrate these points, the rest of this chapter is organized as follows. The first section describes why regulations of banks might be desirable and some of the many different types of regulations used to achieve these goals. The second section reviews the literature on the sources of cross-national variation in regulations. The third section describes who lobbies for what in regards to banking regulations—arguing that banks lobby for capital adequacy standards, as emphasized in the Basel Accords, but against most other types of regulation—and establishes that banks have a collective action advantage. From these two points, testable hypotheses on banking regulations are drawn from Access Point Theory. The fourth section introduces the data and methods used to test these hypotheses and the fourth section presents the results of these tests. The final section concludes by summarizing how the findings support Access Point Theory and what we have learned about the determinants of regulatory variation.

HOW ARE BANKS REGULATED AND WHY?

Bank regulations fall into two main classes: consumer protection and providential regulation. The former is designed to ensure that consumers are not defrauded or preyed upon and include regulations governing bank transparency and disclosure as well limits on fees or interest charged. This chapter focuses on the latter, which are designed to prevent banks from becoming insolvent, that is, to prevent the collapse of banks. I focus on providential regulations (and from here on will use the phrase "bank regulations" to mean only this type of regulation) because consumer protection regulations are typical across a wide range of different industries while providential regulations are more specific to the banking (and other financial) sectors of the economy. Because of this, the politics of the former type

---

2. This is a potentially generalizable point: while, on average, industries will oppose regulations on them and, thus, more access points will lead to fewer regulations, there may exist in other regulatory realms industry-supported regulations. When this occurs, increasing the number of access points will actually increase these types of regulations.

of regulation may be broader than an analysis of the banking sector, although Access Point Theory should be able to explain overall level of consumer protection in society as well. In addition, well-developed literatures in economics, business, and political science focus on providential regulations as these types of regulations are designed to prevent not only the collapse of individual banks but also the possibility of a collapse of the entire national or global banking and financial system. As a result, these regulations are more important nationally and internationally than consumer protection, which focuses on important yet containable issues.[3]

There are many different forms of providential regulations, and countries can choose from a wide menu of options for how to prevent bank collapses and how to minimize the risk of isolated collapses spreading, which presents both a challenge and an opportunity in the empirical testing described below. Though the form and level of regulation differs, all countries currently have some form of providential regulation because the very nature of modern banking creates both the risk of banks collapsing and the risk that these collapses will spread. In other words, the structure of banking creates externalities where the decisions of one bank can affect all other banks such that even the banks themselves recognize that some regulation is necessary to protect them from the actions of bad banks.

This risk derives from the fact that banks are not merely a repository for other people's money: they use the money people deposit to make investments or provide loans to others. As a result, a bank never has the cash on hand to cover even a fraction of their own outstanding liabilities. In other words, if everyone (or, actually, just a small fraction of everyone) who deposited money in a bank withdrew her money within some small time frame, the bank would quickly run out of cash and would not be able to give people their money; that is, the bank would collapse. Thus, if you did not ask for your money quickly enough, you would be left with nothing, giving you an incentive to run to the bank at the first sign of trouble. The expectation that failure is possible therefore might lead to a bank failure even when the bank was solvent. This also accounts for the contagion effect of bank failures: if one bank fails, people might wonder how sound their bank is, and the more banks that fail the more likely people will overreact and demand their money from their bank even if their bank is

---

3. This is not to say that fraud cannot have large-scale effects on the economy, as the Bernie Madoff scandal shows and as the Enron accounting scandal also suggests. However, the goal of consumer protection regulations is to protect the individual consumers while the goal of providential regulations is to protect the financial system. Failures in the former can sometimes be so large as to lead to problems in the latter, but this is rare.

sound. Regulation is seen as necessary to either prevent banks from becoming unsound or to prevent depositors from believing banks are unsound.

There are multiple ways to achieve this purpose. The first is to guarantee that depositors will receive their money back even if the bank fails so that people do not have to run to banks at the first sign of trouble, which should reduce the chances that sound banks fail because of panic and should reduce the contagion effect of bank failures. In the United States, a specific agency, the Federal Deposit Insurance Corporation (FDIC), was created just to serve this role. The FDIC insures all deposits up to a specified amount using a large, permanent fund as backing for deposits in every U.S. bank. The money for this fund is generated through fees on banks. Similar systems exist in many other countries: in fact, 60% of countries in the sample have an explicit deposit insurance system. However, not every deposit insurance system is the same: Britain, for instance, does not have a permanent fund to bail out depositors but rather raises funds as needed through a special levy on banks. In addition, Britain does not have a specific agency overseeing just deposit insurance: before passage of the Financial Services Act in 2000, which reformed British banking regulation, the Bank of England—Britain's central bank—oversaw deposit insurance. Now, the Financial Services Compensation Scheme oversees it, but it also oversees insurance and compensation programs for many other financial activities, such as insurance and mortgage provision (Davies and Green 2008, 50–51). Another common difference between deposit insurance systems is whether reimbursement is capped and whether some form of coinsurance is used, such as in Germany where depositors only receive 90% of their deposit back. Coinsurance and caps are designed to ameliorate a potential downside of deposit insurance: insurance may create a moral hazard by encouraging banks and depositors to engage in risky behavior (Ioannidou and Penas 2010).

In addition, deposit insurance only mitigates the risk of runs on sound banks (and ensures that depositor's own assets are safe); it does not minimize the risks that banks will collapse because they actually are unsound if they lost money on risky investments or if they gave out bad loans or if they poorly managed their money such that they have a liquidity crisis not caused by a bank run. Again, there are multiple options if a country wishes to adopt regulations to reduce bank risk. Banks can be required to keep a certain amount of liquid funds on hand, to prevent liquidity crises but also to serve as a reserve fund in case of investment loss or loan default. This is known as a capital adequacy regulation and is the primary method of regulation adopted in the Basel Accords. The Basel Accords are an international agreement reached by the national bank regulators of the major industrial economies in 1988 in order to increase the stability of the international banking system without undermining the competitiveness of any domestic banking system (Singer 2007). To achieve both goals simultaneously, the Basel Accords set a minimum amount of reserve capital each bank had to hold based upon how large a bank's assets were and how risky their investments were. The Basel Accords were updated in 2004 to better account for differences in risk in the modern economy, but both accords were designed to prevent banks from running too much risk without allowing banks in one country to gain a competitiveness advantage by adhering to low standards. While the benefits of capital adequacy standards should be a more stable banking system and the ability of individual banks to withstand short-term losses, there are also costs to these regulations: by reserving a portion of their assets, banks are forgoing the opportunity to invest that money as well, thus reducing the amount of income they can receive.

Another approach to providential regulation is to prevent banks from engaging in particularly risky types of behavior. For instance, many countries restrict banks from making non-loan investments, or providing insurance, or from purchasing real estate, or from buying or running nonfinancial firms. If all of these restrictions are in place, the only thing banks can do with their capital is provide loans. The Glass-Steagall Act in the United States implemented some of these "activity restriction regulations," creating a clear division between commercial banks, which took in deposits and provided loans, and investment banks, which provided investment services and made their own financial investments. With the repeal of Glass-Steagall in 1999, this division was eliminated as the United States moved away from activity restrictions. In the early '90s, Japan had eliminated its own set of activity restrictions, directly modeled on Glass-Steagall by American administrators during the postwar occupation, by informally allowing banks to conduct more investment activities, usually through subsidiaries. Numerous countries, such as Israel, Indonesia, Taiwan, Turkey, and Mexico, maintain some form of these restrictions. The idea of these restrictions is that certain activities are inherently risky and allowing banks, which serve a crucial purpose for the healthy functioning of a country's monetary system, to take on these risks could lead to a financial crisis. Some have argued, though, that activity restrictions actually increase bank risk since banks without restriction can diversify their activities beyond just loans (Barth et al. 2004). Further, lending is a risky business, too, as is made all too clear by both the Latin American debt crises of the '80s and the current foreclosure crisis. Thus, even limiting banks to the lending business does not inherently eliminate risk. As a result, countries can also regulate how and when loans are provided to try to minimize default risk.

Each of these regulations, though, imposes a cost on banks, either forcing them to pay into a deposit insurance fund (unless this fund is financed through general taxation or some other mechanism), limiting the amount of capital they can invest, or limiting the types of investments they can make. Thus, countries must choose between the safety of the banking system and the profits of the banks. In the modern day global economy, this means choosing between stability and competitiveness, as a country with strong regulations that weaken profits may just cause capital flight to banks in countries with weaker regulations. Countries therefore face two choices: how much and what type of regulation to have.

EXPLANATIONS FOR REGULATORY CHOICES

What explains the variation in how different countries approach these choices? There is surprisingly little research addressing this topic. The economics and finance literatures tend to address the effects of these different regulations while the political science literature is largely rooted in the International Relations subfield and, thus, tends to focus on the international aspects of regulation, such as the negotiation over and adoption of international agreements like the Basel Accords or on the diffusion of regulations from country to country.[4] As a result, there is a surprisingly large gap in our knowledge about the domestic determinants of banking regulations, though the ground is not completely barren on this topic.

For instance, the literature on the Basel Accords provides some guidance on the domestic political determinants of regulations insofar as it focuses on why countries comply with the Accords by creating a minimal capital adequacy level.[5] For instance, Oatley and Nabors (1998) argue that domestic political pressure in the United States by banks to implement regulations that would constrain Japanese banks and "redistribute" profits

---

4. This does not include the large literature spanning both IR and Comparative Politics that studies central bank independence, as recently discussed in Bearce (2008). While central banks often have a role in regulating the private banking system, this literature tends to focus purely on the role of the central banks on monetary policy and is not particularly relevant to the analysis in this chapter.

5. See, for instance, Kapstein (1989) and Simmons (2001).

back to the American banks led the United States to advocate for an international agreement. Thus, as is true for the analysis in this book, one should look to the characteristics of a country that make it more susceptible to banking lobbying. However, domestic-level political influences are frequently ignored in the existing literature. For instance, Singer (2007) provides a comprehensive and interesting account of the international negotiations over the Accords, including why the United States, Britain, and Japan took the positions they did and how the negotiations unfolded. His story about the derivation of state preferences is largely apolitical, though, as it focuses on the dilemma of regulators to balance competitiveness with stability. Similarly, Bernauer and Koubi's (2006) empirical analysis of how much capital banks hold in reserve focuses entirely on variables measuring banking sector structure, economic conditions, and regulatory variables. These and similar pieces do suggest that poor economic conditions encourage countries to adopt stronger regulations, so the empirical analyses below will control for these conditions.

The most extensive examination of the political determinants of variation in cross-national banking regulations is Rosenbluth and Schaap (2003), and the analysis in this chapter draws heavily from their work. Rosenbluth and Schaap focus on the role of electoral rules on prudential regulations, specifically examining the difference between "centripetal" and "centrifugal" electoral laws. These terms are borrowed from Cox (1990) and are used as analogies for laws that tend to create fragmented systems (centrifugal laws, which, so the analogy goes, exert outward force on the party system, causing it to "scatter" into multiple parties) and those that tend to create concentrated party systems (centripetal laws which exert inward force on the party system causing it to concentrate into two parties). For the most part, as both Cox (1990) and Rosenbluth and Schaap (2003) state, centripetal systems tend to be plurality rule and centrifugal systems tend to be PR, so Rosenbluth and Schaap's variables of interest are essentially the PR versus plurality dichotomy discussed in chapter 2.

Their theoretical argument for why this dichotomy matters for banking regulations is similar to that offered by Access Point Theory: centrifugal rules "reinforce the collective-action advantage of well-organized groups" (313) because each political party is small enough to "represent the intense preferences of that group" (314) while centripetal rules lead to large parties that "must appeal to many more voters and ha[ve] no choice but to shave off some of the intense preferences from particular groups" (314). However, as in the trade bias literature, PR systems do not necessarily have more parties than plurality systems. Second, depending on the complexity of society, having three or four parties rather than two may not enable parties to intensely represent any one small group. Finally, even when there are only two parties, if parties are concerned with campaign resources and policy is multidimensional, they can cater to particular intense interests to acquire resources to run their campaigns without necessarily sacrificing the votes of those less intensely interested on this issue. Though Rosenbluth and Schaap find support for their argument that PR systems will have weaker regulations (because they cater to organized banking interests), I argue that, similar to Rogowski's (1987) finding on PR and trade protection, this result is spurious to the number of access points in the system. However, the empirical analyses below will test the possibility that it is the "centrifugal" nature of electoral rules, and not the number of access points, that influence banking regulations by including a dummy variable for PR systems.

The economics and finance approach to the issue of banking regulations tends to focus on the effects of these regulations rather than the causes of them. The collected work of Barth, Caprio, and Levine probably best captures this: they collected the data used in this chapter and in their piece introducing their dataset (Barth et al. 2001), they examine the correlation between different regulatory choices and basic variables measuring, for instance, wealth and region, to determine if there were patterns in who adopted which regulations, but in their own work using their data, they examine which types of regulations "work best" (Barth et al. 2004) and what the link is between regulations and economic "performance" and "stability" (Barth et al. 1999). In general, their findings suggest that regulations that create direct government supervision are inferior to regulations that empower private sector monitoring of banking practices.[6]

This literature investigating the effects of banking regulations often acknowledges that regulations might be endogenous: countries with more risk, for instance, might adopt regulations to minimize this risk. Thus,

---

6. This opposition to direct regulations is fairly common in these literatures. Demirgüç-Kunt et al. (2008a) argue that information provision is the most important regulatory approach to ensure bank soundness rather than capital adequacy or other direct regulations. See also Ashcraft (2007), Cull et al. (2005), and Ioannidou and Penas (2010) while Degryse and Ongena (2007) reviews the literature related to regulation, competition, and performance. This view is by no means universal, though. For instance, Pasiouras et al. (2006) find that heavily regulated banks are better rated and Morrison and White (2005) show formally that strengthening capital requirements can improve bank quality after a crisis in confidence. González (2009) suggests that the impact of regulation depends on the market environment: antitrust regulations reduce economic efficiency in countries that have strong market mechanisms to create discipline but may improve efficiency in countries with weak market mechanisms.

finding that countries with more regulation have more bank failures or crises may not suggest that regulations caused these failures and crises. As a result, this research has investigated what might cause countries to adopt different regulations. However, this is not a question they are interested in theoretically: they only want to identify exogenous instruments that are correlated with level of regulations that cannot be caused by the level of regulation itself. Thus, Barth et al. (2004) and González (2005) include such measures as distance from the equator and religious composition as determinants of regulations but no theoretically informed variables.

The domestic determinants of deposit insurance are one of the few areas where the economics literature has focused theoretically on the political determinants of regulation. Laeven (2004) suggests that political-institutional variables such as democracy or executive constraints do not influence deposit insurance adoption, but does find that when there are many poorly capitalized banks such adoption is more likely. Demirgüç-Kunt et al. (2008b), on the other hand, argue that the level of democracy does influence adoption and, specifically, that more democratic countries should be more likely to adopt deposit insurance and to do so earlier. The causal argument they offer for this finding, though, is at odds with the arguments of Access Point Theory: they suggest that democracies provide more influence to private and minority interests and that increasing the level of democracy allows minority interests that support insurance for private reasons, like risky banks and elderly depositors, to have more influence. Thus, they argue that the more power given to interest groups, the more regulation there should be.

While they do, in fact, find that democracies are more likely to adopt deposit insurance, this does not necessarily support their causal argument. First, it is quite counterintuitive to suggest that autocracies are more likely to implement policies that benefit the majority while democracies, which include some element of majority rule, are more likely to implement policies that benefit only narrow minority interests. In fact, this argument runs completely counter to Selectorate Theory, which argues that democracies are more likely to provide public goods and autocracies more likely to provide only private goods. Second, while Demirgüç-Kunt et al. (2008b) are correct that private and minority interests support deposit insurance, it is also true that private and minority interests oppose deposit insurance, namely larger and less risky banks that are being asked to subsidize the riskier banks by contributing to the insurance pool without being likely to need it. If democracy is more likely to implement minority interests, as Demirgüç-Kunt et al. (2008b) argue, then why are the interests of the large banks excluded? It seems more likely, and more consistent with existing research in political science, that deposit insurance, while providing private benefits to some, also provides (or is believed to provide) the public good of banking stability by preventing contagious bank runs,[7] and thus democracies are more likely to provide insurance as suggested by Selectorate Theory. If this is true, then this raises the broader questions about Selectorate Theory raised in chapter 1: why do some democracies provide more of this particular public good than others? Seen in this view, the results from Demirgüç-Kunt et al. (2008b) are not contradictory to the arguments advanced in this book, but, given the sole focus on level of democracy, also do not provide much insight upon which to build a theory of intra-democratic differences in regulation.

In sum, the existing literatures in both political science and economics provide few explanations of the domestic political determinants of banking regulations and provide virtually no domestic institutional explanations. Thus, not only are banking regulations a good area to test Access Point Theory, as will be described below, but also Access Point Theory might provide us with new answers to an important question that is particularly relevant in the current international economy.

WHO LOBBIES FOR WHAT?

As stated in the previous chapter, the regulated industry will generally have a lobbying advantage because the costs of regulation are concentrated on the industry while the benefits are dispersed. This is also true for banking regulations where, with the exception of deposit insurance funded through general government revenue, costs take the form of lower profits for banks whether it is because they need to pay fees or cannot partake in certain investment activities or cannot invest all of their capital. The benefits are dispersed among all bank depositors and the entire financial system of the country or the world. Thus, for the most part, we would expect banks to have a lobbying advantage and, therefore, more access points should lead to fewer banking regulations.

This is complicated, though, by the fact that banks themselves do derive some benefit from regulations due to the contagion effect. If a "bad bank" collapses, this can raise questions among consumers about the health of their banks, increasing the odds that there will be a run on even a "good

---

7. If a large enough portion of the population has bank deposits then the provision of insurance itself takes on the characteristic of a public good. Certainly, it is a highly dispersed good, whether public or private.

bank." Good banks, therefore, have an incentive to restrain bad banks by preventing them from engaging in overly risky behavior. Yet good banks want to accomplish this without also restraining themselves or limiting their own profits. The best regulation from a good bank's perspective would be one that forces bad banks to do what the good banks are already doing: this forces discipline on the bad banks, making them less likely to collapse and hurt the good banks, while not imposing additional costs on the good banks. If such a regulation exists, then we would expect more access points to lead to more of these regulations while simultaneously leading to fewer regulations that good banks do not support.[8]

What sorts of regulations would we expect banks to support and which would we expect them to oppose? First, we might expect banks to support capital adequacy standards. Although keeping a certain amount of capital in reserve does impose costs on banks, this is a cost that almost all banks choose to pay on their own: virtually all banks have some reserve of uninvested capital because it is simply a good business practice given how banks operate. Without some cushion, any loss on investment or from defaulted loan could send a bank into a liquidity crisis. Healthy banks are likely to look at banks with low reserves as being not only overly risky but also as gaining a competitive advantage over them since these low-reserve banks can receive less return on their investment for each dollar while receiving equal overall return since they are investing more dollars. Thus, healthy banks have a dual incentive to push for higher standards: the reduction of systemic risk and the elimination of this competitive advantage by the risky banks. In fact, Bernauer and Koubi (2006) demonstrate that banks regularly overcomply with capital adequacy standards: the Basel Accords specify that banks must hold 8% of capital in reserve while the average bank in the OECD holds nearly 15% capital in reserve.[9]

---

8. This assumes that the number or lobbying power of good banks is greater than the number or lobbying power of bad banks. If the opposite is true, then more access points will lead to fewer banking regulations of all sorts. Alternatively, if all banks think of themselves as "good banks," that is, do not recognize when they are actually engaging in risky behavior, then more access points will lead to more bank-supported regulations regardless of the actual distribution and power of good and bad banks.

9. This probably understates the amount that banks overcomply, as the 8% standard can be met with both "Tier I" and "Tier II" capital while Bernauer and Koubi's figures only include the amount of Tier I capital held in reserve. Tier I capital are those types of capital that all countries agreed met the Basel standards while Tier II capital are those types of capital that some members believed were not liquid enough or for some other reason should not be used to meet capital adequacy standards. To comply with Basel, banks must have 8% of their assets in reserve capital with at least 4% of their assets in Tier I capital.

Deposit insurance is a more complicated case. If deposit insurance is funded through general revenue or by the depositor, then it provides the benefits of reduced systemic risk without much in the way of additional costs to banks. If deposit insurance is funded through a levy on all banks, though, then the good banks are paying a cost to bail out bad banks; this cost is exacerbated in countries like the United States and Canada where a sizable permanent fund is kept to bail out banks even when there are few bank failures. Contrast this to the British approach, where banks are charged a special levy once a bank fails which will only result in high costs to good banks when there are many or large bank failures. When the banking system is relatively stable, deposit insurance of this type provides little costs so banks, on average, push for this after-the-fact funding mechanism over the pre-funding mechanism in the United States (Davies and Green 2008). Thus, the question of whether banks might prefer deposit insurance regulation depends on the funding mechanism for that regulation. Banks should oppose, though, expensive deposit insurance systems that are funded by the banks themselves while good banks might support cheaper deposit insurance systems and those funded by general government revenue.

Other types of regulations are likely to be opposed by both good and bad banks. Most important, banks are likely to oppose activity restrictions because they prevent them from making potentially lucrative investments. This can be clearly seen by the behavior of U.S. banks once they were allowed to diversify into non-lending investment practices, as they securitized the mortgages and other debt they held and sold these new financial instruments in an attempt to increase the profits on their lending activity. Activity restrictions would have prevented the banks from directly engaging in these practices, which would have limited their exposure when the housing market collapsed, but also would have significantly reduced their profits during the boom. Since even good banks engaged in these investment practices, it is clear that, as opposed to capital adequacy regulations, implementing these restrictions would also constrain the behavior of these good banks. Thus, they are likely to oppose these types of regulations.

In addition to these questions of types of regulation, we can also address the question of how much power is given to regulators. While some banks might prefer some types of regulations, on balance banks will prefer weaker regulators enforcing those rules. For instance, some countries empower regulators to declare banks insolvent, while others do not; some countries allow regulators to suspend dividends or bonuses or management fees; some countries allow regulators to reorganize a bank's management or board. These are not the sorts of powers banks want to put in the hands of regulators even if they are enforcing regulations that they like. Given that most countries have a mix of regulations, not all of which banks are in favor of, makes it even less likely banks would want to have powerful regulators enforcing the rules. Thus, even when banks lobby for certain specific regulations, they will lobby against powerful regulators.

From these considerations, the following specific hypotheses can be drawn:

H5.1: *The more access points there are, the stronger capital adequacy standards will be.*

H5.2: *The more access points there are, the less likely a country is to have deposit insurance.*

H5.3: *The more access points there are, the weaker activity restrictions will be.*

H5.4: *The more access points there are, the fewer powers will be granted to bank regulators.*

DATA AND METHODS

To test the above hypotheses, we need data measuring banking regulations and the enforcement powers of regulators. Barth et al. (2001, 2003, 2008) conducted comprehensive surveys of banking regulators to assess these and other features of a country's banking system and have made the data available for 1999, 2003, and 2007. Unfortunately, because of the data available for the access points variables, only the first survey is usable here, meaning that we will only be able to conduct cross-sectional analyses. Given the sample restriction to democracies and missing data in the independent variables, the sample sizes in the analyses conducted here range from 52 to 55, depending on the exact dependent variable used and the particular specification.

The analyses below are conducted on four different dependent variables, one measuring capital adequacy, one deposit insurance, one activity restrictions, and one supervisory power. For the capital adequacy measure, I use Barth et al.'s Capital Regulatory Index, which they create by examining nine different features of capital regulation: if the country has that regulatory feature, they are given a 1; if they do not have that feature, they are given a 0. Thus, countries with all of the regulatory features—in other words countries with strong capital adequacy regulations—will receive a 9, while countries with none of the features—those with low capital adequacy regulations—will receive a 0. The more regulatory features a country has, the higher the score will be. The first feature is whether a country conforms to the Basel Accords; that is, do they set an 8% minimum amount of capital reserves?[10] The second feature is whether this level of reserves varies with risk; that is, do banks that take on riskier investments have to also keep more currency in reserve? The next three features concern how strict the definition of reserve capital is: if unrealized losses in loans, securities, or foreign exchange are deducted from the capital, banks must keep more capital in reserve if they are suffering these losses; if these losses are not subtracted, less capital is needed. For each of these losses that are deducted from capital, the Capital Regulatory Index increases by 1. The next two features concern what form the capital must take: if the capital must be cash or government securities, then the index increases by 1, and if the capital cannot have been borrowed, the index increases by 1. Finally, if regulators must verify the sources of the capital, the index increases by 1. Thus, the Capital Regulatory Index theoretically goes from 0 to 9, with higher scores indicating stronger capital adequacy regulations. However, no country in the Barth et al. sample scores a 0; that is, all countries have at least one regulatory feature. Further, the country with the lowest score in the Barth et al. sample is Vanuatu, which scores a 1, but it is not included in this chapter's sample. In the sample analyzed below, two countries score a 2: El Salvador and Romania. The United Kingdom and Australia both have all nine features. The median and modal number of features is six, which 15 countries, including the United States and Germany, have. Among major banking countries, Switzerland and France both also receive high scores, 7 and 8 respectively, while Canada has a below average number of features, with 4.

To measure activity restrictions, I use Barth et al.'s "Overall Bank Activity & Ownership Restrictions." This variable measures how restricted four different types of non-lending activities are: the ability of banks to engage in securities; the ability of banks to sell or underwrite insurance; the ability of banks to invest, develop, or manage real estate; and the ability of banks to own and control nonfinancial firms. In each of these four categories, Barth et al. assign a score ranging from 1 to 4 for the level of restrictions: 1 means that "a full range of activities in the given category can be conducted directly in the bank"; 2 means that these activities can be conducted, but "all or some must be conducted in subsidiaries";

---

10. Thus, this measure is a blunt instrument, as overcompliance is counted the same as compliance while having lower-than-Basel reserve requirements is counted the same as having no requirement.

3 means "less than a full range of activities can be conducted in the bank or subsidiaries"; and 4 means that the activity is prohibited (Barth et al. 2001, 13). These four separate indexes are then averaged together to create the overall index with higher numbers equaling more activity restrictions. For instance, if banks are prohibited from conducting any of the above types of activities, they would receive a score of 4; if they were allowed to conduct all four without restriction, they would receive a 1. Aruba and New Zealand both score a 1, while no countries score a 4. A number of countries score a 3.5, which is the highest in the full Barth et al. dataset and in the sample used here. A country that permits all four activities but only in subsidiaries would score a 2 while a country that permits without restriction three of the activities but forbids outright the fourth would also score a 2. Because of this, there is some measurement error as the middle of the range conflates a number of different types of regulation into the same score, but countries that score higher do have more restrictions than those that score lower. The median score for the index is 2.25; the United States and Japan have relatively strong restriction, with scores of 3 and 3.25 respectively, while Germany, Britain, and Switzerland all have almost no restrictions, each having a score of 1.25. France and Canada are only slightly more restrictive with scores of 1.5 to 1.75, respectively. Thus, there is variation not only among all countries but also among the major banking countries.

For deposit insurance, I use a dummy variable constructed by Barth et al. that measures whether a country has an explicit deposit insurance scheme. Sixty percent of the countries in Barth et al.'s dataset and 71% of the subsample used in this chapter have such schemes. There are two major problems with this measure. First, it does not count implicit deposit insurance systems: a country can reimburse depositors at failed banks on an ad hoc basis out of central bank or general treasury funds without an official system to do so. If this reimbursement is regular and expected, it can serve the same function as an explicitly designed system in reducing the probability of bank runs. Second, the measure treats all explicit systems the same. Some systems, though, are stronger than others: for instance, the United States provides full coverage for all deposits up to a certain dollar amount for each depositor (currently $250,000), while other countries have a coinsurance system, such as Germany, which covers only 90% of each depositor's deposits up to a much lower cap past which it covers nothing (currently €50,000, or less than $75,000). If depositors expect to lose some of their deposit if the bank collapses, they have an incentive to withdraw their funds at the first sign of trouble so they can recover all of their deposit, thus reducing the effectiveness of insurance on preventing bank runs.[11] In addition, this measure treats all insurance systems the same regardless of source of funding, even though, as discussed above, banks might support insurance systems with some types of funding but oppose systems with other funding sources. As a result, there is some measurement error in this variable, which makes for a conservative test for the hypothesis; however, if we do not find an effect of access points, it could be because of the quality of the measure rather than that access points have no effect.

Finally, this chapter uses Barth et al.'s Official Supervisory Power Index to measure regulatory power. This variable examines whether regulators and supervisors "have the authority to take specific actions to prevent or correct problems" (Barth et al. 2001, 18). For each of 16 different actions that regulators have the authority to take, a value of 1 is added to the index. If regulators can take all 16 actions, they receive a 16; if none, they receive a 0; if 4, they receive of 4, and so on. The 16 actions are as follows:

1. Supervisors can meet with external auditors without needing the approval of banks.
2. External auditors are legally required to report bank misconduct to the supervisors.
3. External auditors are liable for negligence in their official duties.
4. Supervisors can force a bank to change its internal structure.
5. Supervisors can overrule shareholders on reorganization plans.
6. Supervisors can replace bank management.
7. Supervisors can replace bank directors.
8. Supervisors can suspend bonuses.
9. Supervisors can suspend management fees.
10. Supervisors can suspend dividends.
11. Supervisors can suspend ownership rights.
12. Supervisors can declare a bank insolvent.
13. Deposit insurance agency can sue banks.
14. Off–balance sheet items must be reported supervisors.
15. Directors and managers face automatic civil or criminal sanctions for failure to comply with cease and desist or similar orders from supervisors.
16. Supervisors can order banks to implement measures that will cover losses.

---

11. Coinsurance or reimbursements are typically used both as a cost-saving measure and as a way to reduce the moral hazard of deposit insurance. Depositors might make riskier decisions if they know they will be fully reimbursed.

As can be seen, some of these powers are quite draconian and, as stated above, banks are not likely to want regulators to have many of these powers, even if they support the rules the regulators are trying to enforce. Theoretically, this measure ranges from 0 to 16, but in practice no country has less than a 3 (Singapore) while two countries score 16 (Slovenia and Hungary). The median score is 12, which is fairly close to the maximum, suggesting that most countries vest their regulators with some substantial power. The United States has the highest for any major banking country with 14. Other major banking countries with scores around the median are Japan with a 13, Britain a 12, and Germany an 11. Canada and France are on the low end for major banking countries with scores of 7 and 8, respectively.[12]

Because of the limited size of the sample that results from the pure cross-sectional design, I test the above hypotheses using the access point index variable. Thus, the higher this index, the stronger capital adequacy standards should be, but the weaker activity restriction regulations and regulatory power should be. In addition, the higher this index, the less likely a country should be to have explicit deposit insurance.

The sparseness of the literature on the comparative determinants of regulatory variation provides only limited guidance on what control variables need to be included in the analysis. However, some control variables are obvious, and the literature does suggest the inclusion of a few others. First, PR is included to test the arguments of Rosenbluth and Schaap (2003). GDP and GDP per capita are both included as Barth et al. (2001) find that banking regulations often vary by wealth and size of the economy. Inflation and unemployment are included since Singer (2007) suggests that poor economic conditions might encourage policymakers to increase regulations. Finally, economically open countries might be expected to have fewer regulations if there are concerns that high regulations might hurt the competitiveness of a country's banking sector (Singer 2007). Thus, trade openness, measured by imports plus exports divided by GDP, is included as a proxy for overall economic openness.

Since all of the analyses are cross section only, no time series or panel controls need to be included. The Capital Adequacy, Activity Restriction, and Regulatory Power variables are all ordinal so ordered probit will be used for each of these analyses. The Deposit Insurance variable is binary so regular probit will be used for this analysis. All of the independent

---

12. Barth et al. provide a number of other possible measures of regulatory power, such as number of supervisors per bank and frequency of on-site inspections. Number of access points is not significantly related to these other measures.

variables are lagged one year to eliminate the possibility of reverse causation. The basic model estimated below is as follows:

$$\text{Bank Regulation} = \beta_0 + \beta_1 \text{Access}_{t-1} + \beta_2 \text{PR}_{t-1} + \beta_4 \text{GDP}_{t-1} + \beta_5 \text{GDP/Capita}_{t-1}$$
$$+ \beta_6 \text{Trade Openness}_{t-1} + \beta_7 \text{Unemployment}_{t-1}$$
$$+ \beta_8 \text{Inflation}_{t-1} + \varepsilon. \tag{1}$$

RESULTS

The results of the analyses, presented in table 5.1, largely show support for the above hypotheses: more access points are associated with stronger capital adequacy standards but with weaker activity restrictions and supervisory power. The only finding that does not conform to expectations for Access Point Theory is that the number of access points has no effect on deposit insurance adoption.

Before discussing in more detail how these overall findings fit together, I will describe the results of each analysis, beginning with the results for the regulation that banks support: the Capital Adequacy measure, listed as Model 1 in the table. Here we see that more access points are associated with stronger capital adequacy standards, with the coefficient on the access point index positive and significant at the 0.05 level. A one standard deviation increase in number of access points (2.38 in this sample) results in a roughly 0.5 increase in the Capital Adequacy measure, which in this sample ranges from 2 to 9. The predicted difference between France (which has the highest score on the Access Point index in this sample at 6.9) and Germany (which has an Access Point score of 0.52, which is essentially the mean level in this sample) is about 1¼ steps on the Capital Adequacy scale, which, though less than the actual difference in their levels of regulation (3 steps on the scale), is substantively quite significant. Looking at the control variables, only two are significant: wealthier countries tend to have higher capital adequacy standards and high-inflation countries tend to have lower standards. Both of these results seem logical given that these standards tie up capital that could be invested for more profit: rich countries have more capital to invest and so can afford to invest a lower percentage of it at once (similar to how rich individuals tend to consume less and save more as a percent of their income because they can afford not to consume all of their money) while in high inflation countries, you need a higher nominal rate of return to make a real profit and, thus, might not be able to afford to keep as much capital in reserve.

Table 5.1 THE EFFECT OF ACCESS POINTS ON BANK REGULATION

Variable	Model 1	Model 2	Model 3	Model 4
Access Points	0.22**	-0.12***	-0.11*	0.03
	(0.087)	(0.058)	(0.06)	(0.10)
PR	0.32	-0.26	-0.08	0.32
	(0.38)	(0.33)	(0.36)	(0.50)
GDP	-1.1E-13	2.7E-13***	2.73E-13***	0.00
	(8.3E-14)	(9.4E-14)	(7.9E-14)	(1.3E-12)
GDP per capita	.000042***	-0.000401***	-0.0000097	0.000039*
	(.000015)	(0.000015)	(0.000017)	(0.000021)
Trade Openness	-0.00044	-0.00206	0.0025	0.00067
	(0.0032)	(0.0033)	(0.0039)	(0.0052)
Unemployment	.015	0.047**	-0.02	0.04
	(0.022)	(0.023)	(0.04)	(0.04)
Inflation	-.034***	0.033***	0.005	0.01
	(0.012)	(0.013)	(0.007)	(0.01)
Number of Observations	52	55	55	55
Pseudo R-Squared	0.1577	0.1082	0.0326	0.229

Notes: Robust Standard Errors in Parentheses
***p<.01; **p<.05; *p<.1

Model 2 shows the results for Activity Restrictions and here we see that, as expected, the more access points there are, the fewer restrictions there will be. A one standard deviation change in access points (about 2.36 in this sample) equates to restrictions 0.30 lower. Given that the Activity Restriction scale is the average of four 4-point scales, this equates to about a 1-point change on any of the constituent scales. In other words, for every one standard deviation increase in the number of access points, the level of restrictions for one of the four activities (securities, insurance, real estate, nonfinancial firm ownership) falls by one point. Among the control variables, GDP and inflation are still significant and in the opposite direction as for capital adequacy standards while unemployment is significant and negative in this model. Thus, richer countries and high-unemployment countries tend to have fewer activity restrictions while high-inflation countries tend to have more activity restrictions. The mixed results on the variables measuring the state of the economy suggest that an economic crisis does not increase banking regulations (or, at least, that it takes longer than a year to implement these regulations).

Model 3 reports the results for the supervisor power analysis and finds, as with activity restrictions, that more access points are associated with weaker regulations. Countries with more access points provide significantly fewer powers to their banking supervisors. A one standard deviation change in number of access points is associated with about a 0.27 change in the Supervisory Power measure: this is a smaller effect substantively than those found above as this measure ranges from 0 to 16 (although in this sample, the minimum observed is 5). In fact, the predicted difference between the country with the most access points (France at 6.9) and the one with the fewest (Guyana at -3.2) is just over 1 point on the scale. The only control variable that is significant in this model is GDP: larger economies have stronger supervisory powers, perhaps because they have a more complex banking environment to oversee.

Finally, Model 4 presents the results for the Deposit Insurance variable. Here, we see that number of access points has no influence on whether a country adopts deposit insurance. As discussed above, though, whether banks support deposit insurance depends upon the funding mechanism, and the dependent variable used here does not differentiate. This suggests that the lack of significance may be a result of measurement error: that none of the control variables are significant reinforces this possibility. On the other hand, it is the one coefficient in these analyses that does not match up with theoretical expectations.

Taken together, these results strongly reinforce the idea that when there are more access points, policy will be biased in favor of the side with a lobbying advantage. In the case of banking regulations, we see that it is not simply a case of when there are more access points, there are fewer regulations; instead, we see that there are only fewer regulations of the types opposed by banks. There are, in fact, more regulations of the type supported by banks. No other existing theory can explain this pattern of results. Further, once we control for access points, PR is never significant, despite the expectations of Rosenbluth and Schaap (2003) that electoral rules should determine banking regulations. As in chapter 3 and similar findings with regards to trade policy, this chapter demonstrates that the number of access points is the key institutional factor explaining policy bias and not whether a country has proportional or plurality electoral laws.

CONCLUSION

This chapter continued the examination of the role of access points in policy bias and found, as in the previous chapter, that more access points will lead to regulatory policy that is more biased in favor of industry and against consumers. However, in this chapter, we found that, under certain circumstances, this bias can show itself through *increased* regulation rather than the more standard outcome where more access points will lead to fewer regulations. This calls particular attention to the fact that scholars must be careful in identifying not only which side has the lobbying advantage but also what that side wants. For instance, in chapter 4, we found that, in the aggregate, more access points lead to fewer environmental regulations as, on average, industries will oppose regulation. However, industries may prefer certain regulations: in particular, industries may support market-based regulations like cap-and-trade if they believe that the alternative is a less market-friendly regulatory structure. Thus, if one were to examine the effect of access points on the accession to any particular treaty, researchers will need to be careful to specify the preferences of industry (and activists).

While this chapter, thus, provides a cautionary note to scholars examining access points, it also provides particularly powerful evidence for Access Point Theory: countries with more access points have fewer regulations in general but have more regulations that banks favor. In other words, policy bias is increased by both the regulations that are not there and the exact regulations that are.

In addition to serving as a test of Access Point Theory, this chapter also provides one of the few cross-national examinations of the determinants of variation in banking regulations. The chapter found that how responsive domestic institutions are to interest group pressure explains regulatory outcomes, similar to the arguments of the most extensive existing treatment of this topic, Rosenbluth and Schaap (2003). However, as opposed to that research, this chapter found that it was access points and not electoral rules that determined outcomes and that the effect was not consistent in terms of more or less regulation but rather depended on whether the banks *wanted* a particular regulation.

Further, the chapter found a clear difference between the types of regulations rich countries implemented versus the types poor countries implemented: rich countries tended to have higher levels of capital adequacy standards and were more likely to provide deposit insurance but were less likely to have activity restrictions. Finally, no relationship was found between trade openness and banking regulations, despite the fact that a race-to-the-bottom argument might expect more openness to lead to fewer regulations. While the limited data prevent broad generalizations about these findings, they do point to the potential value of future research on the determinants of banking regulations, particularly as we are able to observe more variation over time and can see how economic conditions, for instance, might influence these changes. However, this chapter does suggest that the response to the financial crisis is not likely to be uniform: while Singer (2007) would suggest that the financial crisis should lead to stronger regulations across the board, Access Point Theory would argue that these are likely to be more bank-friendly regulations in high-access-point countries and more consumer-friendly regulations in low-access-point countries.

PART III

Policy Complexity

CHAPTER 6
Complexity and the Tariff Schedule

This chapter begins the examination of the effects of the number of access points on policy complexity, focusing on the level of complexity in a country's tariff schedule. To briefly review, Access Point Theory predicts that the more access points there are, the more complex policy will be since increasing the number of access points makes lobbying cheaper, which should lead to more lobbying, including lobbying by special interests asking for specific provisions to be entered into policy outcomes to benefit them. When the groups lobbying are predominantly from one side of the policy debate, this will also lead to more bias, as discussed in the previous chapters, but regardless of whether these provisions balance out or not, adding more of them will increase the complexity of policy.

For instance, one of the most important elements of a country's trade policy is its tariff schedule, or the import taxes charged on different products when they enter the country. A tariff schedule can be very simple: Chile, for example, charges a 10% tariff on every product. Other tariff schedules are incredibly complex, like that of the United States where there are hundreds of different tariff lines, some of them ad valorem (or percent of the value of the import) and some of them specific (or based on volume, weight, or number of goods imported.) These tariff lines include quite similar products having vastly different tariff rates; for instance, knit cotton shirts are taxed at 19.7%, unless they are nightshirts, in which case they are taxed at 8.9%, or T-shirts, in which case they are taxed at 16.5%. If the knit shirts are made of synthetic fibers, they are taxed at 32%, and if they are made of natural fiber other than cotton, they are taxed at 14.9%. Interest group politics can be one of the causes of different levels of complexity, as will be discussed in more detail in the next section. Briefly, though, if no interest groups lobby for special treatment for the products they import, export, or compete against, then a single tariff rate might result; however, if some interest groups lobby for lower tariffs on raw materials they import and other interest groups lobby for higher tariffs on goods they compete against, then this can lead to different products having different tariff rates and a more complex tariff schedule.

As discussed in chapter 1, some research, both normative and positive, already exists on tariff complexity, and this chapter builds on this research by providing a richer institutional story for the wide variation in tariff complexity that has been observed. First, a small literature exists in economics that examines tariff complexity from a purely theoretical and largely normative perspective, attempting to answer the question of whether complex or simple (referred to as "uniform" in this literature) tariffs are better from an economic efficiency standpoint. This literature was inspired by the fact that the World Bank frequently advised developing countries to adopt uniform tariffs and, for the most part, has concluded that simple tariff structures (uniform or near-uniform) are better for a number of reasons.[1]

First, simple tariff structures are easier to administer. Fewer customs agents are necessary to classify imports, for instance, and it is unnecessary to attempt to determine the economically optimal tariff rate for each product. Second, simpler tariff structures might encourage more trade and investment, as it will reduce the research costs for companies and investors when deciding to enter a particular market. As Panagariya and Rodrik (1991) point out, though, these benefits are likely to be somewhat limited. More important, they argue, are the "political economy" reasons to move toward a simple tariff, namely that a uniform tariff can lead to lower overall tariff levels either by reducing the demand for high tariffs by industries or by reducing the incentive for policymakers to provide protection to their favored industries. For instance, if there is a uniform tariff

---

1. See Panagariya and Rodrik (1991) for a discussion of World Bank advice. Although a handful of policy-related and country-specific arguments pre-dated the World Bank's advice in the '80s, such as Corden (1957, 1968), it is interesting to note that the World Bank gave this advice before any rigorous research, theoretical or empirical, was conducted to demonstrate the superiority of uniform tariffs and what little research had been conducted on the issue, such as Johnson (1964) and Corden (1971) suggested that the standard argument offered for uniform tariffs at that point, namely that they equalized the rate of protection across industries, was incorrect because the same tariff rate would distort consumption differently for different products.

rate, then an industry that wants more protection for itself must lobby for more protection for everyone, thus creating a free-rider problem as, once the protection is given, every industry benefits whether they lobbied or not. This may be sufficient to cancel out the collective action advantage of protectionists and, at the least, minimize it, thus reducing the overall level of protection. Gatti (1999) argues that uniform tariffs are superior because they limit corruption: if customs agents have discretion in how they categorize imports and there are different tariff lines for different products, they can be bribed into giving more favorable classifications. In addition, a simple tariff might be easier for consumers and voters to understand and, therefore, they may be better able to determine how they are affected by trade policy and hold policymakers accountable for their trade policy positions. Kono (2006) suggests that democracies use relatively more nontariff barriers, which are more complex and harder to understand than even complicated tariff schedules, than non-democracies do exactly because it makes it harder for their voters to hold them accountable for the potential negative effects of protection.

On the other hand, Panagariya (1994, 1996) provides a number of reasons why complex tariffs may be preferred. First, tariffs have important effects on consumption and a uniform tariff rate might lead to larger consumption distortions than a more finely tailored tariff rate that takes into account the differential consumption effects across different products. Second, if tariffs are used for revenue purposes, the Ramsey Rule suggests that a complex tariff will raise more revenue, as discussed in more detail in the next chapter. Panagariya argues, though, that the political economic arguments for uniformity should not be ignored and, therefore, recommends a tariff schedule with three different rates, thus somewhat reducing consumption distortions and somewhat increasing revenue but still providing a tariff structure that might be resistant to free riding and cronyism.

Despite this theoretical literature on the many possible consequences and the potentially large importance of tariff complexity, there has been very little empirical work on the effects of tariff structure and none on the causes of tariff structure. As Kono (2009) points out, this is at least in part due to the fact that there has not existed a good empirical measure of tariff complexity; a deficit which Kono seeks to remedy by creating a measure he terms "tariff specificity" and which I use here. The only empirical works investigating the effects of tariff complexity are Gatti (1999), which showed in a single cross section that complex tariffs are related to higher subjective ratings on a corruption scale, and Ederington and Minier (2002), which demonstrated that very simple and very complex tariffs are associated with higher economic growth while moderately complex tariff were associated with less growth. Both of these studies used the standard deviation of tariff lines as a measure of complexity, which Kono (2009) argues is a flawed measure. First, standard deviation will be correlated with the mean level of the tariff. Second, and more important, a country with two tariff rates applied to all products could have a very high standard deviation if the two rates are far apart while a country with a different tariff rate for every product could have a much lower standard deviation if these rates are tightly clustered around the mean rate. The latter scenario will be a more complex structure than the former. Thus, the standard deviation of tariff rates might provide a good measure of the dispersion of tariff rates but not necessarily of the complexity of those rates. Kono (2009) introduces a new measure of tariff complexity that makes empirical investigation of complexity easier and that I employ here. It is based on how concentrated the tariff schedule is on particular tariff lines, and I describe it in more detail below in the data and methods section. First, though, I describe in more detail how access points lead to more tariff complexity. Then, after presenting the data and methods for the complexity analysis, I present the results of this analysis, showing that countries with more access points have more complex tariff structures. Then, I investigate the effect of tariff complexity on trade patterns to demonstrate that the structure of the tariff has important effects on economic outcomes. Finally, I conclude by summarizing the results and discussing the possibilities of future work on both the causes and effects of tariff complexity.

WHY ACCESS POINTS CAN CAUSE TARIFF COMPLEXITY

As discussed in chapter 2, increasing the number of access points is expected to increase the overall policy complexity as cheaper access provides more opportunity for special interests to lobby for special treatment for their group. In the case of trade policy, this takes the form of lobbying for a different level of protection (either higher or lower) for products produced or imported by their industry. While, as chapter 3 demonstrated, the bulk of this lobbying should be for higher tariff rates to protect domestic industries from foreign competition, thus also increasing policy bias, we should also expect to see industries that use imported raw materials or semifinished products to push for lower tariff rates on the products they import and, possibly, export industries to push for lower tariff rates on the products they export if they believe other countries might reciprocate. Thus, there will be pressure from both sides and if the amount of pressure varies from industry to industry, this can lead to vastly different tariff rates on a wide range of products. Therefore, the basic hypothesis tested in this chapter is that, irrespective of the effect on level of protectionism, *the more access points there are, the more complex trade policy should be.*

This chapter will evaluate trade complexity by examining a country's tariff schedule, which is the list of tariff rates applied to different products. In the modern trade system, these schedules are negotiated during multilateral GATT or WTO rounds where countries offer to lower the maximum tariff rate they can apply to a particular product (known as a tariff bound) in exchange for other countries lowering their tariff bounds on other products. Thus, tariff bounds tend to be stable from year to year with potentially large changes occurring after each completed negotiating round. However, countries are free to charge any rate at or below the bound, as long as they charge this same rate to all WTO members. Frequently, the applied tariff will, thus, be lower than the tariff bound, and these applied tariffs do occasionally fluctuate from year to year. I use variation in applied tariffs here in order to increase the temporal variation and, therefore, the sample size in the analyses below.[2] These tariff schedules allow for some widespread variation in tariff rates as the level of product specification is quite detailed. For instance, fresh or chilled cuts of sheep with bones is a different tariff line from fresh or chilled cuts of sheep without bones, while there are also two categories of frozen cuts of sheep. Surgical rubber gloves and nonsurgical rubber gloves are different product lines as are new tires, used tires, and retreaded tires. There are 17 different product lines for flat-rolled stainless steel and numerous more for hot-rolled or non-alloyed steel. Prior to the GATT/WTO regime, though the tariff

---

2. The gap between the bound and applied tariff is known as the "binding overhang." Almost always, the gap will be positive; that is, the bound tariff will be higher than the applied tariff. It is possible to have a negative gap, that is, higher applied tariffs, and remain within WTO rules, though, if the higher tariff is the result of the use of safeguards measures, which allow countries to temporarily raise tariffs in an industry to give companies a chance to reorganize. Pelc (n.d.) examines the difference between bound and applied tariffs and finds that countries with more access points have lower levels of overhang as the executive will attempt to tie the hands of future policymakers to prevent them from succumbing to pressure from interest groups to further raise tariffs by keeping tariff bounds as close to currently applied tariffs as possible. Pelc uses a different measure (and slightly different definition) of access points than that used here, but this presents an interesting avenue for future research on Access Point Theory as it could be generalizable that strong executives in high-access-point countries might, when possible, create less flexible policy to constrain the ability of other access points to bias policy in the future.

schedules were not negotiated in a multilateral setting with such formalized rules, most countries still had a detailed tariff schedule with high degrees of potential product specification.[3]

In theory, each of these product lines could have a different tariff rate; on the other hand, each of these product lines could have the same tariff rate. As discussed above, Chile has 1 tariff rate for all products, while Georgia has 2 tariff rates with roughly two-thirds of all products assigned to one of these and the other third assigned to the other. Mexico has 23 tariff rates, but 3 of them account for over 90% of all products. China has nearly 50 different rates, with none accounting for more than 10% of all products, and the United States and EU have even more differentiated rate structures. Countries that have 1 tariff rate applied to all products have simple tariff policies; countries that have different rates for each product have complex tariff policies. The next section provides more precise definitions for measuring complexity, but for now it is enough to say that the more specific tariff rates get applied to different products, the more complex tariff rates will be.

Why would increasing the number of access points lead to there being a wider range of different tariff rates in the tariff schedule? When there are few access points, lobbying is relatively expensive such that only the best funded interests or those interests for which trade policy matters the most or who have the closest existing ties with policymakers will lobby for particular trade policies affecting their industry. For instance, perhaps only the automobile industry, steel industry, and sugar industry lobby on trade policy, with the latter two industries asking for protection for their products and the first industry asking for protection for its product but free trade for steel since it purchases foreign steel for use in auto making. This will lead to higher overall protection than if there were no access points and a slightly more complex tariff code: if we assume that policymakers will provide some fixed tariff level (perhaps 0) on all products for which they receive no lobbying, then the tariff code that will result from this scenario will have the bulk of products covered by this single tariff rate but with automobiles and sugar having a higher tariff rate (perhaps even different from each other if they apply a different level of pressure or ask for a different preferred rate) and steel, perhaps, having a still different tariff rate in the middle. (We might assume that the steel industry lobbies more for protection than the automobile industry lobbies for free

---

3. For instance, in the United States. tariffs were set in the U.S. Congress before 1934, but the final omnibus tariff bill would have precise tariff rates applied to a wide range of products. See Destler (2005) for more on this process.

trade on steel as steel is one of only many products they must use to make cars so they will care relatively less about the price of steel than the steel industry will. This process is discussed in more detail in chapter 3 when discussing why protectionists have a collective action advantage.)

If we increase the number of access points further, more industries will find it beneficial to lobby, most asking for protection for their product but some asking for free trade, either on products they import or to extract reciprocal tariff reductions from the countries to which they export. At the minimum, this will lead to fewer products with the default tariff line and more with some alternative tariff, which will increase the complexity under Kono's measurement. This increased complexity will be magnified if, as discussed in the example above, the pressure on some products is partially conflicting, leading to slightly higher than default tariff rates; or if the pressure or preferred rate differs from industry to industry; or if pressure on some products are only from the free-trade side, leading to some products having below default tariff rates. (Obviously, this last case cannot be possible if the default rate is a 0% tariff, especially since export subsidies are forbidden under WTO rules.) However, even if none of these is the case, increasing the number of access points will lead to increased complexity along with increased bias.

DATA AND METHODS

The measure of complexity used in this chapter is borrowed from Kono (2009), which measures the concentration of tariff lines using the familiar Herfindahl-Hirschman Index that has been used to measure, for instance, industrial concentration. The measure is calculated as $\sum s_i^2$ where s is the proportion of all tariff lines that has tariff rate i. When there are relatively few tariff rates that each cover a large number of tariff lines, this index will be high; in fact, when there is one tariff rate for all products it will equal 1. When there are many tariff rates each covering a small number of tariff lines, the index will be low, with a minimum value of 0. For instance, if there are two tariff rates each covering half of the products, the index will equal $(.5)^2 + (.5)^2$ or 0.5. Four tariff rates each covering a quarter of the products would equal $(.25)^2 + (.25)^2 + (.25)^2 + (.25)^2$ or 0.25. Thus, higher scores indicate more uniform tariffs; since the prediction tested here is that higher tariff rates lead to more complex tariff rates, I take the additive inverse of the Herfindahl-Hirschman Index, or $1 - \sum s_i^2$, as my measure of complexity. The measure is calculated using tariff rates at the 6- or 8-digit level on the Harmonized System, which corresponds to either hundreds or thousands of different potential tariff lines, both very fine-grained coding of different products.

Kono (2009) calculates these indexes using the United Nations' Trade Analysis and Information System (TRAINS), which provides data on tariff structure for 113 countries starting in about 1990. However, not all countries provide data in all years, and the gaps between the years provided for the countries are irregular. Further, not all of the 113 countries are democracies, and since EU countries have a common tariff schedule, they are dropped from the analysis.[4] As a result, 56 countries enter the analyses, and there is an irregular panel structure as not all countries have data for all years. Over a dozen countries only have one observation, while about half a dozen, including the United States, Canada, and Japan, have six observations, each. The average country has three observations. Taken together, the sample size in the following analyses is about 170. The average level of complexity in the sample is 0.79, a rather high level of complexity, which roughly corresponds to Guatemala's tariff rate in 2000; the standard deviation in the sample is about 0.25. Chile has the lowest score, 0, as it has a single tariff rate; Mali and Bolivia also have scores under 0.1. The United States has the highest level of tariff complexity, with a score of over 0.99. Canada, Turkey, Norway, Japan, Hungary, and Finland (the latter two before joining the EU) also had complexity scores over 0.95. Ecuador and Bangladesh both had complexity scores right around 0.5, the midpoint of the scale, which roughly means that any two products have a 50–50 chance of sharing a tariff line with each other.

Given the limited amount of data on this complexity variable, this chapter uses the summary access point measure. The expectation is that more access points will lead to higher levels of tariff complexity; thus, the coefficient on the access point variable should be positive and significant. PR is also included as a separate variable with the expectation that it should be insignificant: once we separate out the institutions that tend to vary with PR that influence the number of access points, we should not expect proportional systems to have either more or less complex trade policy. Given the paucity of existing studies of tariff complexity, we have little in the way of guidance for what other variables may influence complexity beyond access point variables. First, though Kono's complexity measure is designed to be independent of tariff level,

---

4. Including them as separate units of observation and including a dummy for EU countries does not appreciably change the results.

it may still be the case that countries with active interest groups may lead to trade policy that is both highly protectionist and highly complex. Thus, the average tariff rate, as reported in Kono's dataset, is included. Further, complex tariff schedules may be more expensive and difficult to administer so that we might expect poorer countries to adopt simpler tariff schedules. In addition, if the World Bank was advising that countries adopt a uniform tariff, then we might expect poorer countries, which were more likely to accept World Bank money and advice than richer countries, to be more likely to have simpler tariffs. Thus, GDP per capita is included. In addition, larger economies might also be more complex and, therefore, need a more complex trade policy. Thus, GDP is included. Finally, trade openness is included, although, as discussed above, it is unclear what effect this should have: countries with a lot of trade may have an incentive to tailor schedules in very specific fashions designed to reduce consumption distortions or they may have an incentive to have simple tariff schedules that limit corruption and prevent importers from being confused. These variables are all drawn from data provided by the Penn World Tables and the World Development Indicators.

The model estimated in the complexity analyses is as follows:

$$\text{Tariff Complexity} = \beta_0 + \beta_1 \text{Access}_{t-1} + \beta_2 \text{PR}_{t-1} + \beta_3 \text{Mean Tariff Rates}$$
$$+ \beta_4 \text{GDP}_{t-1} + \beta_5 \text{GDP/Capita}_{t-1}$$
$$+ \beta_6 \text{Trade Openness}_{t-1} + \varepsilon. \tag{1}$$

Since the complexity measure is continuous, I use OLS regression to estimate the results with panel-corrected standard errors. Because there are so few observations, I do not use fixed country-effects. Also, because tariff complexity is not observed at regular intervals in all countries, I do not include a lagged dependent variable even though there is certainly some persistence in tariff schedules.

RESULTS OF TARIFF COMPLEXITY ANALYSIS

The results of the analysis are presented in table 6.1 and support the core hypothesis of the chapter: more access points lead to more complex tariff schedules. The coefficient on access points is positive and significant, demonstrating that countries with more access points have higher levels of complexity. A one standard deviation increase in the access point measure (about

Table 6.1 THE EFFECT OF ACCESS POINTS ON TARIFF COMPLEXITY

Access Points	0.0165***
	(0.006)
PR	0.133***
	(0.027)
GDP	2.24E-14***
	(6.46E-15)
GDP/Capita	7.33E-06***
	(1.65E-06)
Openness	0.001**
	(0.0005)
Mean Tariff Rate	0.003*
	(0.002)
Constant	0.440***
	(0.073)
N	171
R-Squared	0.209

Notes: ***p<.01; **p<.05; *<p<.1
Panel-Corrected Standard Errors in Parentheses

2.25) leads to an increase of about 0.037 higher complexity. This effect is important in substantive terms: for instance, while only the United States in 1996 had a tariff complexity score over 0.99, another six countries have had tariff complexity scores over 0.953. Thus, a one standard deviation change in the amount of access points can drop a country's expected complexity from the highest in the sample to only the top 15%. Moving from the country in this sample with the fewest access points (Guyana with about -3.2) to the country with the most (India with over 6.75) would increase the complexity of tariffs by 0.16. Though the most important hypothesis is confirmed by these results, the second hypothesis drawn from access point theory is not supported: PR countries have significantly higher levels of tariff complexity than plurality countries. Since there does not seem to be a theoretical link between proportional electoral rules and the provision of specific tariff lines to specific industries, this is probably a sign that the model estimated above is omitting some variable.[5]

---

5. As long as these omitted variables are also not correlated with the access point measure, then we do not need to be concerned about bias in the coefficient on this variable. However, it is certainly possible that the omitted variables *are* correlated with the access point measure. In this case, though, given that the results in this chapter match the results in other chapters, where the models are better specified, we can probably assume that the bias is not too severe.

The control variables also provide some interesting findings, as all of them are significant in this specification. First, average tariff level is significantly related to tariff complexity within this sample and with these controls, despite there being no significant bivariate relationship between the variables in Kono's full dataset and despite the complexity variable having been constructed to be independent of tariff level. In this analysis, countries with higher tariff levels have slightly more complex tariff structure. However, this coefficient is only of borderline significance ($p < .099$) and the result is not particularly robust to other specifications or time-series estimation techniques. Second, we find that larger economies do have more complex tariff rates, as expected, suggesting that complex economies are more likely to craft complex trade policies in order to provide optimal levels of protection for multiple industries needing it. Third, richer countries also have more complex tariff structures, suggesting that lack of administrative capacity or advice from the World Bank is at least partly responsible for simpler tariff structures. Finally, economies that are more open have more complex tariff structures: countries that trade more relative to the size of their economy seem to desire more specific tariff rates that allow them to differentiate between products.

EFFECTS OF TARIFF COMPLEXITY

Does complexity matter? As described in chapter 1, the study of policy complexity is still in its early stages. While an intuitive understanding of the importance of policy bias widely exists, this may not be the case with policy complexity. While it is beyond the scope of this book to offer a detailed examination of the many possible effects of policy complexity, such as for the ability of voters to understand policy and hold their elected officials accountable, this section will provide a preliminary examination of the economic effects of tariff complexity by examining the relationship between tariff structure and trade flows. If we find that countries with complex tariff structures tend to have systematically different amounts of trade, this will suggest that, at the least, the study of trade policy complexity is substantively important and will heighten the need for further examinations of complexity in this and other policy areas.

This section answers the question of whether current tariff complexity affects future trade flows. Theoretically, we might expect complexity to lead to either more or less trade. First, complex tariff schedules may reduce trade by creating a confusing set of rules for potential imports: if there is any uncertainty about which tariff line your product will fall under and if the tariff rates differ between these lines, then this may dissuade you from entering that market. In addition, complex tariff schedules may provide greater opportunity for prohibitory tariffs on many products, pricing out some imports. These prohibitory tariffs may also lead to retaliatory tariffs that limit a country's exports. On the other hand, complex tariffs might allow a country to tailor its tariffs more precisely to maximize protection for certain industries (or maximize government revenue) without pricing out imports in other sectors. In addition, if raw materials and semifinished goods are imported for the manufacture of finished goods that are then exported, a complex tariff schedule will allow for these products to have lower tariff rates than imported finished goods that compete with domestic industry. Thus, complex tariffs might increase exports by allowing export firms to purchase cheaper or more inputs and, thus, sell more goods abroad.

The dependent variable in the analysis below is trade openness, or imports plus exports divided by GDP. This is a standard measure detailing how much a country trades relative to the size of its economy. I include the lagged tariff complexity measure as the main independent variable to test the effect of complexity on openness. I also include a number of standard economic controls that have been used in previous studies of trade policy, as reviewed in Milner (1999) and Busch and Mansfield (Forthcoming). For instance, I include mean tariff rate because higher tariffs are more likely to keep out imports. I include GDP because larger economies are more self-sufficient and less reliant on both imports and exports and GDP/Capita because richer economies are more likely to engage in all forms of economic activity, including trade. I also include unemployment and inflation because trade often decreases in times of economic distress. All of these variables are lagged one year to rule out coterminous effects. Finally, I also include the lagged dependent variable since openness tends to be a persistent variable: open economies typically remain open and closed economies tend to remain closed. The main results are not sensitive to dropping this variable, though. Since trade openness is a continuous variable, I use OLS with panel-corrected standard errors to estimate the following equation:

$$\text{Trade Openness} = \beta_0 + \beta_1 \text{Trade Openness}_{t-1} + \beta_2 \text{Tariff Complexity}_{t-1}$$
$$+ \beta_3 \text{Mean Tariff Rates} + \beta_4 \text{GDP}_{t-1} + \beta_5 \text{GDP/Capita}_{t-1}$$
$$+ \beta_6 \text{Unemployment}_{t-1} + \beta_7 \text{Inflation}_{t-1} + \varepsilon. \qquad (2)$$

The first thing to note in these results, which are presented in table 6.2, is that openness is a heavily trended variable as the coefficient on the

Table 6.2 THE EFFECT OF TARIFF COMPLEXITY ON OPENNESS

Tariff Complexity	3.194*
	(1.698)
Mean Tariff Rate	-0.063
	(0.041)
GDP	2.87E-14
	(1.78E-13)
GDP/Capita	-6.98E-05
	(3.89E-05)
Inflation	0.0009
	(0.001)
Unemployment	-0.018
	(0.117)
Lagged Openness	1.009***
	(0.019)
Constant	-
	-
N	167
R-Squared	0.959

Notes: ***p<.01; **p<.05; *<p<.1
Panel-Corrected Standard Errors in Parentheses

lagged openness level is just about 1.[6] Second, despite the presence of such a strongly trended variable, tariff complexity is significantly related to trade openness: countries with more complex tariffs trade more than countries with simple tariffs. A one standard deviation change in tariff complexity (about 0.25 on the 0–1 scale) is associated with about 0.75% more trade relative to GDP. The United States, with a score of nearly 1, is expected to have over 3% more trade than Chile, with a score of 0. This suggests that consumption distortions introduced by simple tariff rates outweigh the administrative costs and possibility for prohibitory tariffs introduced by complex tariffs. In addition to tariff complexity, only GDP/Capita is also significant, with richer countries, oddly enough, trading

---

6. As Achen (2000) suggests, lagged dependent variables can eat up the explanatory power of other variables and should not always be included in time series and panel regressions. However, dropping the lagged dependent variable does not change the main result that tariff complexity leads to more openness, and the effect of complexity on openness is actually stronger substantively and statistically without the lag. In addition, the coefficient on GDP/capita becomes insignificant in this other specification and the coefficient on GDP becomes significant.

less. Mean tariff rate is almost significant, with countries that have higher tariff rates trading less, as expected. None of the other variables are even close to statistical significance.

CONCLUSION

This chapter performs the first examination of the effect of access points on policy complexity, finding that countries with more access points tend to have more complex tariff structures. In addition, this chapter demonstrates that complexity can have important real-world consequences: more complex tariff structures tend to lead to more trade openness. Taken together, these two sets of findings not only provide strong support for Access Point Theory but also suggest that, though understudied, complexity is an interesting aspect of policy, the causes and effects of which should be better understood.

In addition to its test of Access Point Theory, this chapter also provides us with a number of interesting findings regarding the understudied topic of tariff complexity. First, there is widespread variation in the levels of tariff complexity which is systematically related not only to the economic structure of the country but to the political system as well. While this chapter only focused on the effect of access points on tariff structure, the results suggest that more in-depth analyses of the political determinants, both domestic and international, could be fruitful. For instance, what role has the World Bank played in the move toward simpler tariffs? Did countries that took out loans from the World Bank in the 1980s systematically move to simpler tariffs? Did only some subset of these countries, like those with particular economic structures, follow this advice? Are there differences between democracies and dictatorships on tariff structure as there are on tariff levels? What role does partisanship play?

Another extension that could be even more fruitful would be further analysis of the effects of tariff complexity. The theoretical literature suggests that uniform tariffs should lead to lower levels of corruption, less lobbying for protection, lower levels of tariff revenue, and, though there is debate on this last point, more economic efficiency. Many of these concepts are hard to measure, but given the wide variation in tariff structure, the effect of complexity on amount of trade, and the preexisting theoretical debate, it would be worthwhile to investigate this topic. While those organizations that have advocated uniform tariffs in the past typically also advocate more open trade—and, thus, might want to rethink this advice given the results found here—if it is true that simple tariffs do reduce corruption and the long-term incentive to lobby for protection, then these benefits may outweigh the costs found in this chapter. Only upon having a more complete empirical picture of the effects of tariff complexity can we reach a firmer conclusion on the superiority of complex or simple tariff structures.

CHAPTER 7

Access Points and Tax Code Complexity

Policymakers across the world frequently debate and discuss the topic of tax code complexity. In the United States, critics across the ideological spectrum have called for tax code "simplification:" for instance, think tanks and nonprofits such as the relatively conservative Heritage Foundation and the more liberal Tax Policy Center (affiliated with both the Brookings and Urban Institutes) call for simplification of the tax code.[1] At the level of policymakers and candidates, the most famous call for a simpler tax code is probably Steve Forbes's multiple presidential campaigns centering around a flat tax; however, both Presidents George W. Bush and Barack Obama have pushed to simplify tax codes[2] and a bipartisan bill, the Wyden-Gregg Tax Reform Bill, has been introduced in the Senate to accomplish simplification. Internationally, the United Kingdom created an Office for Tax Simplification in July of 2010 to, in the words of the new Chancellor of the Exchequer, undo "a spaghetti bowl of reliefs and allowances" (Desai 2010). In addition, many countries

---

1. See http://www.heritage.org/research/reports/2010/08/tax-reform for the Heritage Foundation's arguments and http://www.taxpolicycenter.org/briefing-book/improve/simplification/ for the Tax Policy Center's arguments.

2. President Bush created the Advisory Panel on Federal Tax Reform in 2005 with the primary goal of making the tax code simpler. See http://govinfo.library.unt.edu/taxreformpanel/ for the full report and other information. On Tax Day in 2009, President Obama delivered a speech calling for simplification of the "monstrous tax code" and charged Paul Volker's economic advisory committee to investigate ways to achieve this (Weisman and McKinnon, 2009).

around the world, particularly in Eastern Europe, have adopted flat (or, at least, flatter) tax systems in the past decade (Baturo and Gray 2009).

Why do policymakers and policy analysts pay so much attention to how complex the tax code is? Part of the answer is that the public cares a lot about it. Paying taxes is one of the most obvious ways in which a citizen interacts with the government and, depending on how taxes are collected, enables a citizen to most directly see how they (or their bank accounts) are being affected by government decisions. Thus, taxes tend to be one of the most important issue areas for the public. Though the complexity of taxes usually takes a backseat to the level of taxes in terms of public attention, this is not to say that complexity does not matter. Every year in America, as April 15 approaches, most households either pour through complicated forms detailing how they must pay their federal, state, and local taxes or they pay a sizable sum so that someone else does this for them. It is little wonder that U.S. politicians, particularly around Tax Day, frequently vow to simplify this process. In addition, there might be good public policy reasons to simplify the tax code: complex tax codes might be inefficient, might encourage shirking, and might be expensive to oversee.

But if policymakers around the world and across the ideological spectrum have called for simplification, why are tax codes still complex? If simpler tax codes are more efficient and cheaper to administer, why have not all countries moved toward a flat tax? Why do most countries, rather than relying on a single type of tax, mix in income taxes, sales taxes, asset taxes, and other types of taxes? Partly, this is because there are also good public policy arguments in favor of complex tax codes, as will be discussed below. But it is also, at least in part, due to interest group politics.

Who benefits from the spaghetti bowl of reliefs and allowances? In addition to accountants and tax collectors, who might be out of work with simpler tax codes, those receiving the reliefs and allowances benefit. If these complications to the tax code are or can be narrowly tailored, such as a deduction to install solar panels on your home, then this will encourage special interest groups, such as solar panel manufacturers and installers, to lobby for their creation and against their elimination. Thus, the benefits of the complexity often accrue to concentrated interests while the costs, in taxpayer time and frustration, enforcement costs, and possible economic inefficiency, are widely dispersed. This is the classic set up, described in chapter 2, of how increasing the number of access points, by making lobbying cheaper and thus increasing the probability that special interests will lobby for specific provisions benefiting them, leads to complexity. Thus, the more access points there are, the more complex the tax code will be. This explains why the United States, with a relatively high number of access points, continues to have an exceedingly complex tax code despite frequent and bipartisan calls for simplification. And this also explains why Britain, also with a high number of access points, is likely to see little progress from its Office of Tax Simplification. But it also explains why some countries have managed to reform their tax code to simplify them and why other countries never had particularly complex tax codes to begin with.

This chapter examines how access points influence the complexity of tax codes. It provides another test of Access Point Theory, showing how access points can influence complexity in a policy area even when they might not be expected to influence bias. It also provides a detailed and novel account for why variation exists in an important policy area. To accomplish these two tasks, this chapter is organized as follows: The next section discusses the different features of tax codes that can lead to them being either simple or complex. The third section then discusses both the causes and effects of tax code complexity as established in the existing economics and political science literatures on the topics. The fourth section builds on the insights from the existing literature to explain how the number of access points might influence the structure of the tax code and derives testable hypotheses. The fifth section introduces the data and methods used to test these hypotheses, describing the two analyses that will be conducted: an analysis of the length of tax codes and an analysis of composition of the taxes collected. The sixth section presents the results of these analyses and the seventh section concludes.

SIMPLE VERSUS COMPLEX TAX CODES

As Margaret Levi writes in her classic account of why taxation occurs, "Rulers maximize revenue to the state, but not as they please" (1988, 10). In other words, rulers use taxes to appropriate as many resources as they can (either for their own use, to distribute to their supporters, or to pay for policies) but are constrained in doing so, partly by the fact that their constituents generally do not want to pay taxes (or, at least, want to minimize the amount they are taxed.)[3] But rulers have many different choices about how to raise this desired revenue, some of which are not directly related to the overall level of revenue. What are these choices?

---

3. This account is not dissimilar from analyses of the origins and purposes of taxation. Tilly (1990), for instance, argues that the sovereign state was formed as a superior way to raise revenue for warfare; thus, state rulers will try to extract as many resources as they can to fund ever more expensive wars.

Steinmo (1993) suggests that there are five main types of taxes available to the state: income, corporate, consumption, social security, and profit. The OECD provides a similar breakdown, though they differentiate between general consumption taxes (sales or value-added taxes that apply to all or most goods bought) and specific consumption taxes (excise taxes on specific products, like alcohol, gasoline, or tobacco), and they add the category of payroll taxes.[4] Within the OECD, most of these seven types of taxes are used at some level of the government in all countries; aggregating across all OECD countries in 2000, 25% of revenue comes from personal income taxes and another 25% from social security contributions (made either by the employee or the employer); general consumption taxes provide 18% of revenue and specific consumption taxes another 11%; corporate taxes (on profit, revenue, or income) comprise 11.5% of tax revenue with property taxes comprising another 5.5%. Payroll taxes contribute less than half a percent to total tax revenue.[5] With the exception of Mexico, which does not collect income taxes according to the OECD, all of the tax types are employed by every country in the OECD except for social security taxes, which Australia and New Zealand do not collect, and payroll taxes, which only 12 of the current 30 members collect.

Despite the uniformity at these broad levels, wide variation exists in tax codes. First, though most countries use the same six of these categories, there are significant differences in how important each category is in each country. For instance, over 50% of tax revenue in Denmark comes from personal income taxes while less than 10% of Slovakia's tax revenue comes from personal income taxes. The differences are less startling, though still large, in the other categories as can be seen in table 7.1 which shows the distribution of taxes in the OECD countries in 2000 (the most recent year used in the analysis below). Corporate income taxes account for the largest part of revenue in Australia and Norway, at over 20%, while they account for less than 5% of Austrian revenue; property taxes make up over 10% of total revenue in the United States, Korea, Japan, Luxembourg, and the UK[6] while it is only slightly above 1% in Austria, Mexico, and the Czech Republic. General consumption taxes are greater

---

4. These are typically taxes on employers based on the size of their payroll or the size of their workforce rather than the more typical taxes on business based on their income.

5. "Other taxes" make up the last 5%; these taxes include "certain taxes on goods and services and stamp taxes."

6. In every country, these figures represent total taxes in the country at all levels, not just at the national or federal level. The tax code analyses below will only apply to national-level tax laws.

Table 7.1 PERCENT OF REVENUE COLLECTED FROM DIFFERENT TAX SOURCES IN THE OECD IN 2000

Country	Personal Income	Corporate Income	Social Security	Payroll	Property	General Consumption	Specific Consumption	Other
Australia	37.8	20.2	0	1.4	8.8	12	14.1	5.7
Austria	22.1	4.6	34.1	2.8	1.3	16.8	8.1	10.2
Belgium	31.2	7.2	31	0	4.2	16.3	7.1	3
Canada	36.8	12.2	13.6	0.7	9.5	14.2	8.6	4.4
Czech Republic	12.9	9.8	44.2	0	1.4	18.3	11	2.4
Denmark	51.8	6.6	3.6	0.2	3.3	19.3	11.1	4.1
Finland	30.6	12.5	25.2	0	2.4	17.4	10.9	1
France	18	6.9	36.1	1	7	16.9	8.2	5.9
Germany	25.3	4.8	39	0	2.30	18.4	8.8	1.4
Greece	14.7	12.2	30.7	0	6.20	21.5	10.1	4.6
Hungary	18.7	5.7	29.3	1.4	1.7	26.1	13.8	3.3
Iceland	34.8	3.3	7.7	0	7.9	28.5	11	6.8
Ireland	30.4	11.8	13.5	0.2	5.5	22.1	13.9	2.6
Italy	24.8	6.9	28.6	0	4.6	15.4	9.6	10.1
Japan	21.1	13.8	35.2	0	10.5	9.1	8	2.3
Korea	14.6	14.1	16.7	0	12.4	17	19.7	5.5
Luxembourg	18.3	17.8	25.7	0	10.6	14.3	12.5	0.8
Mexico	0	0	16.5	0.2	1.4	18.7	33.4	29.8
Netherlands	15.1	10.1	38.9	0	5.3	17.4	8.9	4.3
New Zealand	43.1	12.4	0	0	5.3	24.9	7.5	6.8
Norway	24.1	20.9	20.9	0	2.3	19.8	9.6	2.4

(continued)

Poland	13.5	7.4	39.5	0	3.5	21.2	13.5	1.4
Portugal	16.7	11.4	30.3	0	3.5	23.4	13.1	1.6
Slovakia	9.9	7.7	41.5	0	1.8	20.4	13.7	5
Spain	18.6	8.9	34.8	0	6.5	17.5	9.6	4.1
Sweden	33.3	7.6	26.4	4.30	3.4	17	7	1
Switzerland	34.9	9	24.3	0.00	9.3	13.1	8	1.4
Turkey	22.2	7.3	18.7	0.00	3.2	24.2	16.4	8
UK	29.3	9.8	17	0.00	11.6	18.1	12.4	1.8
United States	41.9	8.7	23.2	0.00	10.1	7.6	6.3	2.2

Source: OECD Tax Database

than 25% in Hungary and Iceland but less than 10% in the United States and Japan while specific consumption taxes account for over 30% of Mexican taxes but only about 6% of U.S. taxes.

This variation in the structure of the tax contributes to variation in the complexity of the tax code. A tax code with more of these components is more complex than a code with only one component. Despite the fact that most countries have the same number of components, a large literature in economics discussed in more detail below—the "fiscal illusion" literature—argues that tax codes where most of the revenue is collected by one type of tax is simpler than a system where the taxes are spread out across many types of taxes even if both systems have the same number of types of taxes. The concentrated tax system is simpler in this view because most taxpayers likely only interact with the major tax type; the more spread out the tax system is, the more complicated the tax system will appear to taxpayers as they will be interacting with more different types of taxes. In this view of complexity, the more concentrated a tax system is the simpler it is, at least from the point of view of the taxpayer.

Even more diversity is introduced once one examines the many different ways these taxes can be applied. For instance, income taxes can be progressive, flat, or even regressive. General consumption taxes are usually either sales taxes that are applied at the final point of sale or value-added taxes (VATs) that tax a product at every stage of manufacturing and distribution based on how much value is added to the product at that stage. General consumption taxes can also exempt certain goods, most frequently food or clothing. Specific consumption taxes are applied on a wide variety of products, often differing from country to country.

A final source of diversity is particular tax exemptions, deductions, rebates, and similar programs that provide positive or negative incentives for engaging in certain behavior or that reward or punish particular groups through the tax code. Collectively, these are referred to as "tax expenditures"[7] and, more than any of the sources of diversity discussed above, contribute to the complexity of the tax code. While countries that have multiple different types of taxes will have more complex tax codes, on average, than a country with only one type of tax, and countries with

---

7. This phrase was popularized in 1961 by Stanley Surrey, then Assistant Secretary of the Treasury to President Kennedy and also a law professor at Harvard, who argued that using the tax code as a means of creating indirect spending programs led to inefficient revenue collection. Since the tax deductions and loopholes were equated with directly giving money to the recipients of these benefits, they were termed tax "expenditures" as a subset of all government expenditures. See Surrey (1973) for his argument on this issue.

flat income taxes will have less complex taxes, on average, than those with progressive income taxes, the differences between these systems are likely much less than can be introduced by all of the tax expenditures a country can have. These expenditures can serve multiple purposes: first, they can be designed to reward or punish certain people or groups of people; second, they can be designed to encourage activities that (are believed to) have positive social benefits or discourage activities that (are believed to) have negative social benefits; and third, they can be designed to create a "fairer" tax system by recognizing that different individuals have different abilities to pay taxes even if they have the same income. Regardless of the reason, each of these expenditures makes the tax code more complex; given that a country can have a large number of such expenditures, this can create a significant amount of complexity even in a country with only a single flat income tax or a national general consumption tax.

WHY DOES COMPLEXITY MATTER AND WHEN WILL IT EXIST?

Why do some countries have complex tax codes and others simple tax codes? What effect does the complexity of the tax code have? Similar to the trade complexity literature, the existing literature in economics has tended to focus on the second question rather than the first, though existing work in both political science and economics does give us some expectation for what should influence complexity.[8] The economics literature tends to focus on how to best structure taxes to increase the efficiency of the economy, maximize revenue, or lead to some other desirable economic outcome. However, the question of whether simple or complex tax structures are superior has not been resolved.

A number of accounts in both economics and political science argue that complex tax systems will be more efficient than simpler systems. First, the Ramsey Rule (1927) suggests that, at least for consumption taxes, complex taxes will be superior to simple taxes. Taxes on consumption will distort consumption differently for different goods depending on how elastic the demand is for those good, that is, how much demand is affected by price. According to the Ramsey Rule, the ideal tax is one that is inverse to the elasticity for that product; in other words, products that are

---

8. One of the earliest attempts to systematically address both questions is Alt (1983). The following discussion is greatly informed by Alt's analysis as he covered virtually all of the issues addressed below.

very sensitive to price should be taxed less so that the consumption of those products are not over-distorted. Thus, a simple system that taxes all products the same will be inefficient.[9] Second, Franzese (2002b) offers an extension of the Ramsey Rule to all taxation by adding the assumption that taxes face diminished marginal returns: the higher a tax is raised, the less marginal revenue is generated from this tax.[10] In this case, policymakers will want to have multiple different types of taxes, all set at potentially different but relatively low rates, rather than a single type of tax set at a higher rate. Finally, complicated tax systems may be more stable in the face of economic crises: similar to how a diversified investment portfolio insulates an investor from losses when one type of investment loses value, a diversified tax portfolio will insulate a government from declining revenue if an economic downturn only affects a subset of types of economic activity.[11]

On the other hand, much economic research points to the potential downsides of complex tax systems. Yitzhaki (1979), for instance, suggests that complicated taxes create more administrative costs. Similarly, van Velthoven and van Winden (1991) argue that complicated taxes might increase "compliance costs," or the amount of time and effort it takes for taxpayers to pay their taxes. Partially based on this logic, a large body of research argues that complicated taxes will lead to more tax avoidance and tax evasion, thus reducing revenue received.[12] If complicated tax systems do have more administrative costs or if they lead to more tax avoidance, then this will undermine the efficiency of the tax system, although

---

9. Holcombe (2002) suggests that the Ramsey Rule fails to produce optimal taxation once political considerations are taken into account. Allowing differential taxation may allow interest groups to lobby governments for their preferred tax rate, rather than optimal tax rate, on particular products. The deviation from optimal rates caused by lobbying may outweigh the deviation caused by a single tax on all products. While Holcombe correctly posits that tax complexity and interest group activity are related, this book argues that he gets the causal direction backward: it is not that complex tax codes allow for interest group lobbying, it is that interest group lobbying creates complex tax codes.

10. This is not to suggest that there is a Laffer Curve where tax increases reduce revenue, just that a 1% increase in a tax generates less additional revenue when that tax is already high than it would when that tax is low.

11. Misiolek and Perdue (1987) first offered this analogy to portfolio diversification. Misiolek and Elder (1988) review the broader literature on and empirically test implications of the "fiscal stress" approach to tax structure which suggests that complicated tax structure provides more stable revenue in times of "stress."

12. See Alm, Bahl, and Murray (1990) for a review of this literature as well as an empirical test that suggests that only very large changes in the tax structure will have a meaningful effect on the level of tax avoidance.

no research has directly compared this loss of efficiency to the gain of efficiency from following the Ramsey Rule.

In addition to these efficiency concerns, the "fiscal illusion" hypothesis offers another potential downside of complicated tax systems. This argument suggests that complex tax policies are harder for taxpayers to understand, which creates the illusion that they are actually being taxed less than they are. Since they are underestimating how much they, and others, are being taxed, they will underestimate how large the government is which allows the government to grow larger than the taxpayers would wish it to grow, which these analyses always assume is a bad thing.[13] A number of scholars within this research tradition have attempted to test this argument by examining whether complicated tax structures cause growth in government size. To do this, they create a measure of tax complexity based on the composition of the tax structure—how much of what types of taxes a country employs—which they use as their key independent variable. The empirical analysis below will use a similar measure as one of its dependent variables.

In addition to economic effects of complexity, the structure of the tax code also has implications for the fairness of the tax system. The tax literature tends to focus on two different types of fairness, what is referred to as vertical and horizontal equity. Vertical equity is essentially a synonym for progressivity, or the idea that those who can afford to pay more should pay more.[14] Though this concept has recently come under attack from flat tax advocates, vertical equity has been relatively uncontroversial for most of the post–World War II period in most advanced democracies. Even most flat taxes include a standard deduction for every individual which introduces some progressivity into tax collection: the more income you have over the deduction, the slightly higher percentage of your income you will pay in taxes even though all income over the deduction is taxed at the same rate. However, the simplest possible income tax—a flat tax with no deduction—does violate the norm of vertical equity. So too does the simplest possible consumption tax—a flat sales tax on all products—which not only fails to tax those who make more at higher rates but also is actually regressive since poorer individuals spend a larger proportion of their income on consumption. As a result, simpler taxes are often less fair by this notion of vertical equity.

---

13. See Wagner (1976) for the first systematic statement of this argument, Dollery and Worthington (1996) for a review of the literature on fiscal illusion, and Dollery and Worthington (1999) for an empirical test of the argument.

14. Steinmo (1993) provides a discussion of the difference between vertical and horizontal equity.

The desirability of a horizontally equitable tax and whether a complex system is more or less likely to provide it are more debatable points.[15] Part of this debate derives from the fact that even the definition of horizontal equity is not agreed upon by everyone. The basic concept is that a horizontally equitable system implies that similarly situated individuals will pay the same taxes. In other words, an equitable system does not give anyone a special benefit or single out anyone to pay more. However, what does "similarly situated" mean? Some take this to mean that those who earn the same amount should pay the same amount of taxes. In this view of horizontal equity, simpler systems will be fairer as tax expenditures or differentiations between types of income will cause some people with the same income to be paying different amounts of taxes.

On the other hand, another view of horizontal equity holds that it is not merely similar incomes that make people similarly situated but also their broader circumstances. Steinmo (1993, 35) defines horizontal equity exactly opposite to the definition above, stating that "horizontal equity implies that those who are in different circumstances should probably pay different taxes even if their gross income is similar" and illustrating this definition by suggesting that "we take it as self-evident, for example, that a single yuppie who lives on a thirty-thousand-dollar-a-year trust fund and rents a condo in Aspen should probably pay more taxes than a single parent who, on the same income, supports four children and has a house mortgage" (Steinmo 1993, 213). This notion of horizontal equity accords to the belief that it is not those who have the same income who should be taxed the same but rather those who derive the same utility from that income who should be taxed the same. The only way to accomplish this task, if one were to desire to, would be to have a complex tax system that could distinguish between, for instance, earned income and trust fund income or provided deductions for each child or deductions for mortgages. Thus, depending on one's view of the meaning of horizontal equity, either a complex or a simple tax code will be fairer. However, both conceptions of horizontal equity do suggest a strong link between complexity and fairness even if they make opposite predictions about the direction of this link.

While the research described above might suggest factors that policymakers consider when designing the tax code, many fewer works have explored the causes of variation in complexity across countries and over time. We can, however, extrapolate from the factors identified above. For instance, based on the insights provided by Yitzhaki (1979), Hettich and

---

15. See Galle (2008) for a detailed examination of the critiques of horizontal equity as well as a defense of the concept.

Winer (1988) suggest that office-seeking policymakers will want to create extremely complicated tax systems: ideally they would want to create a tax code that taxes each individual differently, based upon how much the taxpayer values the public goods they receive from taxation and how sensitive they are to the costs of taxation. Administrative costs prevent them from implementing such a complicated system, which will lead them to merge similar individuals into classes of taxpayers who are treated the same. From this, we can hypothesize that the more a government cares about remaining in office (or the more accountable they are to the taxpayers), the more complex tax codes will be, while the higher administrative costs are (or the more sensitive a government is to paying these costs), the less complex tax codes will be. In other words, democracies should have more complicated tax codes while poor countries should have simpler tax codes. Similarly, the better a government's administrative capacity, the better able they will be to identify the elasticity of different goods and, thus, set the optimal tax rates based on the Ramsey Rule. Countries with less capacity might choose to implement a simple tax since they know they lack the ability to set an optimal complex tax. Thus, once again, poorer countries might be expected to have simpler tax codes.

In addition to these literatures on tax complexity, the recent political science research on globalization and tax policy also has bearing on why some countries might have more complex tax codes than others. This literature has focused on the possibility that globalization will lead to a race to the bottom, whereby every country lowers its taxes—particularly corporate taxes—to keep mobile capital from investing elsewhere.[16] Though this question is not directly related to the issue of tax complexity, Swank and Steinmo (2002) point out an interesting connection between the effect of globalization on tax rates and tax complexity. Because capital is mobile across borders in a globalized world, countries often need to lower capital taxes, for example, corporate profit taxes, in order to prevent capital flight or attract foreign capital. At the same time, societal demands for spending increase because of rising unemployment and labor dislocations caused by internationalization. Policymakers have sought to lower tax rates on capital without shifting the tax burden to labor or reducing government revenue: the solution to this dilemma, according to Swank and Steinmo, has been to reduce the marginal rates on corporate profits and to eliminate tax expenditures that benefited

---

16. See Garrett (1998), Hays (2003), and Swank (2002) for examples of this research. Most of the analyses suggest that concerns about a race to the bottom are overblown.

reinvestment of profits and other specific corporate activities. As a result, the effective rate of taxation on capital has remained the same despite the reduction in taxes on corporate income. In addition, the elimination of tax expenditures would have simplified the tax code. Thus, we might expect more open economies, which face greater pressure to cut corporate taxes, to have simpler tax codes.

HOW ACCESS POINTS INFLUENCE COMPLEXITY

Despite the great variety in tax codes around the world and the importance of these differences, there are few systematic explanations for this variety, particularly for why some tax codes are more complex than others. Access Point Theory provides new insight into this important area as we would expect countries with more access points to have more complex tax systems. Many of the elements of tax complexity are created by specific provisions that benefit narrow groups. This is especially true of tax expenditures, which are often explicitly designed to benefit specific groups, sometimes even a single company or even individual. More generally, tax expenditures are frequently designed to benefit a specific industry by, for instance, incentivizing the purchase of goods produced by that industry or a specific occupation. As a result, we would expect organized industries or occupational groups to lobby for tax expenditures that benefit their members. The more access points there are, the cheaper lobbying will be, and the more such groups will be able to lobby for their own expenditures.

Thus, Access Point Theory makes the following prediction about tax policy:

Hypothesis 7.1: The more access points there are, the more complex tax policy will be.

Similar to the expectations in other chapters, there is no theoretical reason why proportionality should influence tax complexity once we control for the effect that PR tends to have on number of electoral districts, number of parties, and party discipline. Thus:

Hypothesis 7.2: PR has no effect on the complexity of tax policy.

Notice that Access Point Theory makes no prediction about the level of bias in tax policy. While more access points simultaneously lead to more biased and more complex trade policy, it is only predicted to lead to more complex tax policy. Why? It is not immediately clear that any particular side of a tax policy debate would have a collective action advantage: for instance, if we view tax policy as a dispute between the rich and the poor, then which side derives more concentrated benefits or suffers more concentrated costs from the outcomes of tax policy? One should not expect the rich to create organized interest groups to reduce tax progressivity or the poor to create organized interest groups to increase progressivity. Rather, most countries have a political party representing the rich and one representing the poor: tax progressivity and overall level of taxation are two of the most important elements of the left-right political dimension. In other words, both sides are equally well organized into their relevant political parties.

As a result, we would expect to see lobbying on tax policy to focus on providing specific policies that benefit narrow groups as these groups will want to create policies that benefit them and not those who are not contributing to lobbying. However, we would expect these narrow groups to be drawn from all segments of a country's income distribution. We can see the results of this process by looking at the paradigmatic case of a complex tax system: the United States, with its myriad deductions, credits, exemptions, rebates, and other tax expenditures within the Federal Income Tax, plus all of the other federal taxes and all of the state and local taxes. In fact, Steinmo titles the section introducing U.S. tax policy as "The American Tax System—The Politics of Complexity."

As noted above in the chapter introduction, many policymakers and analysts from across the ideological spectrum currently desire some form of tax simplification and virtually all recent Presidents have at least given lip service to accomplishing this goal. But this is not the first time in American political history that pressure has mounted to reform the tax system in order to reduce the complexity. In the mid-1980s, there was wide recognition that the tax system needed to be reformed and simplified. As a result, President Reagan introduced the Tax Reform Act of 1986, which collapsed the number of tax brackets and eliminated a number of deductions and both corporate and personal tax shelters.[17] However, for all the changes to the tax system made by this Act, and for all the attention on the problem of complexity in the preexisting tax system, it is hard to argue that the Tax Reform Act of 1986 actually simplified the tax code. As Steinmo (1993, 232) points out:

---

17. See Slemrod (1992) for a detailed discussion of the Act and its effects on complexity. He concludes that, at least in term of compliance costs for personal income tax, the Act made the tax code more complex.

There were a huge number of highly particularist measures retained for specific groups, industries, cities, regions of the country, and even individuals. A partial list of these includes reindeer hunters, chicken farmers, watchmakers, pen manufacturers, ministers, military personnel, timber growers, oil and gas investors, state and municipal bond investors, some commodity investors, building rehabilitators, steel manufacturers, tuxedo rental companies, firms with Puerto Rican owners, solid waste facilities, the estate of James H. W. Thompson, dependents of MIA's, foster parents, certain Indian tribes, the Miami Dolphins, Cleveland, Chicago, Memphis, and northern New Jersey.

Taken together, Steinmo (1993, 168) argues that "rather than simplify the tax code, the 1986 act took an already incredibly complex tax code and made it even more complicated." However, examining this partial list of expenditures also makes it clear that not only did wealthy groups, like the Miami Dolphins and oil and gas investors, gain benefits from this increased complexity, but so too did less wealthy groups, like reindeer hunters and ministers and dependents of MIAs.[18] Thus, the added complexity from all of these expenditures did not increase the bias of the tax system as no one side systematically benefitted from these expenditures over another side.

Steinmo suggests that it was the "institutional fragmentation" of the U.S. system that led to this complexity, arguing that the high number of veto points in the U.S. system made it necessary to create compromises that added to complexity. But, it should be noted, for all the veto points there were, none of them vetoed reform. For all the stability that high veto points are supposed to add, massive tax reform was accomplished. Access Point Theory argues that it is not the veto points that led to the complexity but rather the access points: it was not that so many policymakers had to consent for policy to pass but that so many policymakers could be lobbied by special interests that enabled chicken farmers, Midwestern cities, oil-men, and others to insert specific provisions and add complexity to a reform that was intended to create simplicity. While it is true that the United States has a notoriously complex tax code and also has among the highest number of access points, it is less clear how systematic this story is. How complex is the U.S. tax code in comparison to other countries? Or is it just more complex than observers within America wish it were? If it is

---

18. We also see from this list that tax expenditures can be used to incentivize activities that a country might believe have larger societal benefits and not just to provide narrow benefits to particular groups. For instance, this list includes incentives to become foster parents and rewards for joining the military. Thus, complexity is not entirely driven by interest group lobbying.

relatively complex, do other high-access-point countries have similarly complex systems while low-access-point countries have simpler systems? The next section describes methods to answer these questions.

DATA AND METHODS

With the exception of the analyses discussed above about flat tax adoption, no one has empirically examined in a systematic fashion the determinants of tax code complexity. This presents two questions that need to be answered before conducting the analysis in this chapter: how do we measure tax code complexity and what independent variables need to be included? I take up these two questions in turn here.

I measure tax complexity in two different ways. First, the fiscal illusion literature suggests that tax systems that are concentrated around one type of tax are simpler than systems that are dispersed around multiple different types of taxes. This is a similar measure of complexity as that for tariff complexity discussed in the last chapter and, empirically, the measure is constructed in the same way using a Herfindahl-Hirschman Index. To construct my measure, I use the eight different tax categories used by the OECD as described above and calculate the index as Σs_i^2 where s is the proportion of all tax revenue collected through i type of tax. Because a Herfindahl-Hirschman Index is a measure of concentration and I want a measure of dispersion as my measure of complexity, I take the additive inverse of this sum (or $1 - \Sigma s_i^2$) such that higher values correspond with more complex systems. As in tariff complexity, a system that gets all of its revenue from one source will have a score of 0 while a system that gets all of its revenue equally from all eight sources will get a score of 1. The more prominent one or two types of taxes are and the fewer types of taxes a country has, the lower the score will be. The data for this variable is taken from the OECD's Tax Database, which provides the amount collected of each different type of tax in OECD countries between 1965 and the present, with data reported at five-year intervals. The analysis below on this variable conducts panel analysis on these data, though the time-series gaps are left in the sample.

This measure of complexity, though the standard in the economics literature, only captures one source of complexity. Most important, it does not measure the extent that tax expenditures are used within a tax system. To augment the analyses using the tax concentration measure, I also construct a measure of tax complexity that takes into account all possible sources of complexity. To create this more comprehensive measure, one could create a set of coding rules measuring elements of each of these features and then create an index of tax code complexity by examining each tax code for these features. However, it is not immediately clear which features are most important for complexity: are all tax expenditures equally complex? How many additional tax expenditures within a personal income tax equal the level of complexity of adding a general consumption tax? Is the difference in complexity between a flat tax and a progressive tax the same as the difference in complexity between a sales tax and a VAT? Rather than create potentially arbitrary coding rules, this chapter instead adapts the methodology used by Huber and Shipan (2002) for measuring bureaucratic autonomy. Huber and Shipan argue that longer laws will contain more text limiting the discretion of bureaucratic agencies to implement policy however they see fit. Hence, longer laws constrain autonomy and discretion while shorter laws provide room for discretion. Their measure of discretion is thus the page length of various laws. In order to compare lengths of laws across different languages, they create a "verbosity index" to account for the fact that some languages take more space to describe the same thing than other languages. This index uses various EU laws (which are identical in every EU country and published in every official language of the EU) to create a ratio between the number of pages each law takes up in each language compared to the number of pages the law takes up in English.

While Huber and Shipan provide strong evidence that length of laws measures limits on discretion, the connection between length and complexity is even more intuitively clear. First, each type of tax that is applied in a country must be described in law; therefore, a country with only an income tax will, on average, have a shorter tax code than one that has both an income and consumption tax. Second, and more important, every tax expenditure must be enumerated in the law, adding to the length of the law for every expenditure. While a short law might give discretion to the bureaucracy, as Huber and Shipan suppose, it might also just be clearly expressing how a simple law must be applied. However, a short law cannot be complex. The one complicating factor is that a long law might be long because it is complex or because the authors of the law included, for example, background information or language about the desired effects of the law. On the other hand, Huber and Shipan claim that the laws they examine contain few of these sorts of extraneous elements. Thus, I use the length of a tax law as a proxy for complexity of the tax law, specifically by counting the number of words in the country's tax laws. Though this measure more accurately captures the major source of complexity—tax expenditures—only one observation per country is available and not all countries are represented in the sample, thus limiting the sample size. I therefore conduct separate analyses using both dependent variables as the strength of each of these variables offsets the weakness of the other.

The data for the tax-code-length analysis is obtained from the World Bank–run website doingbusiness.com, which includes a "law library" containing the text of tax laws for nearly 120 countries.[19] If a country has multiple laws governing the collection of taxes, such as a law on income tax and another on consumption taxes, then the website contains the text of each of these laws and I combine these laws into a single document. Many of these texts are provided in English translation, although many others are provided only in their native language (or French translation). I count the number of words in the law, using the English version when available. If no English language version is available, then I count words in the native language (or French) version and then convert these numbers to an equivalent number of English words by constructing a verbosity index similar to the one designed by Huber and Shipan.[20] Since every official document of the European Union is published in every recognized language of the EU, I construct this verbosity index using three tax laws recently passed by the EU.[21] For each of the laws, I create the ratio of number of words in each language compared to the number of words in English and then construct the verbosity index by averaging these three ratios.[22] Finally, I multiply the word counts for each country's tax code by the verbosity index for the language in which the tax code was written. All of the tax codes in the sample are available in official EU languages, so I do not have to drop cases or substitute verbosity indexes for similar languages as Huber and Shipan do. The longest tax code after this conversion is that of the United States, with 3,866,392 words, confirming the conventional wisdom that the U.S. tax law is particularly complex. The shortest tax codes are the Ivory Coast's,

---

19. Not all of these countries are democratic or have data available for all of the independent variables, so not all appear in the analyses below.

20. My verbosity index differs slightly from Huber and Shipan's in that they are counting the number of pages taken up by a law and I am counting the number of words in the law. This difference is inconsequential substantively; I count words merely because the tax laws are found online rather than in preprinted form.

21. The three laws are Council Directive 2006/138/EC, which covers the application of the VAT to radio and television services; Council Directive 2008/8/EC, which covers the definition of supplier location for taxation on services; and Council Directive 2009/69/EC, which covers tax evasion on imports. These three were chosen because they were recently passed, cover common EU taxation issues (rather than country-specific issues), and varied in their length.

22. The verbosity indices were quite similar for each of the three laws used, with correlations ranging from .975 and .99 between each of them.

Mali's, and Benin's, each with 6,035 words.[23] Britain, Canada, and Australia also have tax codes of over a million words,[24] while Bangladesh, Norway, and Senegal all have tax codes with fewer than 15,000 words. The mean number of word counts is 323,661 words (slightly higher than Germany's and France's) with a standard deviation of 776,115 words. Given the fact that this data is extremely skewed, I take the natural log of the word count: the mean of this transformed variable is 11.7 with a 1.7 standard deviation, a minimum value of 8.2 and a maximum value of 15.2, in other words, a more normally distributed variable.

In order to test the above hypotheses, I include the access point summary index described in chapter 2, to test Hypothesis 7.1, and the PR dummy, to test Hypothesis 7.2. Previous analyses provide little in the way of guidance for important control variables, and given the paucity of observation in the analyses below, I only include those that appear most important. First, the globalization literature exemplified by Steinmo and Swank suggests that countries that are open to trade are forced to lower their capital tax rates and compensate for the lost revenue by eliminating tax expenditures, thus simplifying the tax code. As a result, I include trade openness—measured as imports plus exports divided by GDP—and expect the coefficient on this variable to be negatively signed. Second, I include GDP per capita based on the argument presented in the second section of this chapter that administrative costs and administrative capacity can explain tax code complexity: poorer countries, which have less administrative capacity and are more sensitive to administrative costs, might be more likely to implement simpler tax policies to minimize these costs. Third, I include GDP as a control based on the idea that larger economies and societies might need more complex policies to govern them. Finally, a dummy variable for EU membership is included as some taxation in EU countries is handled at the EU level, thus eliminating the need for some tax language in national laws and concentrating national tax revenue into those categories not taxed at the EU level. As a result, it is expected that the coefficient on this variable will be negative.

Given that the dependent variables are for practical purposes continuous, I estimate the models using OLS regression and include robust or

---

23. These three countries are all part of the West African Economic and Monetary Union which has, among other things, harmonized their indirect taxation policies.

24. This pattern may suggest that there is something about British heritage that influences tax code complexity, but New Zealand has less than 50,000 words and Ireland less than 25,000.

panel-corrected standard errors to account for possible heteroskedasticity. In the word count analysis, I have only one observation of the dependent variable per country, so no country fixed-effects or time-series controls can be included.[25] The limited sample size also prevents the inclusion of too many control variables and raises a number of other issues that will be addressed in the results section below.[26] Finally, all of the independent variables are lagged one year to account for the possibility of contemporaneous causation. The basic model estimated below is as follows:

$$\text{Tax Complexity} = \beta_0 + \beta_1 \text{Access}_{t-1} + \beta_2 \text{PR}_{t-1} + \beta_3 \text{EU} + \beta_4 \text{GDP}_{t-1} + \beta_5 \text{GDP/} \\ \text{Capita}_{t-1} + \beta_6 \text{Trade Openness}_{t-1} + \varepsilon. \tag{1}$$

RESULTS

The results of the analysis are reported in table 7.2 and are very supportive of Access Point Theory. Model 1 in the table is the word count analysis. In this model, the access point index variable is positive and significant, meaning that more access points lead to longer word counts. In addition, the number of access points has a very large substantive impact as a 1-point increase in the index leads to a 55% increase in the length of the tax code and a one standard deviation change in the number of access points (about 2.6) leads to an over 140% increase in the length of the tax code. In addition, the coefficient on PR is insignificant, suggesting that proportionality alone has no influence on tax code complexity.

---

25. The tax codes were adopted in different years in each country. In fact, in many countries, multiple laws, each passed in different years, comprise their tax code. As a result, it is not immediately obvious which year should be used for the independent variables. Since countries can choose to change their tax policies in any year, I assume that the tax policy they have in any given year is the tax policy they want to have in that year. Thus, any year could be used. I choose to estimate the analyses using data from the year 2000, the most recent year for which we have all of the independent variables. However, all of the results reported below are essentially the same regardless of the year estimated. In fact, the access point variable is always positive and significant, even in those years for which we have fewer than 20 observations.

26. The concentration analysis does include multiple observations in each country, so fixed-effects can be used here. But the rather small number of observations per country (at most six) means that inclusion of a dummy variable for each country would use up a large number of degrees of freedom. Except for the coefficient on GDP, which becomes insignificant, the results are robust to including country fixed-effects. They are also robust to include year fixed-effects as well, suggesting that common temporal patterns are not influencing the results.

Table 7.2 THE EFFECT OF ACCESS POINTS ON TAX CODE
COMPLEXITY

Variable	Model 1	Model 2
Access Points	0.439***	-0.004***
	(.109)	(0.001)
PR	0.769	-0.026***
	(0.635)	(0.008)
GDP	3.48E-13***	-5.39E-15**
	(1.1E-13)	(2.11E-15)
GDP per capita	1.18E-5	6.54E-7***
	(2.38E-5)	(2.27E-7)
Trade Openness	0.003	-0.0003***
	(0.006)	(.00003)
EU	-0.761	0.0103**
	(0.654)	(0.004)
Constant	10.058***	0.266***
	(0.889)	(0.014)
Number of Observations	32	120
R-Squared	.567	.095

Notes: Model 1 is word count analysis with robust standard errors in parentheses
        Model 2 is concentration analysis with panel-corrected standard errors in parentheses
***p<.01; **p<.05; *<p<.1

The only control variable that is significant is GDP: larger countries have longer tax codes, perhaps because their more complex economies and societies demand more complex tax codes to govern them. This finding also echoes the finding in the trade complexity literature, where larger economies had more complex tariff schedules. This suggests the more generalizable conclusion that large countries will have more complex policies overall. Neither GDP per capita nor trade openness was significant; in fact, the coefficient on trade openness was positively signed, the opposite of what we might have expected from the Swank and Steinmo (2002) results. Finally, although the coefficient on EU is negative, as expected, it does not quite reach statistical significance.

The small sample size of this analysis does raise a number of questions about the validity of these results. First, the small sample limits the number of control variables one can include. Though the model estimated above includes all of the variables suggested by Access Point Theory and by previous analyses of tax complexity, many control variables typically found in the tax literature were not included. Including unemployment, inflation, and economic growth (one variable at a time) does not change the results reported here. Second, lack of statistical power in these analyses leads to a conservative test of the hypotheses. Thus, the fact that access points are so strongly significant despite the small sample size should reinforce our confidence that the number of access points is influencing the length of the tax code. On the other hand, we should be careful about concluding that the insignificant variables, such as PR and trade openness, really have no influence on complexity. Finally, a small sample like this one is particularly sensitive to outliers: if one country has a different relationship between an independent variable and the length of the code than the other countries, this can skew the results dramatically. However, reestimating the model while dropping each country from the sample one at a time does not change the results: access points and GDP remain positive and significant in every estimation while none of the other variables become significant, though the EU becomes only marginally insignificant when Britain is dropped from the sample. This suggests that no one country, such as the United States with by far the longest tax code and among those countries with the highest number of access points, is driving the results. In fact, even if all of the English-speaking countries with long tax codes—the United States, Great Britain, Canada, and Australia—are dropped, access points remain positive and significant even though the sample size now drops to 28 and the variation in the dependent variable is truncated. In other words, neither outliers nor omitted variable bias seems to be causing the results in this chapter: access points have a dramatic and powerful effect on how long a country's tax code is.

This finding is reinforced by the results from Model 2, the concentration analysis, which does not suffer from the same extreme sample size issues (though at 120 observations across 27 different countries, the sample is not particularly large in this analysis either). Once again, access points are positive and significant: the more access points there are, the more dispersed taxes will be across multiple types of taxes. In other words, high-access-point countries will have more complex tax systems. In this analysis, all of the other variables are significant, including PR, which also has a positive effect on complexity, contradicting the finding in the word count analysis, though it is unclear what it is about proportionality that leads to less concentrated tax collection. GDP is also positive and significant in this analysis, as it was above, suggesting that larger countries have more complex tax codes. EU countries have simpler tax codes, as expected, but the other two control variables are in the opposite direction as predicted: rich countries have simpler tax systems and open economies have more complex tax systems. Despite these inconsistent results on the control variables, the main finding of this chapter is consistent: access points significantly contribute to tax code complexity.

CONCLUSION

This chapter concludes the empirical tests of Access Point Theory. As in the previous chapters, we find strong support for the theory: increases in the number of access points are associated with more complexity in tax policy. However, as opposed to the area of trade policy where access points increase both bias and complexity simultaneously, we only expect access points to increase complexity in tax policy since no one side has a collective action advantage in tax policy. As a result, while narrow groups will lobby for narrow policy provisions benefiting only them, the sum total of all these narrow provisions will not be systematically biased toward the rich or toward the poor, or any other large group. Therefore, this chapter demonstrates that access points influence policy complexity even when it is not expected to influence policy bias.

This chapter also provided one of the first empirical tests of the cross-national determinants of tax code complexity. In addition to the number of access points, we also found that larger countries have more complex tax codes while we found inconsistent results for wealth and trade openness. In order to conduct this test, this chapter created a new measure of tax code complexity (the number of words in the tax code) and constructed a cross-national counterpart for a measure often used at the state level (the concentration index). Hopefully, the creation of these measures will spur additional research on the causes and consequences of tax code complexity.

CHAPTER 8
Conclusion

This book provided a detailed and generalized version of Access Point Theory and then provided numerous empirical tests of the theory across a wide range of policy areas. Access Point Theory argues that increasing the number of access points decreases the costs of lobbying by inducing competition among the access points for the benefits that lobbyists provide. This will lead to more lobbying, which will lead to more complex policies when policies can be narrowly tailored to benefit specific groups and to more biased policies when one side of a policy debate has a lobbying advantage. The empirical sections demonstrated that Access Point Theory successfully explains bias in trade policy and environmental and banking regulation, and complexity in trade and tax policy. In addition, the empirical chapters provided new insight into the causes of variation in a number of policy outcomes, such as the type of banking regulations employed or the complexity of the tax code. Thus, this book has demonstrated the power of Access Point Theory: not only does it provide a new explanation for how political institutions affect policy outcomes, but it can also be used to explain important policy decisions made by democracies. This chapter explains the numerous additional areas of research to which Access Point Theory can be applied and lays out a road map for a future research agenda on the interaction of institutions and interest groups in the policymaking process.

WHAT ELSE CAN ACCESS POINT THEORY EXPLAIN?

While this book demonstrated how Access Point Theory explains bias and complexity in a wide range of policy areas, the theory can actually explain much more than just these areas and these outcomes. Future work should focus on how the number of access points can explain bias and complexity in other policy areas, how it can explain other policy outcomes besides bias and complexity, and how it can explain lobbying behavior.

Other Policy Areas

The empirical chapters of this book examined how Access Point Theory can explain bias in trade policy and environmental and banking regulations, and complexity in trade and tax policy. This is only the start of the many different policy areas where Access Point Theory makes predictions. As discussed in chapters 4 and 5, regulatory politics in general should see increased bias with more access points. Just as countries with many access points have fewer environmental regulations and more bank-friendly banking regulations, they should also have weaker consumer safety and health regulations, for instance, and should also have more industry-friendly regulations over such industries as insurance, real estate, and other professions. On the other hand, areas where both sides are organized, such as worker safety regulations, particularly in countries with strong unions, should not exhibit this pattern.

In addition, Access Point Theory has strong predictions for pork barrel politics. As described in Weingast, Shepsle, and Johnsen (1981), distributive spending is the classic example of a case where the benefits are concentrated—in this case on the recipients of the pork—while costs are dispersed on every taxpayer. Thus, proponents of (particular) pork should be better organized than opponents of (overall) pork. Cheaper lobbying will allow these special interests to more easily lobby for their pet project which should increase the amount of pork in the budget. The problem with testing this application of the theory is that good cross-national measures of pork are difficult to come by. Were such a measure available, though, Access Point Theory should be able to explain the political determinants of the variation across countries and over time. Similarly, as described in chapter 1, welfare state complexity might also be explained by the number of access points, though a lack of a consistent and systematic cross-national measure of welfare state complexity prevents easy analysis of this question.

The lobbying advantage that generates bias in all the policy areas examined in this book and mentioned so far in this chapter derives from one side having a collective action advantage. However, lobbying advantages can be created by other mechanisms, which might yield additional policy areas within which Access Point Theory can generate predictions. For instance, some groups might have an inherent resource advantage: if one side of the policy debate is wealthier than the other, then it will better be able to bear the costs of lobbying. In this case, it is not that it is more efficient in lobbying or has lower costs for other reasons, as it does when there is a collective action advantage, just that it has a greater ability to pay the same price for access than the disadvantaged side does. More access points might, therefore, be related to more regressive policies that favor the rich over the poor and smaller welfare states. Another possibility might be that policymakers might be systematically more receptive to certain groups. For instance, underrepresented minorities may have a harder time gaining access to government leaders in polarized societies. In countries with many access points, we might expect there to be more bias against minorities, that is, less minority protection and perhaps more oppression, than in countries with few access points. Future work should, therefore, systematically explore the many possible sources of lobbying advantages and apply Access Point Theory to the issues areas where these advantages are strongest.

How Policymakers Respond to Access Points

In addition to bias and complexity, Access Point Theory can also likely explain other policy outcomes, though the theory would need to be extended to fully demonstrate the causal logic linking number of access points to these outcomes. However, I sketch here a preliminary explanation for how Access Point Theory might explain two such additional outcomes: constraint and delegation. The logic for both of these rests on the assumption that policymakers know that having a high number of access points systematically leads to more biased and more complex policies. If this fact is known to policymakers, and they wish to mitigate the bias and complexity, they may take action to insulate themselves or other policymakers from interest group pressure. This can be accomplished, of course, through constitutional reform that changes the institutions of the country and, thus, the number of access points, but constitutional reform is difficult and time-consuming, and I am aware of no cases of such reform motivated by a desire to limit interest group access. However, there are relatively easier methods to limit this access that policymakers can and have tried: constraint and delegation.

As discussed in chapter 3, the classic story of how the RTAA was passed, dating back to Schattschneider (1935), is that Congress recognized that when they set tariff rates themselves, a logroll resulted that led to higher overall tariff rates than anyone wanted. Thus, they delegated power to the President to break this logroll and enable lower tariff rates. In other words, Congress delegated power from a high-access-point institution (themselves) to a low-access-point institution (the President), thereby reducing the weighted number of access points as described in chapter 2, and reducing the bias of policy. Although Hiscox (1999) and others have raised legitimate questions about how deliberate this actually was in the case of the RTAA, chapter 3 found that delegation did lead to fewer access points, less lobbying, and lower tariff rates. More recently, in debates over fast-track authority, policymakers have actively argued that delegation to the President makes it less likely that interest groups can lobby for protection. They have even renamed fast-track authority "Trade Promotion Authority" to reflect this understanding. In addition, this story of delegation is likely more generalizable than just trade policy in the United States. Epstein and O'Halloran (1999) provide a compelling account of Congress's choice to delegate power in the United States, arguing, among other things, that delegation to the President is more likely in cases of unified government and in policy areas that are "informationally intense." Access Point Theory might suggest that if one were to try to generalize this argument to other countries, these findings would be most true in countries with a large number of access points. In other words, countries with few access points will receive less benefit from delegation than countries with many access points, so delegation should occur less often, and information intensity and unified government should have less influence on the decision.

Second, if policymakers are aware that a high number of access points leads to bias, they may try to constrain future policymakers from implementing biased policy. This was discussed in chapter 6 with regards to Pelc's (n.d.) arguments about tariff overhang: all countries in the WTO create tariff schedules where they agree to maximum tariff rates (bound tariffs) that are higher than the rates they actually use (applied tariffs.) This difference between bound and applied tariffs is called an overhang and represents an intentional element of flexibility: countries can increase their tariff rates to the bound level in times of economic distress without violating their WTO agreement. However, this flexibility is likely to be abused in countries with many access points, as interest groups lobby to push tariffs to the bound level even when the economy is not struggling. Leaders in high-access-point countries may therefore try to constrain future policymakers by not negotiating a large overhang. Thus, we would expect more access points to be associated with less overhang.

A similar story of constraining future policymakers is often told in the central bank independence literature, as exemplified by Bernhard (1998). Leaders may be worried that future policymakers will attempt to manipulate monetary policy for electoral gain, thus creating inflation. Therefore, they delegate power to an independent central bank to constrain future policy-makers' ability to influence monetary policy. This might be more important in high-access-point countries since low inflation can be seen as a public good while the benefits of expansionary monetary policy are somewhat more concentrated on those currently in the labor market and, particularly, on those with jobs that are in marginal or risky sectors of the economy; thus, proponents of expansion may have a collective action advantage over opponents, leading to more expansionary (and inflationary) policy in high-access-point countries. As a result, we might expect more access points to be associated with more central bank independence. All of these hypotheses are preliminary, but they point to the idea that scholars studying policy outcomes other than just bias and complexity may benefit from asking how the number of access points might influence those outcomes as well.

Lobbying Behavior

While this book has largely focused on the effects of access points on policy outcomes, Access Point Theory also provides predictions on the behavior of political actors, most obviously on the decisions of interest groups to lobby. The causal story underlying Access Point Theory is that more access points lead to cheaper lobbying which leads to more lobbying. Further, if one side has a lobbying advantage, then more access points should lead to a larger increase in lobbying for this advantaged side over the disadvantaged side. If this causal story is accurate, then not only should we observe more biased and complex policies when there are more access points, but we should also observe more active interest groups and more biased involvement of interest groups. Chapter 3 demonstrated that this was true in the case of trade lobbying in the United States before and after delegation to the President, providing support for the microfoundations of the theory. However, we can also use this theory to explain the behavior of lobbyists cross-nationally. For instance, countries with more access points should have more active lobbyist and special interest activities.

The main problem with a cross-national examination of lobbying behavior is the paucity of data on cross-national lobbying. Most countries do not record interest group contributions and legislative testimony in as much detail as the United States does. One area where we do have a significant amount of data, though, is EU lobbying, where the European Union Commission keeps track of who registers as a lobbyist or sets up an office in Brussels to lobby the EU. Bernhagen and Mitchell (2009) analyze the decisions of large corporations to lobby the EU and find that these decisions are largely based on how important regulatory policy is to the firm: if the firm has large profits but is part of an industry that is exposed to regulations, it will lobby the EU more often. In addition, though, we would expect domestic-level variables to influence these decisions, especially the number of access points. European corporations that wish to influence European policy have two choices: they can lobby the European Union to change EU-level policy or they can lobby their national government, either to change relevant national policy or to vote on their behalf at the EU level. If it is easy to lobby their home government—for example, if there are many access points—then we would expect relatively more national-level lobbying and relatively less EU-level lobbying. If it is hard to lobby the home government—for example, if there are few access points—then we would expect relatively less national-level lobbying and relatively more EU-level lobbying. While data on national-level lobbying is scant or nonexistent we can test Access Point Theory at the EU level: all else equal, corporations based in low-access-point countries will be more likely to actively lobby the EU than corporations based in high-access-point countries. A similar logic could be used to explain lobbying choices in other multilevel governments, such as the decision to lobby at the federal, state, or local level in the United States.

EXTENSIONS TO THE THEORY

In addition to the empirical extensions of Access Point Theory described above, a number of theoretical extensions are also possible, two of which are detailed here: combining Access Point and Veto Player Theories and extending Access Point Theory to nondemocratic systems.

Combining Access and Veto Points

As described in chapter 1, there is significant overlap between Access Point Theory and Veto Player Theory: each theory counts the number of certain types of policymakers and argues that this count influences important policy outcomes. Further, many of the institutions that contribute to more access points, such as number of parties and federalism, also contribute to more veto players. The two theories also occasionally make either the same prediction or make predictions that are contradictory to each other. Most of the time, though, the two theories will serve as complements: they make predictions unrelated to each other as they focus on different policy outcomes. Veto Player Theory only predicts that more veto points lead to more policy stability and that fewer veto points lead to less stability: it does not predict what the status quo will be if it is stable or how policy will change if it can change. Access Point Theory, on the other hand, only predicts what policy will look like if it can change (or what the original status quo was) but cannot predict how possible this change is.

In this way, the two theories might be fruitfully combined, with Veto Player Theory predicting whether policy change is possible and Access Point Theory predicting the direction and magnitude of change. To test this possibility, we would want to interact a summary measure of veto players and a summary measure of access points. As the number of veto players decreases, the number of access points will matter more. When there are too many veto players, access points should be irrelevant as no matter how interest groups may lobby to change policy, the policy cannot be changed. Given that the empirical chapters did not conduct such an interactive analysis, the analyses in these chapters were probably undercounting the importance of the number of access points since they were combining both situations where access points could matter and those where they could not, not because interest groups did not want to exploit their access to push for policy provisions that would benefit them but because change was impossible.

Another way to combine the two theories is to view Access Point Theory as specifying the preferences of the different veto players. Veto Player Theory is only able to make predictions about final policy if we know who the agenda setter is and what he and the other veto players want. Access Point Theory provides an explanation of what is likely to emerge from the agenda-setting process. While we still may need to assume what the preferences of some of the veto players are (especially those who are not also access points), combining the theories in this way would enable us to predict what alternative to the status quo these veto players might need to veto. In summary, while both Veto Player and Access Point Theory make important and interesting predictions about the policymaking process, these insights could be expanded by combining the two theories into one multistage model of the policymaking process.

This book intentionally only applied Access Point Theory to democratic systems. This choice is not because I do not believe that access matters in non-democracies, just that it might matter differently. Democratic systems are designed to be representative, and its leaders are accountable to the citizens through regular election. Further, democratic systems provide the freedom necessary for societal groups to form and try to influence policy and, though this book focuses on why some groups might do this better than others, democracies rarely systematically prevent groups from trying to do so. Some or all of these features may be absent in autocracies. If policymakers are not accountable to the people, will this lead to more or less power to interest groups? If interest groups are restricted from forming, will it matter how much access would be provided to them if they did? These concerns suggest that one should be very careful in comparing the amount of access points in democracies and dictatorships, and trying to predict policy differences that result from this. For instance, even though most democracies have more access points than most non-democracies, Access Point Theory would not predict that democracies should be more protectionist.

However, while I would caution against comparing the number of access points across regime types, I believe future research should investigate the effect of the number of access points in non-democracies. Research has recently focused on institutional differences within non-democracies, particularly on the variation in elections and legislatures and other methods of power-sharing within dictatorships. This attention to systematically unpacking authoritarianism is quite new, and it opens up the possibility of measuring the number of access points in dictatorships. Most prominently, Gandhi (2008) examines when dictatorships allow legislatures and opposition parties to exist and, potentially, exercise some power, and argues that these power-sharing systems, under certain circumstances, contribute to the dictator remaining in power.[1] In making this argument, Gandhi collected extensive data on dictatorial institutions, which could be utilized to examine the number of access points in dictatorships. It could be argued that legislatures and opposition parties provide additional access points to dictatorial regimes even when they have little actual power.[2] Thus, dictatorships with these institutions

---

1. See also Gandhi and Lust-Okar (2009) for a review of the literature on elections in dictatorships and Vreeland (2008) for an application of how dictatorial institutions influence the decision to sign human rights treaties.

2. They would need to have some power, or they would not be relevant and, therefore, would not be access points. But Gandhi (2008) demonstrates that these institutions are not always mere "window dressing."

should have more access points and more biased and complex policies than dictatorships without these institutions. In constructing this Access Point Theory of dictatorships, we would need to be careful to also distinguish systems where citizens are free to form groups and ones where this ability is limited as the number of access points should only matter in countries where some freedom of association is allowed. Care must be taken, therefore, in extending this theory to non-democracies but, though this book only focused on access points in democracies, there is no theoretical reason to believe that the theory could not also be extended to dictatorships. Once this is done, we can begin to examine the causes of variation in trade policy, regulatory policy, and bias and complexity in other policies within dictatorships. While this book has often argued that the causes of such variation in democracies are understudied, these topics are unstudied within dictatorships. The work of Gandhi (2008) and others, when combined with Access Point Theory, thus opens up the possibility of greatly expanding our knowledge of policymaking in many countries around the world.

CONCLUDING THOUGHTS

The primary purpose of this book is to lay out a research agenda investigating the role of access points on policymaking. To accomplish this, I presented a generalized version of Access Point Theory, empirically tested the theory across a wide range of policy areas, and then sketched out avenues for future research. While doing this, the book has also accomplished a number of other goals. First, it described two broad characteristics of policy, bias and complexity, one of which has been understudied—complexity—and the other of which has tended to only be studied in isolation within particular policy areas. Hopefully, this book spurs more research on the causes and consequences of complexity as well as attention to the general factors that cause bias across policy areas. Second, though the domestic causes of variation in the level of protection, that is, trade bias, have been extensively examined and a significant amount of research has also investigated variation in environmental regulations, the other policy areas examined in this book have been subjected to less empirical testing. As such, this book has shed light on a number of important policy areas, such as why countries have different banking regulations and the determinants of tax code structure. Even in the areas where existing research is most extensive, Access Point Theory provides new insights and resolves existing debates, such as whether and how delegation to the President influenced U.S. trade policy and what types of democratic institutions contribute to more environmental institutions. Finally, this book makes no claim that access points are the only, or even necessarily the most important, feature of institutions, just that access points often matter. So, too, will other underlying institutional features for other types of policy outcomes. Hopefully, this book makes clear the potential value in analyzing institutions in this way and encourages additional theorizing about the general features of institutional configurations.

In summary, while this book has developed a general theory that can explain much in politics, there is still much more to be explained, both by Access Point Theory and by other institutional theories. Institutions determine the rules by which the game of politics is played, and these rules significantly matter. Focusing on these rules and how they differ from country to country thus helps us understand why the politics and policies of different countries vary so greatly even in the face of pressure from globalized forces. Though this book is not the first step in understanding the role of institutions, nor do I expect or want it to be the last, this book should move our understanding forward and help us to understand what causes countries to choose different policies.

REFERENCES

Achen, Christopher H. 2000. Why Lagged Dependent Variables Can Suppress the Explanatory Power of Other Independent Variables. Unpublished manuscript, University of Michigan, Ann Arbor.

Alm, James, Roy Bahl, and Matthew M. Murray. 1990. Tax Structure and Tax Compliance. *Review of Economics and Statistics* 72 (4): 603–613.

Alt, James E. 1983. The Evolution of Tax Structure. *Public Choice* 41 (3): 181–222.

Antweiler, Werner, Brian R. Copeland, and M. Scott Taylor. 2001. Is Free Trade Good for the Environment? *American Economic Review* 91 (4): 877–908.

Ashcraft, Adam B. 2007. Does the Market Discipline Banks? New Evidence from Regulatory Capital Mix. *Journal of Financial Intermediation* 17 (4): 543–561.

Austen-Smith, David, and John R. Wright. 1994. Counteractive Lobbying. *American Journal of Political Science* 38 (1): 25–44.

Bailey, Michael, Judith Goldstein, and Barry R. Weingast. 1997. The Institutional Roots of American Trade Policy: Politics, Coalitions, and International Trade. *World Politics* 49 (3): 309–338.

Baldwin, Robert E. 1985. *The Political Economy of U.S. Import Policy*. Cambridge, MA: MIT Press.

Barth, James R., Gerald Caprio, Jr., and Ross Levine. 1999. Financial Regulation and Performance. Santa Monica, CA: Milken Institute.

———. 2001. The Regulation and Supervision of Banks around the World: A New Database. World Bank Policy Research Working Paper #2588.

———. 2003. *Rethinking Bank Regulations: Till Angels Govern*. Washington, DC: World Bank.

———. 2004. Bank Regulation and Supervision: What Works Best? *Journal of Financial Intermediation* 13 (2): 205–248.

———. 2008. Bank Regulations Are Changing: For Better or Worse? *Comparative Economic Studies* 50 (3): 537–563.

Baturo, Alexander, and Julia Gray. 2009. Flatliners: Ideology and Rational Learning in the Adoption of the Flat Tax. *European Journal of Political Research* 48 (1): 130–159.

Bearce, David. 2008. Not Complements, But Substitutes: Fixed Exchange Rate Commitments, Central Bank Independence, and External Currency Stability. *International Studies Quarterly* 52 (4): 807–824.

Beck, Nathaniel. 1991. Comparing Dynamic Specification: The Case of Presidential Approval. *Political Analysis* 3: 51–87.

Beck, Nathaniel, and Jonathan N. Katz. 1995. What to Do (and Not to Do) with Time-Series Cross-Section Data. *American Journal of Political Science* 89 (3): 634–647.

Beck, Thorsten, George Clarke, Alberto Groff, Philip Keefer, and Patrick Walsh. 2001. New Tools in Comparative Political Economy: The Database of Political Institutions. *World Bank Economic Review* 15 (1): 165–176.

Bennedsen, Morten, and Sven E. Feldmann. 2001. Information Lobbying and Political Contributions. Unpublished paper.

Bernauer, Thomas, Anna Kalbhenn, Vally Koubi, and Gabrielle Ruoff. 2008. International Entanglement and Contingent Behavior as Determinants of International Cooperation: Explaining Global Environmental Treaty Ratifications, 1950–2000. Unpublished manuscript.

Bernauer, Thomas, and Vally Koubi. 2006. On the Interconnectedness of Regulatory Policy and Markets: Lessons from Banking. *British Journal of Political Science* 36 (4): 509–525.

———. 2009. Effects of Political Institutions on Air Quality. *Ecological Economics* 68: 1355–1365.

Bernhagen, Patrick, and Neil J. Mitchell. 2009. The Determinants of Direct Corporate Lobbying in the European Union. *European Union Politics* 10 (2): 155–176.

Bernhard, William. 1998. A Political Explanation of Variations in Central Bank Independence. *American Political Science Review* 92 (2): 311–328.

Bowler, Shawn, David M. Farrell, and Richard S. Katz, eds. 1999. *Party Discipline and Parliamentary Government*. Columbus: Ohio State University Press.

Bueno de Mesquita, Bruce, Alastair Smith, Randolph M. Siverson, and James D. Morrow. 2003. *The Logic of Political Survival*. Cambridge, MA: The MIT Press.

Busch, Marc L., and Edward D. Mansfield. Forthcoming. Trade: Determinants of Policies. In *The International Studies Compendium Project*, edited by Robert A. Denemark et al. Oxford: Wiley-Blackwell.

Carey, John. 2003. Discipline, Accountability and Legislative Voting in Latin America. *Comparative Political Studies* 35 (2): 191–211.

Carey, John, and Matthew S. Shugart. 1995. Incentives to Cultivate a Personal Vote: A Rank Ordering of Electoral Formulas. *Electoral Studies* 14 (4): 417–439.

Chang, Eric, Mark Kayser, Drew Linzer, and Ronald Rogowski. Forthcoming. *Electoral Systems and the Balance of Consumer-Producer Power*. New York: Cambridge University Press.

Chang, Eric, Mark Kayser, and Ronald Rogowski. 2008. Electoral Systems and Real Prices: Panel Evidence for the OECD Countries, 1970–2000. *British Journal of Political Science* 38 (4): 739–751.

Congleston, Roger D. 1992. Political Institutions and Pollution Control. *Review of Economics and Statistics* 74 (3): 412–421.

Corden, W. Max. 1957. The Calculation of the Cost of Protection. *Economic Record* 33 (1): 29–51.

———. 1968. Australian Economic Policy Discussion in the Post-War Period: A Survey. *American Economic Review* 58 (3): 88–138.

———. 1971. *The Theory of Protection*. Oxford, UK: Clarendon Press.

Cox, Gary W. 1990. Centripetal and Centrifugal Incentives in Electoral Systems. *American Journal of Political Science* 34 (4): 903–935.

———. 1997. *Making Votes Count: Strategic Coordination in the World's Electoral Systems*. New York: Cambridge University Press.

Cull, Robert J., Lemma W. Senbet, and Marco Sorge. 2005. Deposit Insurance and Financial Development. *Journal of Money, Credit, and Banking* 37 (1): 43–82.

Davies, Howard, and David Green. 2008. *Global Financial Regulation: The Essential Guide*. Malden, MA: Polity Press.

DeBoef, Suzanna. 2000. Modeling Equilibrium Relationships: Error Correction Mechanisms with Strongly Autoregressive Data. *Political Analysis* 9 (1): 78–94.

DeBoef, Suzanna, and Jim Granato. 1999. Testing for Cointegration When Data Are Near-Integrated. *Political Analysis* 8: 99–117.

DeBoef, Suzanna, and Luke Keele. 2005. Taking Time Seriously: Dynamic Regression. Unpublished manuscript.

Degryse, Hans., and S. Ongena. 2007. The Impact of Competition on Bank Orientation, *Journal of Financial Intermediation* 16 (3): 399–424.

Demirgüç-Kunt, Asli, Enrica Detragiache, and Thierry Tressel. 2008a. Banking on the Principles: Compliance with Basel Core Principles and Bank Soundness. *Journal of Financial Intermediation* 17 (4): 511–542.

Demirgüç-Kunt, Asli, Edward J. Kane, and Luc Laeven. 2008b. Determinants of Deposit Insurance Adoption and Design. *Journal of Financial Intermediation* 17 (3): 407–438.

Desai, Sumit. 2010. Osborne Tackles "Spaghetti Bowl" Tax Code. Reuters, July 20, 2010. Available at http://uk.reuters.com/article/idUKTRE66I5WP20100720.

Destler, I. M. 2005. *American Trade Politics*. 4th ed. Washington, DC: Institute for International Economics.

Dinda, Soumyananda. 2004. Environmental Kuznets Curve Hypothesis: A Survey. *Ecological Economics* 49: 431–455.

Dollery, Brian E., and Andrew C. Worthington. 1996. The Empirical Analysis of Fiscal Illusion. *Journal of Economic Surveys* 10 (3): 261–297.

———. 1999. Tax Complexity and Fiscal Illusion: An Empirical Evaluation of the Heyndels and Smolders Approach. *Public Finance* 51 (4): 522–533.

Drope, Jeffrey M., and Wendy L. Hansen. 2004. Purchasing Protection? The Effect of Political Spending on U.S. Trade Policy. *Political Research Quarterly* 57 (1): 27–37.

Ederington, Josh, and Jenny Minier. 2002. Tariff Uniformity and Growth. *Policy Reform* 5 (2): 56–73.

Ehrlich, Sean D. 2004. *Access to Protection: Democratic Institutions, Interest Group Politics, and International Trade Policy*. Ph.D. diss., University of Michigan, Ann Arbor.

———. 2007. Access to Protection: Domestic Institutions and Trade Policies in Democracies. *International Organization* 61 (3): 571–605.

———. 2008. The Tariff and the Lobbyist: Political Institutions, Interest Group Politics, and U.S. Trade Policy. *International Studies Quarterly* 52 (3): 427–446.

———. 2009a.Constituency Size and Support for Trade Liberalization: An Analysis of Foreign Economic Policy Preferences in Congress. *Foreign Policy Analysis* 5 (2): 215–232.

———. 2009b. How Common Is the Common External Tariff? Domestic Influences on European Union Trade Policy. *European Union Politics* 10 (1): 115–141.

Enelow, James M., and Melvin J. Hinich. 1984. *The Spatial Theory of Voting: An Introduction*. Cambridge: Cambridge University Press.

Epstein, David, and Sharyn O'Halloran. 1999. *Delegating Powers*. New York: Cambridge University Press.

Franzese, Robert J. 2002a. Electoral and Partisan Cycles in Economic Policies and Outcomes. *Annual Review of Political Science* 5: 369–421.

———. 2002b. *Macroeconomic Policies of Developed Democracies*. New York: Cambridge University Press.

Franzese, Robert J., Karen Long Jusko, and Irfan Nooruddin. 2007. Party Unity and the Effective Constituency in Distributive Politics. Unpublished manuscript.

Gallarotti, Guilio M. 1985. Towards a Business Cycle Model of Tariff. *International Organization* 39 (1): 155–187.

Galle, Brian. 2008. Tax Fairness. *Washington and Lee Law Review* 65: 1323–1380.

Gandhi, Jennifer. 2008. *Political Institutions under Dictatorship*. New York: Cambridge University Press.

Gandhi, Jennifer, and Ellen Lust-Okar. 2009. Elections under Authoritarianism. *Annual Review of Political Science* 12: 403–422.

Garrett, Geoffrey. 1998. *Partisan Politics in the Global Economy*. New York: Cambridge University Press.

Gatti, Roberta. 1999. Corruption and Trade Tariffs, or a Case for Uniform Tariffs. *Policy Research Working Paper*. Washington, DC: The World Bank Group.

Gilligan, Michael. 1997. *Empowering Exporters: Reciprocity, Delegation, and Collective Action in American Trade Policy*. Ann Arbor: University of Michigan Press.

Gleditsch, Nils P., and Bjorn O. Sverdrup. 2002. Democracy and the Environment. In *Human Security and the Environment: International Comparison*, edited by Edwin Paper and Michael Redclift, 45–70. London: Elgar.

Gonzáles, Francisco. 2005. Bank Regulation and Risk-Taking Incentives: An International Comparison of Bank Risk. *Journal of Banking and Finance* 29 (5): 1153–1184.

———. 2009. Determinants of Bank-Market Structure: Efficiency and Political Economy Variables. *Journal of Money, Credit, and Banking* 41 (4): 735–754.

Goodhart, Lucy. 2008. Trade Protection as Pork: Districts and Electoral Laws as Determinants of Trade Policy. Paper presented at the annual meeting of the Midwest Political Science Association.

Greene, William H. 2000. *Econometric Analysis*. 4th ed. Upper Saddle River, NJ: Prentice Hall.

Grossman, Gene M., and Elhannan Helpman. 1994. Protection for Sale. *American Economic Review* 84 (4): 833–850.

———. 2002. *Interest Groups and Trade Policy*. Princeton, NJ: Princeton University Press.

———. 2004. A Protectionist Bias in Majoritarian Politics. Unpublished manuscript.

Hacker, Jacob S. 2002. *The Divided Welfare State: The Battle of Public and Private Social Benefits in the United States* Cambridge: Cambridge University Press.

Hall, Richard L. 1996. *Participation in Congress*. New Haven, CT: Yale University Press.

Hallerberg, Mark, and Patrick Marier. 2004. Executive Authority, the Personal Vote, and Budget Discipline in Latin American and Caribbean Countries. *American Journal of Political Science* 48 (3): 571–587.

Hankla, Charles R. 2006. Party Strength and International Trade. *Comparative Political Studies* 39 (9): 1133–1156.

Hansen, John Mark. 1991. *Gaining Access: Congress and the Farm Lobby, 1919–1981*. Chicago: University of Chicago Press.

Hays, Jude C. 2003. Globalization and Capital Taxation in Consensus and Majoritarian Democracies. *World Politics* 56 (1): 79–113.

Henisz, Witold. 2010. The Political Constraint Index (POLCON) Database. Available at http://www-management.wharton.upenn.edu/henisz/.

Hettich, Walter, and Stanley L. Winer. 1988. Economic and Political Foundations of Tax Structure Economic and Political Foundations of Tax Structure. *The American Economic Review* 78 (4): 701–712.

Hiscox, Michael. 1999. The Magic Bullet? The RTAA, Institutional Reform, and Trade Liberalization. *International Organization* 53 (4):669–698.

———. 2002. *International Trade and Political Conflict: Commerce, Coalitions, and Mobility.* Princeton, NJ: Princeton University Press.

Holcombe, Randall G. 2002. The Ramsey Rule Reconsidered. *Public Finance Review* 30 (6): 562–578.

Huber, John D. 1996. *Rationalizing Parliament: Legislative Institutions and Party Politics in France.* New York: Cambridge University Press.

Huber, John D., and Charles R. Shipan. 2002. *Deliberate Discretion? The Institutional Foundations of Bureaucratic Autonomy.* New York: Cambridge University Press.

Ioannidou, Vasso P., and Maria Fabiana Penas. 2010. Deposit Insurance and Bank Risk-Taking: Evidence from Internal Loan Rankings. *Journal of Financial Intermediation* 19 (1): 95–115.

Johnson, Harry G. 1964. Tariffs and Economic Development: Some Theoretical Issues. *Journal of Development Studies* 1 (1): 3–30.

Kapstein, Ethan B. 1989. Resolving the Regulator's Dilemma: International Coordination of Banking Regulations. *International Organization* 43 (2): 323–347.

Karol, David. 2002. Divided Government and U.S. Trade Policy: Much Ado about Nothing? *International Organization* 54 (4): 825–844.

———. 2007. Does Constituency Size Affect Elected Officials' Trade Policy Preferences? *Journal of Politics* 69 (2): 470–482.

Katzenstein, Peter J. 1977. Domestic Structures and Strategies of Foreign Economic Policy. *International Organization* 31 (4): 879–920.

———. 1985. *Small States in World Markets: Industrial Policy in Europe.* Ithaca, NY: Cornell University Press.

Kayser, Mark, and Ronald Rogowski. 2002. Majoritarian Electoral Systems and Consumer Power: Price-Level Evidence from the OECD Countries. *American Journal of Political Science* 46 (3): 526–539.

King, Gary, Michael Tomz, and Jason Wittenberg. 2000. Making the Most of Statistical Analyses: Improving Interpretation and Presentation. *American Journal of Political Science* 44 (2): 347–361.

Kingdon, John W. 1989. *Congressmen's Voting Decisions.* Ann Arbor: University of Michigan Press.

Kono, Daniel Y. 2006. Optimal Obfuscation: Democracy and Trade Policy Transparency. *American Political Science Review* 100 (3): 369–384.

———. 2009. One Policy for Each or One for All? A New Measure of Trade-Policy Particularism. Unpublished manuscript. UC-Davis, CA.

Krasner, Stephen D. 1978. United States Commercial and Monetary Policy: Unraveling the Paradox of External Strength and Internal Weakness. In *Between Power and Plenty: The Foreign Economic Policies of Advanced Industrial States*, edited by Peter J. Katzenstein, 51–87. Madison: University of Wisconsin Press.

Laeven, Luc. 2004. The Political Economy of Deposit Insurance. *Journal of Financial Services Research* 26 (3): 201–224.

Lake, David A. 1988. The State and American Trade Strategy in the Pre-Hegemonic Era. *International Organization* 42 (1): 33–58.

Lasswell, Harold D. 1958. *Politics: Who Gets What, When, and How.* New York: Meridian Books.

Levi, Margaret. 1988. *Of Rule and Revenue.* Berkeley: University of California Press.

Li, Quan, and Rafael Reuveny. 2006. Democracy and Environmental Degradation. *International Studies Quarterly* 40 (4): 935–956.

——. 1999. *Patterns of Democracy: Government Forms and Performance in Thirty-Six Countries.* New Haven, CT: Yale University Press.

Lindner, Laura A. 1993. "Repealing" the Glass-Steagall Act: A Japanese Lesson in Economic Strategy. *Wisconsin International Law Journal* 11: 495–529.

Lohmann, Susanne, and Sharyn O'Halloran. 1994. Divided Government and U.S. Trade Policy. *International Organization* 48 (4): 595–632.

Magee, Stephen P., William A. Brock, and Leslie Young. 1989. *Black Hole Tariffs and Endogenous Policy Theory: Political Economy in General Equilibrium.* Cambridge: Cambridge University Press.

Mansfield, Edward D., and Marc L. Busch. 1995. The Political Economy of Non-Tariff Barriers: A Cross-National Analysis. *International Organization* 49 (4): 723–749.

Mayer, Wolfgang. 1984. Endogenous Tariff Formation. *American Economic Review* 74 (5): 970–985.

McGillivray, Fiona. 1997. Party Discipline as a Determinant of Endogenous Tariff Formation. *American Journal of Political Science* 41 (2): 584–607.

Midlarsky, Manus. 1998. Democracy and the Environment: An Empirical Assessment. *Journal of Peace Research* 35 (3): 341–361.

Milner, Helen V. 1988. *Resisting Protectionism: Global Industries and the Politics of International Trade.* Princeton, NJ: Princeton University Press.

——. 1998. *Interests, Institutions, and Information: Domestic Politics and International Relations.* Princeton, NJ: Princeton University Press.

——. 1999. The Political Economy of International Trade. *Annual Review of Political Science* 2: 91–114.

Milner, Helen V., and B. Peter Rosendorff. 1997. Democratic Politics and International Trade Negotiations: Elections and Divided Government as Constrains on Trade Liberalization. *Journal of Conflict Resolution* 41 (1): 117–146.

Misiolek, Walter S., and Harold W. Elder. 1988. Tax Structure and the Size of the Government: An Empirical Analysis of the Fiscal Illusion and Fiscal Stress Arguments. *Public Choice* 57 (3): 233–245.

Misiolek, Walter S., and D. G. Perdue. 1987. The Portfolio Approach to State and Local Tax Structures. *National Tax Journal* 40: 111–114.

Mitchell, Brian R. 1995. *International Historical Statistics.* New York: Stockton Press.

Mitchell, Ronald B. 2002–2008. International Environmental Agreements Database Project (Version 2007.1). Available at http://iea.uoregon.edu/.

Monroe, Burt L. 1994. Understanding Electoral Systems: Beyond Plurality vs. PR. *PS: Political Science and Politics* 27 (4): 677–682.

Moravcsik, Andrew. 1997. Taking Preferences Seriously: A Liberal Theory of International Politics. *International Organization.* 51 (4): 513–553

Morrison, Alan D., and Lucy White. 2005. Crises and Capital Requirements in Banking. *American Economic Review* 95 (5): 1548–1572.

Neilson, Daniel L. 2003. Supplying Trade Reform: Political Institutions and Liberalization in Middle-Income Presidential Democracies. *American Journal of Political Science* 47 (3): 470–491.

Neumayer, Eric. 2002. Do Democracies Exhibit Stronger International Environmental Commitment? A Cross-Country Analysis. *Journal of Peace Research* 39 (2): 139–164.

——. 2003. Are Left-Wing Party Strength and Corporatism Good for the Environment? A Panel Analysis of 21 OECD Countries, 1980–1998. *Ecological Economics* 45 (2): 203–220.

Nousiainen, Jaako. 2000. Finland: The Consolidation of Parliamentary Government. In *Coalition Governments in Western Europe*, edited by Wolfgang C. Muller and Kaare Strom, 264–299. Oxford: Oxford University Press.

Oatley, Thomas, and Robert Nabors. 1998. Redistributive Cooperation: Market Failure, Wealth Transfers, and the Basle Accords. *International Organization* 52 (1): 35–54.

Olson, Mancur. 1971. *The Logic of Collective Action: Public Goods and the Theory of Groups*. Rev. ed. New York: Schocken Books.

——. 1982. *The Rise and Decline of Nations: Economic Growth, Stagnation, and Social Rigidities*. New Haven, CT: Yale University Press.

Organization for Economic Cooperation and Development. 2004. *OECD Environmental Data Compendium*. Paris: OECD.

Ostrom, Elinor. 2003. How Types of Goods and Property Rights Jointly Affect Collective Action. *Journal of Theoretical Politics* 15 (3): 239–270.

Pahre, Robert. 2004. House Rules: Institutional Choice and United States Trade Negotiations. *Conflict Management and Peace Sciences* 21 (3): 195–213.

Panagariya, Arvind. 1994. Why and Why-Not of Uniform Tariffs. *Economic Studies Quarterly* 45 (3): 227–245.

——. 1996. The Economics and Politics of Uniform Tariffs. Unpublished manuscript. University of Maryland, College Park.

Panagariya, Arvind, and Dani Rodrik. 1991. Political Economy Arguments for Uniform Tariff. *Policy, Research, and External Affairs Working Papers* Washington, DC: World Bank Group.

Panayotou, Theodore. 2000. Economic Growth and the Environment. Unpublished manuscript, Center for International Development at Harvard University.

Pasiouras, Fotios, Chrysovalantis Gaganis, and Constantin Zopounidis. 2006. The Impact of Bank Regulations, Supervision, Market Structure, and Bank Characteristics on Individual Bank Ratings: A Cross-Country Analysis. *Review of Quantitative Finance and Accounting* 27 (4): 403–438.

Pastor, Robert A. 1980. *Congress and the Politics of U.S. Foreign Economic Policy 1929–1976*. Berkeley: University of California Press.

Payne, Rodger A. 1995. Freedom and the Environment. *Journal of Democracy* 6 (3): 41–55.

Pelc, Krzysztof J. n.d. Why the Overhang? Explaining the Gap between Bound and Applied Tariff Rates. Unpublished manuscript.

Perrson, Torsten, and Guido Tabellini. 2000. *Political Economics: Explaining Economic Policy*. Cambridge, MA: MIT Press.

Poloni-Staudinger, Lori. 2008. Are Consensus Democracies More Environmental? An Examination of Majoritarian and Consensus Democracies and Environmental Effectiveness. *Environmental Politics* 17 (3): 410–430.

Prakash, Aseem, and Matthew Potoski. 2006. Racing to the Bottom? Globalization, Environmental Government, and ISO 14001. *American Journal of Political Science*, 50 (20): 347–361.

Przeworski, Adam, Michael E. Alvarez, Jose Antonio Cheibub, and Fernando Limongi. 2000. *Democracy and Development: Political Institutions and Well-Being in the World, 1950–1990*. Cambridge: Cambridge University Press.

Ramsey, Frank P. 1927. A Contribution to the Theory of Taxation. *Economic Journal* 37: 47–61.

Ringquist, Evan J., and Tatiana Kostadinova. 2005. Assessing the Effectiveness of International Environmental Agreements: The Case of the 1985 Helsinki Protocol. *American Journal of Political Science* 49 (1): 86–102.

Rogowski, Ronald. 1987. Trade and the Variety of Democratic Institutions. *International Organization* 41 (2): 203–223.

——. 1999. Institutions as Constraints on Strategic Choice. In *Strategic Choice and International Relations*, edited by David A. Lake and Robert Powell, 115–136. Princeton, NJ: Princeton University Press.

Rosenbluth, Frances, and Ross Schaap. 2003. The Domestic Politics of Banking Regulation. *International Organization* 57 (2): 307–336.

Schattschneider, E. E. 1935. *Politics, Pressure and the Tariff: A Study of Free Private Enterprise in Pressure Politics, as Shown in the 1929–1930 Revision of the Tariff.* New York: Prentice Hall.

——. 1960. *The Semisovereign People.* New York: Holt, Rinehart, and Wilson.

Scruggs, Lyle. 1999. Institutions and Environmental Performance in 17 Western Democracies. *British Journal of Political Science* 29 (1): 1–31.

——. 2001. Is There Really a Link Between Neo-Corporatism and Environmental Performance? Evidence for the 1990's. *British Journal of Political Science* 31 (4): 686–692.

Seddon Wallach, Jessica, Alejandro Gaviria, Ugo Panizza, and Ernesto Stein. 2002. Political Particularism around the World. Unpublished manuscript.

Siaroff, Alan. 1999. Corporatism in 24 Industrial Countries: Meaning and Measurement. *European Journal of Political Research* 36 (2): 175–205.

Simmons, Beth. 2001. The International Politics of Harmonization: The Case of Capital Market Regulations. *International Organization* 55 (3): 589–620.

Singer, David Andrew. 2007. *Regulating Capital: Setting Standards for the International Financial System.* Ithaca, NY: Cornell University Press.

Slemrod, Joel. 1992. Did the Tax Reform Act of 1986 Simplify Tax Matters? *The Journal of Economic Perspectives* 6 (1): 45–57.

Solsten, Eric, ed. 1995. *Germany: A Country Study.* Washington, DC: GPO for the Library of Congress.

Steinmo, Sven. 1993. *Taxation and Democracy.* New Haven, CT: Yale University Press.

Surrey, Stanley S. 1973. *Pathways to Tax Reform: The Concept of Tax Expenditures.* Cambridge, MA: Harvard University Press.

Swank, Duane. 2002. *Global Capital, Political Institutions, and Policy Change in Developed Welfare States.* New York: Cambridge University Press.

Swank, Duane, and Sven Steinmo. 2002. The New Political Economy of Taxation in Advanced Capitalist Democracies. *American Journal of Political Science* 46 (3): 642–655.

Taylor, Michael, and Hugh Ward. 1982. Chickens, Whales, and Lumpy Goods: Alternative Models of Public-Goods Provision. *Political Studies* 30: 350–370.

Tilly, Charles. 1990. *Coercion, Capital, and European States, AD 990–1992.* Cambridge, MA: Blackwell.

Trefler, Daniel. 1993. Trade Liberalization and the Theory of Endogenous Protection. *The Journal of Political Economy* 101 (1): 138–160.

Trubowitz, Peter. 1998. *Defining the National Interest: Conflict and Change in American Foreign Policy*. Chicago: University of Chicago Press.

Truman, David B. 1951. *The Governmental Process: Political Interests and Public Opinion*. New York: Knopf.

Tsebelis, George. 2002. *Veto Player: How Political Institutions Work*. Princeton, NJ: Princeton University Press.

Tsebelis, George, and Jeannette Money. 1997. *Bicameralism*. New York: Cambridge University Press.

Van Velthoven, Ben, and Frans Van Winden. 1991. A Positive Model of Tax Reform *Public Choice* 72 (1): 61–86.

Von Stein, Jana. 2008.The International Law and Politics of Climate Change: Ratification of the United Nations Framework Convention and the Kyoto Protocol. *Journal of Conflict Resolution* 52 (2): 243–268.

Vreeland, James. 2008. Political Institutions and Human Rights: Why Dictatorships Enter into the United Nations Convention against Torture. *International Organization* 62 (1): 65–101.

Wagner, Richard E. 1976. Revenue Structure, Fiscal Illusion, and Budgetary Choice. *Public Choice* 25 (1): 45–61.

Walti, Sonja. 2004. How Multilevel Structures Affect Environmental Policy in Industrialized Countries. *European Journal of Political Research* 43: 599–634.

Ward, Hugh. 2006. International Linkages and Environmental Sustainability: The Effectiveness of the Regime Network. *Journal of Peace Research* 43 (2): 149–166.

Weingast, Barry R., Kenneth A. Shepsle, and Christopher Johnsen. 1981. The Political Economy of Benefits and Costs: A Neoclassical Approach to Distributive Politics. *Journal of Political Economy* 89 (4): 642–664.

Weisman, Jonathan, and John D. McKinnon. 2009. Obama Calls for Simpler Tax Code. *Wall Street Journal*, April 16, 2009.

Wilson, James Q. 1989. *Bureaucracies: What Government Agencies Do and Why They Do It*. New York: Basic Books.

Yitzhaki, Shlomo. 1979. A Note on Optimal Taxation and Administrative Costs. *The American Economic Review* 69 (3): 475–480.

INDEX